Complex Sample Survey Estimation in Static State-Space

Raymond L. Czaplewski

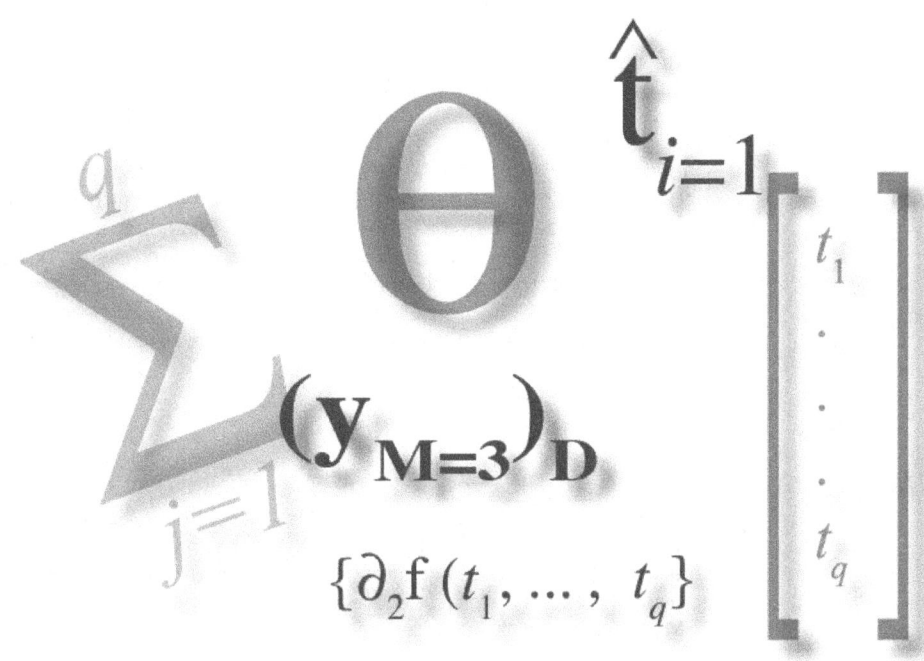

United States Department of Agriculture / Forest Service

Rocky Mountain Research Station

General Technical Report RMRS-GTR-239

July 2010

Abstract

Increased use of remotely sensed data is a key strategy adopted by the Forest Inventory and Analysis Program. However, multiple sensor technologies require complex sampling units and sampling designs. The Recursive Restriction Estimator (RRE) accommodates this complexity. It is a design-consistent Empirical Best Linear Unbiased Prediction for the state-vector, which contains all sufficient statistics for the sampled population. RRE reduces a complex estimator into a sequence of simpler estimators. Also included are model-based pseudo-estimators and multivariate Taylor series approximations for covariance matrices. Together, these provide a unified approach to detailed estimation in large, complex sample surveys.

Keywords: FIA, sampling, recursive, Pythagorean regression, EBLUP, remote sensing

Author

Raymond L. Czaplewski is a Research Mathematical Statistician with the USDA Forest Service, Rocky Mountain Research Station (RMRS), in Fort Collins, CO. He is a member of the RMRS Inventory, Monitoring, and Analysis Program and the Interior West Forest Inventory and Analysis (FIA) program, with headquarters in Ogden, UT. He was an RMRS Project Leader with the national FIA program, a Program Analyst with the Bighorn National Forest, and a Wildlife Planner with the Wyoming Game and Fish Department. He received his Ph.D. from Colorado State University in quantitative range science, his M.S. degree from University of Wyoming in systems ecology, and his B.A. degree from Northwestern University in biology. His professional interests include statistical estimators for sample surveys that integrate time-series of remotely sensed observations with FIA field data.

Acknowledgments

Detailed technical reviews by Jean Opsomer, Ph.D., Jianqiang Wang, Ph.D., and David Turner, Ph.D., improved the original draft of this manuscript. Steen Magnussen, Ph.D., also provided valuable suggestions. Any remaining errors or omissions remain the sole responsibility of the author.

Contents

Introduction

The USDA Forest Service, Research and Development branch, through its Forest Inventory and Analysis (FIA) program, is committed to delivering current, consistent, and credible information about the status, condition, and trends of America's forests (Gillespie 1999; Van Deusen and others 1999; Smith 2002; Bechtold and Scott 2005; McRoberts 2005; Patterson and Reams 2005; Reams and others 2005; Scott and others 2005). The FIA strategic plan for 2007 to 2011 (USDA Forest Service 2007) charts the course for continuous improvement in the near term. The FIA plan details plans to utilize the latest technologies to acquire data through remote sensing, field activities, primary forest product studies, utilization studies, and landowner surveys. FIA plans to elevate its emphasis on remote sensing and field data to analyze the location, status, and trends in land use, land cover, and fragmentation.

The 2007 FIA strategic plan identifies opportunities to expand its service to the nation after full implementation of the base FIA program, which is described in its 1998 strategic plan (USDA Forest Service 1998). Development and implementation of these opportunities are not included in the current or target funding for FIA. However, FIA can provide the leadership necessary to pursue these opportunities through research and development, innovation, strategic partnerships, and cost sharing with other programs.

One key opportunity is to increase the role of remote sensing to improve cost effectiveness and data quality. One of many options might include a shift in FIA investments toward observations with remotely sensed data. However, verification of remotely sensed data with sufficient field data remains essential. A shift toward more remotely sensed observations is most compelling in the Interior West, interior Alaska, and other regions with forests dominated by open canopies, lower levels of stocking, and lower productivity. FIA leadership envisions using high-resolution, remotely sensed imagery and light detection and ranging (LiDAR) technology. Other sensors include Moderate Resolution Imaging Spectro-radiometer (MODIS) with 250-m pixels (Justice and others 2002), Landsat (30-m pixels), and IKONOS satellites (1-m pixels). Lower-resolution satellite data, such as MODIS and Landsat, are suitable for synoptic, wall-to-wall, full-coverage, thematic mapping. Sampling is needed for higher resolution, remotely sensed data such as IKONOS, small-footprint LiDAR, and large-scale aerial photography.

Another key opportunity is to enhance support to the National Forest System (NFS) within the U.S. Forest Service. FIA could extend its sampling grid of field plots to all NFS lands, not just to those that meet the definition of forest. This expansion would also require an inventory compilation package be developed for NFS business needs, including mid-level vegetation map products. This is consistent with the FIA guiding principle to develop inventory methods and new techniques that will assist NFS in meeting the requirements of the National Forest Management Act. Remote sensing might reduce the cost of this ambitious strategy.

A remote sensing module might support other opportunities for FIA service. A rapid assessment capacity could be developed within FIA to provide emergency surveys of resource impacts within days or weeks following a major environmental disturbance such as a wildfire, storm, hurricane, or sudden insect or disease outbreak (Van Deusen and others 1999).

Urban trees and forests affect quality of life of urban populations, which constitute approximately 80 percent of the U.S. population. Urban forestry is especially important to states with increasing populations. However, the FIA system does not include urban forests. A systematic approach to collecting and reporting data on status and trends of trees and forests in urban settings is another strategic opportunity. The FIA sample frame could be expanded to urban settings. The Federal role would best remain at the strategic scale, but an FIA system could serve as a platform for institutions to intensify to the individual city level. In principle, remote sensing technologies could contribute to a cost effective solution in urban settings.

FIA has the opportunity to help build a national rangeland inventory. The 2002 House Interior Appropriations Committee report (USDA Forest Service 2007) included language directing the Secretaries of Agriculture and the Interior to collaborate in implementing a rangeland monitoring system. There is an ongoing effort to explore this opportunity in partnership with the USDA Forest Service's National Forest System, the USDA Natural Resources Conservation Service's National Resources Inventory, and the USDI Bureau of Land Management. Remote sensing technologies offer a potential contribution to cost-effective implementation. The feasibility of this major undertaking might be improved with remotely sensed data. This too is an FIA strategic priority (USDA Forest Service 2007).

FIA also has the strategic opportunity to monitor wildlife habitat to mitigate concerns about management actions on species viability. However, standard FIA indicators, plot size, and measurements protocols can miss important habitat features. The geographic scale of a habitat feature for many wildlife species might not match the scale of an FIA field plot. Enhancements or embellishments might be necessary to the traditional FIA design and processing procedures. Synoptic remote sensing methods might produce geospatial data on certain habitat features with sufficient accuracy. Other habitat features require higher resolution observations that are feasible with a sample of large-scale aerial imagery or small-footprint LiDAR data that cover sampling units 5 acres to 2500 acres in size. Holthausen and others (2005) provide a detailed assessment of strategic monitoring of wildlife populations that could be linked to the FIA program.

There is another strategic opportunity to conduct strategic-level monitoring of status and trends on all treed land. Indicators could be developed for ecosystem health, biodiversity, carbon sequestration, wildlife corridors and habitat, narrow riparian features, windrows, and agroforestry stands. Some indicators might be reliably measured with high-resolution remote sensing technologies.

Integrating new technologies is critical to the efficient implementation of the FIA program (Van Deusen and others 1999). One focus of the 2007 FIA strategic plan is to build technology partnerships with other national programs that produce data related to FIA objectives. These national programs include: National Resources Inventory conducted by the USDA Natural Resources Conservation Service; the Multi-Resolution Land Characterization Consortium and its National Land Cover Data products, which are coordinated by the USGS Earth Resources Observation and Science Center; the GAP Analysis Program by the USGS Biological Resources Division; NASA; and NOAA (USDA Forest Service 2007). Most opportunities for improved technologies involve sharing costs and logistical burdens to use remotely sensed data from satellites and low-altitude aircraft more efficiently and effectively in order to facilitate broad-scale applications of Geographical Information Systems.

FIA plans to increase capacity to conduct research and development on techniques that improve how data are collected, analyzed, and disseminated (USDA Forest Service 2007). Potential research areas include improved sampling and estimation procedures, better linkages to small-area or tactical assessments, development of improved geospatial analytical tools, and better mechanisms for making data and results available to the public. The highest priorities are to improve efficiency of FIA, expand the scope of FIA, and develop new product lines that demonstrate value added to FIA. An emphasis on national techniques will increase FIA involvement in internally directed extramural research that will increase the knowledge and uses of FIA data.

Accomplishing these strategic FIA objectives will likely require statistical estimators that combine annual time-series of FIA field data with separate time-series of remotely sensed data from different sensors with different resolutions in order to estimate status, trends, and location by class for land use/land cover/ fragmentation change analysis (de Gruijter and others 2006). This report is one attempt to advance these programmatic objectives. It describes a suite of statistical estimation methods that accommodate complexities inherent to using diverse remote sensing technologies. It is a unified and cohesive approach to estimation. These methods rely upon the extensive literature on Kalman filtering, and they build upon recent developments by Knottnerus (2003) that are closely related to the static Kalman filter.

Outline

This paper is organized as follows. The section "Stratification in FIA" includes the limitations of FIA's post-stratification estimator. The next section, "Recursive Restriction Estimator (RRE)", introduces the core estimation concepts used throughout this report. This section illustrates the algebraic identity between the Generalized Least Squares survey estimator and the Kalman filter. These concepts are applied with Recursive Restriction Estimation in complex sampling designs using the following examples.

The first example is "Two-Phase Sampling for Continuous Variables with a Sample at Phase 1". It considers the case of a large sample of points that are measured with high-resolution remote sensing at Phase 1 (P1) and a small sub-sample of these points that are measured by a field crew. It is similar to FIA methods used in the 1960s to 1990s. This example does not include pre-stratification, but it does apply to the case of double-sampling for stratification with equal inclusion probabilities among strata. This example illustrates estimation in state-space with the static Kalman filter, although it requires only a single recursion of the RE object, which is a special case of RRE.

The second example is "Two-Phase Sampling for Continuous Variables with a Census at Phase 1". Rather than a sample of points at Phase 1, this example uses one or more censuses of remotely sensed pixels at Phase 1. A special case of this design is used by FIA throughout the United States. However, this FIA estimator, which uses temporally indifferent post-stratification, captures only a portion of the available auxiliary pixel data (see "Stratification In FIA,"). RRE is a more capable alternative. Computation of optimal RRE weights requires inversion of a covariance matrix, which is the partition of the sample covariance matrix for the auxiliary variables. However, whenever the auxiliary data at the population level are known constants, this covariance matrix is singular or ill-conditioned, and the inversion is infeasible. This example introduces one form of RRE that solves this numerical problem. The vector of census constraints, which contains the exact population totals for all auxiliary variables, is processed recursively, one element at a time. The RRE sequentially applies the scalar inverse of the sample variance for each auxiliary variable rather than attempt an infeasible matrix inversion. This section also demonstrates RRE is equivalent to optimal calibration.

The third example is "Three-Phase Sampling for Continuous Variables". It starts with the previous example and then adds a third phase, which is an equal-probability sub-sample of the Phase 2 (P2) sample. This example is directly relevant to the FIA design that includes the Phase 3 (P3) Forest Health Monitoring plots. It uses all remotely sensed data and the Phase 2 field measurements to improve population estimates for the Phase 3 variables. Sequential RRE is a simple solution to this otherwise complex estimation problem. Simplicity is achieved by first using RRE with the remotely sensed data to improve population estimates of variables that are measured with FIA Phase 2 field protocol. In the next step, the RRE object combines the results of the first step with the Phase 3 sub-sample. This two-step process is an example of a different type of recursion. The primary purpose is to simplify the estimator rather than solve numerical problems. However, the dimensions of the multivariate vectors can become large, posing numerical risks and other problems. This example includes a sub-optimal RRE alternative that uses smaller matrix dimensions to be more numerically robust in.

The fourth example is "Single-Phase Sampling for Continuous Variables with Cluster Plots". This section introduces an RRE for experimental designs such as the FIA Nevada Photo-based Inventory Pilot (NPIP) study. NPIP uses a 50-acre photo-plot, which is a cluster of 49 points that are measured with a sample of high-resolution aerial photography. One of these 49 points is the center of a standard FIA Phase 2 field plot. RRE uses the sample of photo-interpreted measurements to improve precision of population estimates from the sample of Phase 2 field measurements. The previous examples consider remotely sensed data from independent samples at the different phases. That type of independence does not exist when remotely sensed and field measurements are made within the same cluster plot in this two-stage design.

The fifth example is "Two-Phase Sampling for Continuous Variables with Cluster Plots". This is based on the previous NPIP example with the addition of a large, independent sample of 50-acre cluster plots. This large Phase 1 sample is measured with photo-interpretation of the same type of high-resolution aerial photography; there are no field measurements made within this Phase 1 sample of cluster plots. Furthermore, this example includes wall-to-wall, full-coverage data from spaceborne sensors. RRE is a simple solution to this complex design.

All of the examples assume the remotely sensed data are continuous variables. Each continuous variable is represented by a single element in a multivariate vector. The section "Categorical Variables" expands the scope of RRE. A polychotomous variable with C categories may be readily transformed into a vector of C dichotomous variables and then used directly with the estimators in previous sections. Rather than a single element for a continuous variable, there will be C elements for a categorical variable. If there are two polychotomous categorical variables, then a C_1-by-C_2 contingency table of cross-classifications is possible. Each of the $C_1 \times C_2$ dichotomous cross-classifications would require a separate vector element. This can produce vectors and covariance matrices with large dimensions, which often lead to numerical problems. Sub-optimal alternatives are discussed.

The section "Robust Numerics" briefly covers the subject of numerical round-off error and the need for robust algorithms. U-D factorization, which uses the modified Gram-Schmidt orthogonalization, is an example. Optimal sample survey estimation is hindered by numerical problems that have been solved by engineering statisticians. The Kalman filtering literature offers an abundance of reliable solutions

FIA relies on "expansion factors" to simplify post-stratified estimation in FIA's large database. FIA expansion factors are analogous to calibration weights, which, likewise, are widely used in large government survey programs to conveniently improve statistical efficiency with auxiliary information. FIA expansion factors and calibration weights modify the design weights for each Primary Sampling Unit (PSU) to incorporate the auxiliary data, such as the population census of predictions for remotely sensed pixels. The section "Optimal PSU Expansion Values for Each FIA Plot" develops analogous methods for the RRE. This method assigns a vector of expansion values to each PSU. The RRE expansion vector for each PSU uses the auxiliary data specifically observed for that PSU. The sum of RRE expansion values for each PSU in the sampled population will exactly equal the estimated vector of population totals from the RRE. The RRE covariance matrix is similarly expressed as the sum of expansion value vector cross-products at the PSU level. This solves problems with the FIA database that are identified by Scott and others (2005). Further development is needed for FIA plot expansion factors from RRE algorithms.

The section "Multivariate Vector of FIA Study Variables" describes the core variables being estimated by FIA. In principle, all these variables can be simultaneously estimated with RRE. Multivariate FIA response variables enable pseudo-estimators for other FIA statistics in later sections. However, it is always possible to estimate one study variable at a time, which is the situation in FIA.

The section "Multivariate Vector of Auxiliary Variables" briefly covers the different types of remotely sensed and geospatial variables that might improve precision of FIA statistics. RRE can simply accommodate the complex sampling designs required to utilize auxiliary information from these diverse technologies.

Next, a series of examples illustrate various pseudo-estimators. These are transformations of vector estimate from a design-based estimator. They depend upon multivariate estimation and are not generally feasible with the usual univariate estimators. The section "Linear, Small-Area, Synthetic Estimator with Census Predictors" is an example of a multivariate transformation for small-area estimation with inverse calibration (Tenenbein 1972; Brown 1982). The example uses a complex version of the NPIP design (discussed in "Single-Phase Sampling for Continuous Variables with Cluster Plots"), which uses a small sample of 50-acre photo-plots that surround a 1-acre FIA field plot, a large sample of 50-acre photo-plots that do not include a field plot, and wall-to-wall remotely sensed data. However, the same pseudo-estimation methods apply to any RRE estimate and its covariance matrix. The small areas in this example are individual 6000-acre FIA hexagons, which FIA uses for national-scale geospatial presentations. These pseudo-estimators are consistent in that the sum of small-area estimates over all small areas equals the RRE estimates for the total population. This would support a geospatial presentation database based on FIA hexagons.

The section "Non-Linear Pseudo-Estimators" covers more examples that are relevant to FIA. Computation of these non-linear transformations is straightforward. However, the estimator for the associated covariance matrix requires multivariate Taylor-series transformations. The sub-section "Product Estimator: Missing Data Imputation" is a simple example in which the first-order Taylor-series produces an exact model-based estimator for the covariance matrix. The example uses model-based imputation of FIA biomass accretion estimates for lands that are too dangerous to measure by a field crew and for private lands for which the landowner has denied legal trespass to an FIA field crew. The example assumes classifications of wall-to-wall pixels from a spaceborne sensor are available for all lands. These remotely sensed data serve as predictors of the missing FIA field measurements. The model assumes that the expected biomass accretion for each remotely sensed category is independent from the missing data status. Given these model assumptions, it readily produces variance estimates for population totals that include both the sampling and estimation errors for the measured sampling units and prediction error from the model for missing data.

The sub-section "Ratio Pseudo-Estimator: Volume per Estimated Unit Area of Forest Cover" considers the ratio operator, which is a more complex non-linear transformation. The example is estimation of wood volume per forested acre. The pseudo-estimator is the population estimate of total wood volume divided by the estimated total area of forest. The covariance matrix for this pseudo-estimator uses the first-order Taylor-series approximation. The sub-section "Recursive Object-Oriented Simplification of Taylor-Series Approximations" presents several techniques that simplify derivation of multivariate Taylor-series approximations for covariance matrices. The sub-section "A Model-Based Estimator for Small-Domain Predictions" is a more complex example of multivariate pseudo-estimators that combines both linear and non-linear transformations. It uses the Taylor-series simplifications given in the previous sub-sections. The example uses unbiased estimates of tree volume with expensive measurements of upper-stem diameters on a small sub-sample of FIA Phase 2 field plots. It assumes inexpensive volume estimates for Phase 2 plots are biased by volume equations that are fit to historical data, which no longer represent the current sampled population. This is a form of calibration in which an expensive, unbiased estimate from a small sample is empirically used to correct for measurement bias in a less-expensive estimate from a large sample. The calibration is performed for many small-domains. The sum of estimates for all domains is consistent with the estimate for the population total. The sub-section "Second-Order Taylor-Series Approximation to

Assess Bias" considers the error in first-order Taylor-series approximations by computing the second-order approximation. Recursive methods presented in previous sub-sections simplify derivation of the second-order approximation.

The final sections depart from mathematical statistics and concentrate on application topics. The section "Accuracy and Registration of Remotely Sensed Data" explores the degree of association required between the study variables and the remotely sensed auxiliary variables. The "Discussion" covers the following topics: the advantages of RRE compared to post-stratification, Risk management with complex sampling designs, and seminal literature. "Future Research and Development" briefly discusses the next steps needed to implement RRE confidently with the FIA database. "Conclusions" follows.

Stratification in FIA

FIA is a pioneer in the use of remotely sensed data for stratification to improve efficiency of its statistical products (e.g., Bickford and others 1963). Today, this is exclusively accomplished with the post-stratification statistical estimator (Scott and others 2005). FIA applies post-stratification with full-coverage, remotely sensed thematic maps of forest versus non-forest cover produced with wall-to-wall Landsat data (e.g., Hoppus and Lister 2002; Nelson and others 2007). Hansen and Wendt (2000) and McRoberts and others (2002) further stratify based on edge conditions between the following remotely sensed classifications of forest and non-forest: forest, forest edge, non-forest edge, and non-forest. McRoberts (2006) uses a related approach with four strata that are based on predictions of the proportion forest area in each Landsat pixel from a logistic regression model. These stratifiers separate heterogeneous edge conditions from more homogeneous conditions within the interior of stands. Most stratification schemes help isolate many of the most serious classification errors that are caused by misregistration between FIA plots and their corresponding pixels. A relatively small frequency of misclassification errors can degrade the statistical efficiencies offered by remote sensing (Czaplewski and Patterson 2001, 2003).

Certain FIA areal summary statistics are constrained to match administrative records for geopolitical entities. These include Census Bureau statistics for total area of each county, regardless of terrestrial land cover, and the area of significant water bodies by county. Areal constraints used by FIA also include major land ownership categories. FIA cross-classifies remotely sensed pixel data and these administrative areal statistics, and this merged cross-classification is applied with the post-stratification estimator to impose areal control. The result is numerous strata, many of which have very small samples of FIA sample plots. Stratification is best used to reduce variance in sample estimates. However, FIA also uses stratification to impose areal control for administrative statistics. Areal control does not necessarily produce variance reduction. Stratification for areal control and remotely sensed data produces numerous small strata that contain few FIA plots.

Prior to 1999, FIA would survey all field plots in a state, produce statistical and analytical reports, and then move to the next state in the regional survey sequence. Each state was re-surveyed every 7 to 15 years (Gillespie 2000). FIA documents cite this as a periodic survey. These periodic surveys served the states well shortly after the full survey was completed. However, confidence in the data decreased as the data aged more than five years (American Forest Council 1992:1-15). The Agricultural Research Extension and Education Reform Act of 1998 directed all FIA units to change these statewide periodic systems into a nationally consistent annual survey system (Gillespie 1999). Beginning in 1999, FIA responded to this Congressional direction by systematically subdividing its sampling frame into 5 to 10 separate panels. Each panel includes 10 to 20 percent systematic sample of all FIA field plots in each state. Ideally, a single panel is fully measured during a single year (Van Deusen 2002). However, this subsampling frequency introduces an unintended consequence—it further aggravates problems that are inherent with detailed stratification and very small, within-stratum sample sizes.

One solution to the relatively small sample size in each annual FIA panel is to merge field data from multiple years. A time-series of panel measurements is treated as though it was measured during a single year. Post-stratification uses a single set of remotely sensed images (Bechtold and Scott 2005) rather than an annual time-series of remotely sensed data. However, changes in plot conditions between acquisition of the remotely sensed data and the most recent field measurements are not distinguishable from prediction errors with remotely sensed data. This type of disagreement between field data and remotely sensed classifications will reduce the statistical efficiency from stratification. The loss in efficiency will be rapid as the agreement deteriorates (Czaplewski and Patterson 2001, 2003), regardless of the cause (i.e., classification error versus change in land cover). This means that the value of remotely sensed data slowly diminishes in dynamic landscapes, which are exactly the types of domains that often have the greatest need for current monitoring data. These same areas could benefit the most from remotely sensed data if the limits from post-stratification can be mitigated.

Inaccurate variance estimates can be common for strata that have rare or common attributes. For example, if all plots sampled in a forest stratum are truly forest, then the estimated variance for forest cover will be zero in that stratum. Even though the stratum has some non-forest cover, the stratum estimate for non-forest area would be zero with zero variance. Likewise, if a particular condition exists in a stratum but not in the sample for that stratum, then the sample survey estimate will be zero with zero estimated sampling error. This is known as a sampling zero in the analysis of contingency tables. The frequency of this type of error in realized variance estimates increases as the number of strata increases because within-stratum sample sizes become small (e.g., $4 \leq n_h \leq 10$), as recommended by Scott and others (2005). Seminal references recommend larger sample sizes (e.g., $20 \leq n_h$; Särndal and others 1992:251, 267; de Gruijter and others 2006:118).

Stratification on remotely sensed data for both variance reduction and areal control has another undesirable consequence. FIA field plots frequently straddle stratum boundaries, which compromises the assumed independence of sampling errors among strata in the post-stratification estimator (Hahn and others 1995; Bechtold and Scott 2005). FIA treats a single plot that straddles multiple strata as if it is partially included in each stratum. The plot expansion factors are used to account for "mixed-condition" plots (Scott and others 2005). This means that the variance estimators FIA uses assume that this departure from underlying statistical assumptions of stratification does not cause substantial bias in variance estimators. Van Deusen (2005) found that these "variance estimates will often be optimistic when weighted estimators are applied to arbitrary population subsets." Scott and others (2005) reported that "FIA is evaluating the frequency of plots that straddle NFS boundaries and may switch to the ratio-of-means estimators described by Zarnoch and Bechtold (2000), if necessary."

The following example attempts to clarify the current situation. Auxiliary variables are available from different sources of remotely sensed and geospatial data. The post-stratification estimator used by FIA (Scott and others 2005) requires cross-classification of multiple sources of categorical auxiliary data (Zhang 2000). For example, consider two such sources: (1) a detailed thematic map of five forest types that uses remotely sensed data; and (2) a map of five ecoregions, each of which is associated with different components of potential natural vegetation (Bailey 2004). Cross-classification produces 25 potential strata. Further, assume there are 1000 FIA field plots (i.e., a typical FIA inventory unit), of which 100 are measured each year in a single panel. If only one of the potential sources of auxiliary data is used for post-stratification, which has five categories, then there would be an average of $(100/5) = 20$ FIA plots in each stratum. If both sources of auxiliary data are used in post-stratification, there would be an average of $[(100/5)/5] = 4$ FIA plots in each cross-classified stratum. Twenty FIA plots might be sufficient for estimating conditions in a single stratum, but five FIA plots might not be sufficient for reliably estimating conditions in a single cross-classified stratum. Because the number of strata is limited by the FIA sample size, the number of categories created through cross-classification is also limited. Inevitably, different cross-classified categories must be merged, or some thematic information must be ignored, in order to create strata with sufficient sample sizes. Furthermore, stratification reduces the information in continuous remotely sensed data into categorical values (Mandallaz 2008:89). For example, remotely sensed data can predict continuous variables that are correlated with relevant variables, such as total biomass, but some of that remotely sensed information is lost when categorized into an ordinal variable.

Recursive Restriction Estimator (RRE)

The Recursive Restriction Estimator (RRE) refers to the sequential application of the Restriction Estimator (RE), in which the RE output from one recursion is used as input to the next recursion. RRE is a special case of the Kalman filter, namely the static Kalman filter. The Kalman filter was originally developed as a multivariate time-series estimator for dynamic stochastic systems. In contrast, the static Kalman filter is not used for time-series applications. Rather, it is used here to estimate more precisely a vector of population totals at one point in time, which is considered the static "state" of the system. The Kalman filter, either in a time-series or static application, is a sequential recursive estimator in multivariate state-space.

Pollock (2003) reviews the history of recursive estimation. Gauss originally published the concept of recursive least squares during 1821 to 1826. Gauss refers to augmentation with new observations, which is essentially recursive least-squares estimation. Recursive estimation was rediscovered by Kalman (1960) and Kalman and Bucy (1961), which soon spawned the vast amount of literature on the Kalman filter. Kalman and Bucy cast recursive estimation into the state-space model with time-varying parameters, which complicates the mathematics but expands the applications.

Knottnerus (2003) provides a detailed treatise on estimation for complex sample surveys. His unifying "standard sampling model" uses Pythagorean regression, and he demonstrates the intimate connection between Pythagorean regression and the Kalman filter. Knottnerus further illuminates the relationships among regression theory, systems theory, and sampling theory. Similar connections in more applied settings are made by Czaplewski and others (1988), Czaplewski (1989, 1990, 1996, 1999, 2000, 2001, in prep.[b]), and Czaplewski and Thompson (2009).

State-Space

State-space is a mathematical model of a stochastic process. The state-space concept of the Kalman filter originated in electrical engineering for applications in astronautical navigation systems (Jazwinski 1970). It has been extended to a large number of different stochastic processes, including those that evolve over both time and space (Wikle and Cressie 1999). Harvey and Todd (1983) equate state-space to "structural" or "unobserved components" time-series models. In the context of probability sampling, the stochastic structure is defined by the probability distributions of the various random sampling and measurement errors (Särndal and others 1992:21, 515, 538, 606; Knottnerus 2003:11). The U.S. Bureau of Labor Statistics has used the state-space perspective for two decades in longitudinal panel surveys (Tiller 1992; Pfeffermann and Tiller 2006).

Kalman (1960) used the state-space paradigm to describe a dynamic stochastic system: "The fundamental concept is the notion of the state. By this is meant, intuitively, some quantitative information (a set of numbers, a function, etc.) which is the least amount of data one has to know about the past behavior of the system in order to predict its future behavior." Jazwinski (1970) defines the state-space as a family of random variables or vectors. The state-vector is described by Maybeck (1979:26, 112) as "the set of n variables, the values of which are sufficient to describe the system ... completely." State-space is "memoryless" in the sense that the state at time t fully contains all sufficient information about the past (Kalman and others 1969); it is not necessary to store past information. Otherwise, the dimensions of the estimation problem would be larger, as in most other time-series models.

In the context of the static Kalman filter, the state-space of the multivariate time-invariant system contains all relevant quantitative information, namely the population parameters, about a sampled population. In a simple design, the state-space, or the vector of population parameters, includes the primary study variables. In a complex sampling design, the state-space is enlarged to include complex auxiliary parameters at the population or domain levels. Auxiliary variables are generally inexpensive, correlated to some degree with the study variables, and, therefore, available to improve estimates of the study variable (Särndal and others 1992:220, 304, 397).

In the methods that follow, the state-space does not explicitly include individual population elements, sampling units, or inclusion probabilities, although those essential concepts in sample surveys are used for unbiased, design-based estimation of a state-vector and its covariance matrix during execution of the RE (Sugden and Smith 2002; Knottnerus 2003:357). The sequential processing of time-series information in the **dynamic** Kalman filter is replaced in the **static** Kalman filter with sequential processing of information from different components of a complex sample survey, such as different stages or phases. Because the Kalman filter is memoryless, the static Kalman filter need not store all auxiliary information as it sequentially processes individual components of a complex sample survey. This reduces the dimensions of the sequential multivariate estimator.

Recursive Estimation

Meinhold and Singpurwalla (1983) describe the recursive process as "the evolution of a series of regression functions, each having a potentially different intercept and regression coefficient; the evolution stems from a learning process involving all the data." The dynamic Kalman filter is a recursive estimator that uses two prior vector estimates: (1) a model-based estimate of the current state-vector based on the best estimate at the previous time step; and (2) a current direct measurement (e.g., design-based sample estimate of population totals) for a linear transformation of the same state-vector. The Kalman filter combines both estimates into a more precise estimate of the current state-vector using a multivariate composite estimator. Assuming unbiased measurements of the current state-vector, unbiased estimators for the state-vector at the previous time period, and unbiased model predictions of the current state based on the previous state, the Kalman filter removes all information available from the current time and all previous time steps. Given these assumptions, the remaining random residual estimation errors are "white noise" and are independent of all previous estimation errors (Knottnerus 2003:311). The recursion process is repeated at the next time step as the state of the stochastic system changes and new measurements of the system become available. There is no need to process any past information beyond the previous time step because the Kalman filter estimate contains all previous information. In other words, the Kalman filter is memoryless in that it propagates all sufficient statistics for the problem conditional on the realized independent observations.

The Kalman filter is seldom applied in sample surveys. Contributions by Knottnerus (2003), Knottnerus and van Duin (2006), Sõstra (2007), and Sõstra and Traat (2009) are among the few exceptions. More often, the application of the Kalman filter is in the context of time-series estimation with longitudinal panel surveys (e.g., Harvey 1978; Tam 1987; Tiller 1992; Jones 1993; Frees 2004; Oud 2004; de Gruijter and others 2006; Pfeffermann and Tiller 2006). These authors use models at the level of individual population elements or sampling units. However, state-space perspective (e.g., Rosenbrock and MacFarlane 1972) is equally valid. For example, Czaplewski and Thompson (2009) estimate the state of a large forest with the state-vector defined as the number of trees in several different condition categories within the entire sampled population. Individual sampling units in a probability survey are used in the measurement vector as estimates of these population parameters, but otherwise, they do not explicitly appear in the time-series model within the Kalman filter.

The Basic Idea

The Merriam-Webster Dictionary defines a recursion process as the "succession of elements (as numbers or functions) by operation on one or more preceding elements according to a rule or formula involving a finite number of steps." In the context of RRE, the recursion starts with exactly two elements, called objects here, of a complex survey design. For example, consider FIA research on the Nevada Photo-based Inventory Pilot Study (Frescino and others 2009a), in which a sample of high-resolution aerial photography is added to the existing design of FIA Phase 2 field samples and the wall-to-wall, full-coverage census of Landsat satellite pixels.

- The Phase 1 Object is a relatively large probability sample of PSUs. Each PSU is measured with two protocols: (1) remotely sensed vector measurements from a spaceborne, earth-observing satellite sensor and (2) vector measurements based on photo-interpretation of a sample of high-resolution aerial photography. The spaceborne sensor protocol is inexpensive, but it contains considerable measurement error relative to photo-interpretation. However, measurements from the spaceborne sensor are correlated to some degree with more accurate photo-interpreted measurements. Standard, design-based methods produce sample survey estimates for the vector of population totals and its covariance matrix. This is used as the state vector in the Kalman filter, which is discussed in more detail below. The state-vector includes a partition for the variables measured with the spaceborne sensor protocol. The remaining partition contains the variables measured with the photo-interpretation protocol. The covariance matrix includes a diagonal partition for the covariances among variables measured with the spaceborne protocol and another diagonal partition for variables measured with photo-interpretation. The remaining off-diagonal partition contains the estimated sample cross-covariances among the population estimates for the spaceborne and photo-interpreted variables.

- The "Census Object" is based on 30- by 30-m pixels, each of which is measured with the same spaceborne sensor protocol as in Phase 1. The photo-interpretation protocol in Phase 1 is **not** used in the census. This is a true census because the set of remotely sensed pixels fully covers the entire sampled population. Enumeration of the spaceborne measurements for each and every pixel in the sampled population produces a vector constant of population totals for variables measured with the spaceborne protocol. The covariance matrix for the population totals exactly equals **zero** because there are no sampling errors. This vector constant contains the auxiliary information, and it is called the measurement vector in the Kalman filter.

- The RE combines the measurement vector from the Census Object with the state-vector from the Phase 1 Object. Depending on the magnitude of the off-diagonal cross-covariances among the spaceborne and photo-interpreted variables from the Phase 1 sample, the RE population estimate for the photo-interpreted variables will be more precise than the corresponding design-based estimates from the Phase 1 Object alone. This is a design-based calibration estimator, which is discussed in the section "Relationship to an Optimal Sample Survey Estimator."

- The RE vector estimate contains a partition that corresponds to the spaceborne variables. That partition will exactly equal the measurement vector from the remotely sensed census. Its corresponding partition in the RE covariance matrix is exactly **zero**. The remotely sensed census statistics essentially constrain the RE estimator. (See Knottnerus 2003:Chapter 12 on the General Restriction Estimator) The RE estimate for the photo-interpreted variables contains all information contributed by the correlation with the spaceborne variables. Therefore, the partitions for the spaceborne variables may be deleted from further consideration. The remaining partition of improved population estimates for the photo-interpreted variables is redefined as the measurement vector in the second recursive process, which follows.

So ends the first recursion. Now, an example of the second recursive process, in which the RE results from the first recursion are combined with another independent design object:

- The Phase 2 Object is a probability sample of PSUs with a relatively small sample size. Each Phase 2 PSU is measured with two protocols: (1) the same photo-interpretation of high-resolution aerial photography used in Phase 1 (above) and (2) expensive, on-the-ground vector measurements made by FIA field crews. Measurements from the photo interpretation are reasonably well correlated with certain field measurements. FIA uses these field measurements as the minimum acceptable protocol for data quality of its statistical tables. As with the Phase 1 object above, standard design-based methods produce a sample survey estimate for the vector of population totals and its covariance matrix from Phase 2. This is used as the new definition of the state-vector during this second recursion. The off-diagonal partition of its covariance matrix contains the estimated sample cross-covariances among the population estimates for photo-interpreted and FIA field variables from the small Phase 2 sample.

- The Composite Object is identical to the partition of RRE vector estimate from the first recursion that corresponds to the photo-interpreted variables. Its covariance matrix is the corresponding partition from the outcome of the first recursion. Because the Composite Object fully incorporates all relevant information from the census in the first recursion, the size of this covariance matrix is smaller than the corresponding partition in the design-based Phase 1 estimate. The Composite vector estimate is redefined as the measurement vector for this second recursion. It does not contain any elements for variables measured with the FIA field protocol in Phase 2.

- The RE combines the measurement vector from the Composite Object with the state-vector from the Phase 2 Object. Because the off-diagonal cross-covariances among the photo-interpreted and field variables from the Phase 2 sample are non-zero, RRE population estimates for the FIA field variables will be more precise than the corresponding design-based estimates from the Phase 2 Object alone. The RRE partition that corresponds to the photo-interpreted variables is less precise in the first recursion relative to the outcome of the second recursion because the latter gains strength from the Phase 2 sample. The remaining partition that corresponds to the FIA field variables contains all information available from the Census, Phase 1, and Phase 2 objects. Unless needed for other purposes, the partition for the photo-interpreted variables may be discarded because all relevant information has been filtered out and incorporated into RRE for the partitions corresponding to the FIA field variables.

Therefore, the design-consistent Empirical Best Linear Unbiased Estimator (EBLUE) of population estimates for the FIA field variables is achieved through two recursive steps. The census of remotely sensed spaceborne measurements improves the population estimates for the photo-interpreted variables in the first recursion. The second recursion uses these improved estimates results to further improve population estimates for the FIA field variables. The recursive method separates the complexity of the sampling design into simpler objects that are sequentially combined with RRE. As briefly discussed in the following section "Relationship to an Optimal Sample Survey Estimator," RRE is also a multivariate recursive calibration estimator in state-space.

Now, the focus shifts to the details of the composite estimator. The univariate composite estimator is a conditionally unbiased statistical method that combines a weighted sum of two separate, previously calculated statistical estimates into a single, more efficient estimate (e.g., Cochran 1977:346, 355). The more precise of the two previously calculated estimates is weighted more heavily. The scalar weights are computed to produce an approximately minimum variance estimator. The less familiar Restriction Estimator (RE) combines two previously calculated vector estimates, which need not have equal dimensions, with a matrix of optimal weights computed with the estimated covariance matrix for each vector estimate. In the context of multilevel sampling, the composite estimator is used to combine estimates sequentially from the various sampling phases or stages. Sampling units are segregated into independent samples for each phase or stage (Magnussen 2003, including references to Card 1982; Cochran 1977; Tenenbein 1972), and the multivariate composite estimator is used to combine pairs of stages, phases, censuses, or prior composite estimates into a more efficient estimate of the variables of interest. But first, the univariate composite estimator will be used as an introduction to the more complex multivariate composite estimator.

The Univariate Composite Estimator

The univariate composite estimator is well known in sample survey applications, such as sampling over time, small-area estimation, and adaptive sampling (e.g., Särndal and others 1992:371; Schreuder and others 1993:321; Binder and Hidiroglou 1988:190; Valliant and others 2000:400; De Gruijter and others 2006:226; Gregoire and Valentine 2007:388). Czaplewski and Thompson (2009) provide a tutorial description of the univariate Kalman filter in the context of time-series data that assists intuitive understanding. The univariate composite estimator is presented here with notation that is a slight modification of Särndal and others (1992:371).

Assume t_X and t_Z are two unbiased estimators of the same univariate population total t for the sampled population (e.g., total woody biomass or total forest area). As an example, consider two independent estimates from simple random sample 1 ($s = 1$) and an independent simple random sample 2 ($s = 2$):

$$\bar{y}_X = \sum_{i \in (s=1)} \frac{y_i}{n_X} \qquad\qquad \bar{y}_Z = \sum_{i \in (s=2)} \frac{y_i}{n_Z}$$

$$\hat{t}_X = A\bar{y}_X \qquad\qquad\qquad \hat{t}_Z = A\bar{y}_Z \qquad\qquad (1)$$

$$\hat{V}(\hat{t}_X) = A^2 \left(\frac{1}{n_X - 1}\right) \sum_{i \in (s=1)} \frac{(y_i - \bar{y}_X)^2}{n_X} \quad\Bigg|\quad \hat{V}(\hat{t}_Z) = A^2 \left(\frac{1}{n_Z - 1}\right) \sum_{i \in (s=2)} \frac{(y_i - \bar{y}_Z)^2}{n_Z}$$

Let the linear combination of the two estimators be the weighted (i.e., constant "k," $0<k<1$) sum of the two prior estimates. From Särndal and others (1992:Eq. 9.9.3), the composite estimator is defined as t_{RE} is:

$$\hat{t}_{RE} = k\,\hat{t}_X + (1-k)\,\hat{t}_Z$$

$$= \hat{t}_Z + k\left(\hat{t}_X - \hat{t}_Z\right).$$

$$= \begin{bmatrix} k \ \vert \ 1-k \end{bmatrix} \begin{bmatrix} \hat{t}_X \\ \hat{t}_Z \end{bmatrix}$$

(2)

The variance estimator for the composite estimate (Särndal and others 1992:Eq. 9.9.4) in Eq. 2 is:

$$\hat{V}\left(\hat{t}_{RE}\right) = k^2\hat{V}\left(\hat{t}_X\right) + (1-k)^2\,\hat{V}\left(\hat{t}_Z\right) + 2k\,(1-k)\,\hat{C}\left(\hat{t}_X,\hat{t}_Z\right)$$

$$= \hat{V}\left(\hat{t}_Z\right) - k\left[\hat{V}\left(\hat{t}_Z\right) + \hat{C}\left(\hat{t}_X,\hat{t}_Z\right)\right]$$

$$= \begin{bmatrix} k \ \vert \ 1-k \end{bmatrix} \begin{bmatrix} \hat{V}\left(\hat{t}_X\right) & \vert & \hat{C}\left(\hat{t}_Z,\hat{t}_X\right) \\ \hline \hat{C}\left(\hat{t}_X,\hat{t}_Z\right) & \vert & \hat{V}\left(\hat{t}_Z\right) \end{bmatrix} \begin{bmatrix} k \\ 1-k \end{bmatrix}$$

(3)

where C is the scalar cross-covariance among the random errors from the two estimators. Because the two samples are independent in this example, $C = 0$, and:

$$\hat{V}\left(\hat{t}_{RE}\right) = k^2 V\left(\hat{t}_X\right) + (1-k)^2\,\hat{V}\left(\hat{t}_Z\right)$$

$$= \begin{bmatrix} k \ \vert \ 1-k \end{bmatrix} \begin{bmatrix} \hat{V}\left(\hat{t}_X\right) & \vert & 0 \\ \hline 0 & \vert & \hat{V}\left(\hat{t}_Z\right) \end{bmatrix} \begin{bmatrix} k \\ 1-k \end{bmatrix}$$

The unbiased minimum variance univariate composite estimator is achieved with the following k weighting constant (Bierman 1977):

$$k = \frac{V\left(\hat{t}_Z\right) + C\left(\hat{t}_X,\hat{t}_Z\right)}{V\left(\hat{t}_X\right) + V\left(\hat{t}_Z\right) + 2C\left(\hat{t}_X,\hat{t}_Z\right)}$$

$$= \left(V\left(\hat{t}_Z\right) + C\left(\hat{t}_X,\hat{t}_Z\right)\right)\left(\left\{V\left(\hat{t}_X\right) + V\left(\hat{t}_Z\right) + 2C\left(\hat{t}_X,\hat{t}_Z\right)\right\}^{-1}\right)$$

(4)

If the two estimates of t_X and t_Z are independent, then $C = 0$ and Eq. 4 simplifies to:

$$k = \frac{V\left(\hat{t}_Z\right)}{V\left(\hat{t}_X\right) + V\left(\hat{t}_Z\right)}$$

(5)

(See Cochran (1977:346), Maybeck (1979:12-14), and De Gruijter and others (2006:226).) Relatively large deviations from the optimal scalar weight (k) in Eq. 5 do not substantially degrade the efficiency of the composite estimator (Schaible 1978). Therefore, a sub-optimal weight computed from sample estimates of the variances is expected to perform well in most univariate cases:

$$k = \frac{\hat{V}\left(\hat{t}_z\right)}{\hat{V}\left(\hat{t}_x\right) + \hat{V}\left(\hat{t}_z\right)} \tag{6}$$

The theoretical estimator in Eq. 5 is the Best Linear Unbiased Estimator (BLUE). The applied estimator in Eq. 6 is a sub-optimal Empirical Best Linear Unbiased Estimator (EBLUE) (Militino and others 2008). Because both estimators t_x and t_z are design-consistent, their weighted sum is also design-consistent.

As seen from Eq. 6, the univariate composite estimator weights each independent estimate inversely proportional to its relative variances. The most precise estimate (least variance) receives the greatest weight, although the less precise estimate does receive a positive weight.

If the first estimator is twice as precise as the second (i.e., $V(\hat{t}_x) = V(\hat{t}_z)/2$) and each estimator is mutually independent, then the first estimate will be weighted more heavily (Eq. 6) by a factor of $k = (2/3)$, while the second estimate, which is less precise, will receive the lesser weight of $(1 - k) = (1/3)$:

$$
\begin{aligned}
\hat{V}\left(\hat{t}_{\mathrm{MvCE}}\right) &= \left(\frac{2}{3}\right)^2 \hat{V}\left(\hat{t}_x\right) + \left(1 - \frac{2}{3}\right)^2 \left[\hat{V}\left(\hat{t}_z\right)\right] + 2\left[\left(\frac{2}{3}\right)\left(1 - \frac{2}{3}\right)\right]0 \\
&= \left(\frac{4}{9}\right)\hat{V}\left(\hat{t}_x\right) + \left(\frac{1}{9}\right)\left[2\,\hat{V}\left(\hat{t}_x\right)\right] \\
&= \left(\frac{2}{3}\right)\hat{V}\left(\hat{t}_x\right) \\
&= \left(\frac{1}{3}\right)\hat{V}\left(\hat{t}_z\right)
\end{aligned}
\tag{7}
$$

The estimated variance for the resulting composite estimate (Eqs. 3 and 6) would be less than the variance of either independent estimate by itself (Eq. 7).

As another example, if both estimators are independent and equally precise (i.e., $V(\hat{t}_x) = V(\hat{t}_z)$), then each estimate receives an equal weight of $k = 0.5$. The composite estimate would have an estimated variance that is one-half of either independent estimate by itself (Eqs. 3 and 6).

The Restriction Estimator (RE) Object

The Restriction Estimator (RE) is a generalization of the univariate estimator in Eqs. 2 to 6. The RE is also a special case of the static Kalman filter (Maybeck 1979:114; Gregoire and Walters 1988; Czaplewski 2000). RE is a "static linear model" in the terminology of Maybeck (1977:114). It is a special case of the Kalman filter in Eqs. 9 through 12. Like the Kalman filter, RRE is: (1) a recursive formulation of the Bayes estimator (e.g., Jazwinski 1970:145; Maybeck 1979:205), (2) the minimum mean square error predictor (e.g., Jazwinski 1970:149; Maybeck 1977:232), and (3) a maximum likelihood estimator when joint densities are all Gaussian (e.g., Jazwinski 1970:207; Maybeck 1977:234). Duncan and Horn (1972), Diderrich (1985), Gregoire and Walters (1988), and Piepho and Ogutu (2007) demonstrate the close relationship between the Kalman filter and Theil and Goldberger's (1961) mixed estimator. As a special case of the Kalman filter, RRE is an iterative least-squares approach to estimation (Jazwinski 1970:276; Bierman 1977). Based on a matrix inversion lemma employed by earlier authors, Diderrich (1985) and Czaplewski (2001) illustrate the algebraic equivalency between the generalized least squares estimator and the composite estimator in this context (Householder 1964; Maybeck 1979:213). Knottnerus (2003:315, 326) uses the perspective of Pythagorean regression and the matrix inversion lemma to make the strong connection between the Kalman filter and estimators for complex sample surveys. This includes constraints on the estimands. De Gruijter and others (2006) give a more contemporaneous exposition on the Kalman filter in the context of sampling in time and space for monitoring of natural resources. Because the sample survey applications considered here are temporally static, the terms "RRE" and "static Kalman filter" are used synonymously.

The following illustration uses the seminal work by Maybeck (1979) on the Kalman filter as an introduction to RE. Blending the notation of Maybeck (1979:246-247) with that of Särndal and others (1992:Appendix A), the stochastic model for two multivariate design-based sample matrix estimates as:

$$\hat{\mathbf{t}}_{XY(1)} = \mathbf{t}_{X(0)} + \boldsymbol{\varepsilon}_W \qquad\qquad \hat{\mathbf{t}}_{Z(1)} = \mathbf{H}\,\mathbf{t}_{XY(1)} + \boldsymbol{\varepsilon}_V$$

$$\mathrm{E}[\boldsymbol{\varepsilon}_W] = \mathbf{0} \qquad\qquad \mathrm{E}[\boldsymbol{\varepsilon}_V] = \mathbf{0}$$

$$\mathrm{E}[\boldsymbol{\varepsilon}_W\boldsymbol{\varepsilon}_W'] = \mathbf{V}(\hat{\mathbf{t}}_{XY(1)}) = \mathbf{P}(1) = \mathbf{Q}(1) \quad \mathrm{E}[\boldsymbol{\varepsilon}_V\boldsymbol{\varepsilon}_V'] = \mathbf{V}(\hat{\mathbf{t}}_{Z(1)}) = \mathbf{R}(1) \qquad (8)$$

$$\mathrm{E}[\boldsymbol{\varepsilon}_W\boldsymbol{\varepsilon}_V'] = \mathbf{C}(\hat{\mathbf{t}}_{XY(1)}, \hat{\mathbf{t}}_{Z(1)}) = \mathbf{C}(1)$$

where $\mathbf{t}_{XY(1)}$ is the $(q_X + q_Y)$-by-1 state-vector of population totals for the q_X auxiliary variables (X) and q_Y study variables (Y), and $\mathbf{t}_{Z(1)}$ is the q_Z-by-1 measurement vector of population totals from a linear transformation (matrix constant $\mathbf{H}$) of population parameters for all measurement protocols for variables X and Y. The state-vector $\mathbf{t}_{XY(1)}$ and measurement vector $\mathbf{t}_{Z(1)}$ (Eq. 8) may have different dimensions (i.e., $q_{XY} \neq q_Z$) or the same dimensions (i.e., $q_{XY} = q_Z$). The RE (below) will combine vector estimates of $\mathbf{t}_{XY(1)}$ and $\mathbf{t}_{Z(1)}$ into a more precise, minimum-variance estimate of the full $(q_X + q_Y)$-by-1 state-vector . This structure follows that used by Knottnerus (2003:335) for the regression estimator as a partitioned restriction estimator.

The notation in Eq. 8 follows: $\boldsymbol{\varepsilon}_W$ is the q_{XY}-by-1 vector of random estimation errors with q_{XY}-by-q_{XY} covariance matrix ; $\mathbf{H}$ is the q_Z-by-q_{XY} matrix of known constants that identify the linear transformation of $\mathbf{t}_{XY(1)}$ that produces $\mathbf{t}_{Z(1)}$; $\boldsymbol{\varepsilon}_Z$ is the q_Z-by-1 vector of random estimation errors for the sample estimate of the auxiliary variables with q_Z-by-q_Z covariance matrix ; and is q_{XY}-by-q_Z cross-covariance matrix between $\boldsymbol{\varepsilon}_W$ and $\boldsymbol{\varepsilon}_Z$.

Translation of remaining notation used by Maybeck (1979:246-247) in Eq. 8 follows: the time-series transition matrices $\boldsymbol{\Phi} = \mathbf{G} = \mathbf{I}$ (i.e., q_{XY}-by-q_{XY} identity matrix); the q_{XY}-by-q_{XY} covariance matrices $\mathbf{P}(0) = \mathbf{0}$ (i.e., the zero matrix) and $[\mathbf{P}(1) = \boldsymbol{\Phi}\mathbf{P}(0)\boldsymbol{\Phi}' + \mathbf{G}\mathbf{Q}(1)\mathbf{G}' = \mathbf{Q}(1)]$; and the input control vector $\mathbf{B}\times\mathbf{u} = \mathbf{0}$ (i.e., q_{XY}-by-1 zero vector). Given the abbreviated stochastic model in Eq. 8, the minimum variance composite estimator follows equations 5-115 through 5-117 for the Kalman filter in Maybeck (1979:247). Notation starts with that of Maybeck (1979) and is followed with equivalent notation that is a facsimile of Särndal and others (1992).

The q_{XY}-by-q_Z gain matrix $\mathbf{K}$, which is a matrix extension of the univariate weighting constant k in Eq. 4 (Maybeck 1979:Eq. 5-115), is:

$$\mathbf{K} = [\mathbf{P}(1)\mathbf{H}' + \mathbf{C}(1)]\left([\mathbf{H}\mathbf{P}(1)\mathbf{H}' + \mathbf{R}(1) + \mathbf{H}\mathbf{C}(1) + \mathbf{C}'(1)\mathbf{H}']^{-1}\right)$$

$$= \begin{bmatrix} \hat{\mathbf{V}}_X(\hat{\mathbf{t}}_{XY})\mathbf{H}' \\ + \hat{\mathbf{C}}(\hat{\mathbf{t}}_{XY}, \hat{\mathbf{t}}_Z') \end{bmatrix} \left(\begin{bmatrix} \mathbf{H}\,\hat{\mathbf{V}}(\hat{\mathbf{t}}_{XY})\mathbf{H}' + \hat{\mathbf{V}}(\hat{\mathbf{t}}_Z) \\ + \mathbf{H}\,\hat{\mathbf{C}}(\hat{\mathbf{t}}_{XY}, \hat{\mathbf{t}}_Z) + \hat{\mathbf{C}}(\hat{\mathbf{t}}_{XY}, \hat{\mathbf{t}}_Z)'\mathbf{H}' \end{bmatrix}^{-1} \right) \qquad (9)$$

Use of estimated covariances in Eq. 9 does not affect the asymptotic variance (Knottnerus 2003:336).

Using the gain matrix $\mathbf{K}$ in Eq. 9, the RE (Maybeck 1979:Eq. 5-116) is:

$$\hat{\mathbf{t}}_{RE} = \hat{\mathbf{t}}_{XY} + \mathbf{K}\left(\hat{\mathbf{t}}_Z - \mathbf{H}\,\hat{\mathbf{t}}_{XY}\right)$$

$$= \begin{bmatrix} \hat{\mathbf{t}}_X \\ \hat{\mathbf{t}}_Y \end{bmatrix} + \mathbf{K}\left(\hat{\mathbf{t}}_Z - \mathbf{H}\begin{bmatrix} \hat{\mathbf{t}}_X \\ \hat{\mathbf{t}}_Y \end{bmatrix}\right)' \tag{10}$$

The gain matrix $\mathbf{K}$ is the matrix of approximately optimal weights on the residual difference between the Phase 1 and Phase 2 population estimates for the auxiliary variables. See Knottnerus (2003:335-357) for a comparison of the Kalman filter with the minimum variance regression estimator.

Eq. 10 is the multivariate extension of the univariate composite estimator in Eq. 2. The corresponding covariance matrix (Maybeck 1979:Eq. 5-117) is:

$$\mathbf{V}\left(\hat{\mathbf{t}}_{RE}\right) = \mathbf{P}(1) - \mathbf{K}\left[\mathbf{H}\mathbf{P}(1) + \mathbf{C}(1)\right]$$

$$= \hat{\mathbf{V}}\left(\hat{\mathbf{t}}_{XY}\right) - \mathbf{K}\left[\mathbf{H}\,\hat{\mathbf{V}}\left(\hat{\mathbf{t}}_{XY}\right) + \hat{\mathbf{C}}\left(\hat{\mathbf{t}}_{XY},\hat{\mathbf{t}}_Z\right)\right] \tag{11}$$

which is the multivariate extension of the univariate composite estimator in Eq. 3. (The covariance matrix in Eq. 11 is expressed in a more familiar form in the next section.)

Special cases of the RE are algebraically identical to optimal sample survey estimators, as shown in the next section for two-phase sampling. More general expressions of the RE may be applied to more complex designs, such as two-stage sampling. Examples include "Single-Phase Sampling for Continuous Variables with Cluster Plots". The sequential application of the RRE addresses even more complex designs. One example is "Two-Phase Sampling for Continuous Variables with Cluster Plots", which uses photo-interpretation and sub-sampling for field measurements for a small sample of cluster plots, photo-interpretation (without field measurements) for a large independent sample of cluster plots, and a census of pixels from a spaceborne sensor. Furthermore, because RRE is a special case of the Kalman filter, the methods that follow are compatible with time-series estimators for longitudinal surveys.

Relationship to an Optimal Sample Survey Estimator

While the structure of the covariance matrix estimator in Eq. 11 is familiar in the Kalman filtering literature, it is much less familiar in the sample survey literature. The major exception is Knottnerus (2003). He simplifies estimators for complex sample survey designs through the Pythagorean regression form of Generalized Least Squares regression. Chapter 2.8 in Knottnerus' book demonstrates that Pythagorean regression is algebraically equivalent to the static Kalman filter.

A special case of the RE Eq. 11 is algebraically identical to the minimum variance Generalized Least Squares regression estimator in the sample survey literature. Let the vector $\mathbf{t}_Z$ be estimated from a Phase 1 sample or census. Let vector $\mathbf{t}_{XY}$ be estimated from an independent Phase 2 sample. Assume the first q_X-by-1 partition of the state vector $\mathbf{t}_{XY}$ represents the population totals for the auxiliary variables ($\mathbf{t}_X$) and the remaining q_Y-by-1 partition represents the population totals for the study variables ($\mathbf{t}_Y$). Furthermore, Let the vectors $\mathbf{t}_Z$ and $\mathbf{t}_X$ represent the same remotely sensed auxiliary variables (i.e., $\mathbf{t}_Z = \mathbf{t}_X$), the only difference being that $\mathbf{t}_Z$ is estimated from the Phase 1 sample and $\mathbf{t}_X$ is estimated from the Phase 2 sample; therefore, $\mathbf{H} = [\mathbf{I} \mid \mathbf{0}]$ in Eqs. 9 through 11. Furthermore, $\mathbf{C}(1) = \mathbf{0}$ in Eqs. 9

through 11 because the Phase 1 and Phase 2 samples are independent. Thus, Eqs. 9 through 11 simplify to:

$$\hat{\mathbf{t}}_{RE} = \hat{\mathbf{t}}_{XY} + \mathbf{K}\left[\hat{\mathbf{t}}_{Z} - \mathbf{H}\,\hat{\mathbf{t}}_{XY}\right]$$

$$\hat{\mathbf{V}}\left(\hat{\mathbf{t}}_{RE}\right) = \hat{\mathbf{V}}\left(\hat{\mathbf{t}}_{XY}\right) - \mathbf{K}\,\mathbf{H}\left[\hat{\mathbf{V}}\left(\hat{\mathbf{t}}_{XY}\right)\right] \quad (12)$$

$$= \left(\mathbf{I} - \mathbf{KH}\right)\left[\hat{\mathbf{V}}\left(\hat{\mathbf{t}}_{XY}\right)\right]\left(\mathbf{I} - \mathbf{KH}\right)'$$

where

$$\hat{\mathbf{V}}\left(\hat{\mathbf{t}}_{XY}\right) = \left[\begin{array}{c|c} \hat{\mathbf{V}}\left(\hat{\mathbf{t}}_{X}\right) & \hat{\mathbf{C}}\left(\hat{\mathbf{t}}_{X},\hat{\mathbf{t}}_{Y}\right) \\ \hline \hat{\mathbf{C}}\left(\hat{\mathbf{t}}_{X},\hat{\mathbf{t}}_{Y}\right) & \hat{\mathbf{V}}\left(\hat{\mathbf{t}}_{Y}\right) \end{array}\right] \quad (13)$$

After combining Eqs. 9 and 13, the q_{XY}-by-q_Z gain matrix of optimal weights equals:

$$\mathbf{K} = \left[\begin{array}{c|c} \hat{\mathbf{V}}\left(\hat{\mathbf{t}}_{X}\right) & \hat{\mathbf{C}}\left(\hat{\mathbf{t}}_{X},\hat{\mathbf{t}}_{Y}\right) \\ \hline \hat{\mathbf{C}}\left(\hat{\mathbf{t}}_{X},\hat{\mathbf{t}}_{Y}\right) & \hat{\mathbf{V}}\left(\hat{\mathbf{t}}_{Y}\right) \end{array}\right]\left[\begin{array}{c} \mathbf{I} \\ \mathbf{0} \end{array}\right]\left(\left[\begin{array}{cc} \mathbf{I} & \mathbf{0} \end{array}\right]\hat{\mathbf{V}}\left(\hat{\mathbf{t}}_{XY}\right)\left[\begin{array}{c} \mathbf{I} \\ \mathbf{0} \end{array}\right] + \hat{\mathbf{V}}\left(\hat{\mathbf{t}}_{Z}\right)\right]^{-1}\right)$$

$$= \left[\begin{array}{c} \hat{\mathbf{V}}\left(\hat{\mathbf{t}}_{X}\right) \\ \hline \hat{\mathbf{C}}\left(\hat{\mathbf{t}}_{Y},\hat{\mathbf{t}}_{X}\right) \end{array}\right]\left(\left[\hat{\mathbf{V}}\left(\hat{\mathbf{t}}_{X}\right) + \hat{\mathbf{V}}\left(\hat{\mathbf{t}}_{Z}\right)\right]^{-1}\right) \quad (14)$$

$$= \left[\begin{array}{c} \hat{\mathbf{V}}\left(\hat{\mathbf{t}}_{X}\right)\left(\left[\hat{\mathbf{V}}\left(\hat{\mathbf{t}}_{X}\right) + \hat{\mathbf{V}}\left(\hat{\mathbf{t}}_{Z}\right)\right]^{-1}\right)' \\ \hline \hat{\mathbf{C}}\left(\hat{\mathbf{t}}_{Y},\hat{\mathbf{t}}_{X}\right)\left(\left[\hat{\mathbf{V}}\left(\hat{\mathbf{t}}_{X}\right) + \hat{\mathbf{V}}\left(\hat{\mathbf{t}}_{Z}\right)\right]^{-1}\right) \end{array}\right]$$

The equations for the matrix $\mathbf{K}$ in Eq. 14 and the covariance matrix estimator in Eq. 12 may be combined as follows:

$$\hat{\mathbf{t}}_{RE} = \hat{\mathbf{t}}_{XY} + \left[\begin{array}{c} \hat{\mathbf{V}}\left(\hat{\mathbf{t}}_{X}\right)\left(\left[\hat{\mathbf{V}}\left(\hat{\mathbf{t}}_{X}\right) + \hat{\mathbf{V}}\left(\hat{\mathbf{t}}_{Z}\right)\right]^{-1}\right)' \\ \hline \hat{\mathbf{C}}\left(\hat{\mathbf{t}}_{Y},\hat{\mathbf{t}}_{X}\right)\left(\left[\hat{\mathbf{V}}\left(\hat{\mathbf{t}}_{X}\right) + \hat{\mathbf{V}}\left(\hat{\mathbf{t}}_{Z}\right)\right]^{-1}\right)' \end{array}\right]\left[\hat{\mathbf{t}}_{Z} - \left[\begin{array}{cc} \mathbf{I} & \mathbf{0} \end{array}\right]\hat{\mathbf{t}}_{XY}\right] \quad (15)$$

Because the objective is to improve estimates of the study variables with the auxiliary variables, our ultimate interest is limited to the partition of the vector estimate in Eq. 15 that corresponds to the study variables ($\mathbf{t}_Y$).

$$\hat{\mathbf{t}}_{RE_{\,Y}} = \begin{bmatrix} \mathbf{0} & \mathbf{I} \end{bmatrix} \hat{\mathbf{t}}_{RE}$$

$$= \begin{bmatrix} \mathbf{0} & \mathbf{I} \end{bmatrix} \begin{bmatrix} \hat{\mathbf{t}}_X \\ \hat{\mathbf{t}}_Y \end{bmatrix} + \begin{bmatrix} \mathbf{0} & \mathbf{I} \end{bmatrix} \begin{bmatrix} \hat{\mathbf{V}}\,\hat{\mathbf{t}}_X \left(\begin{bmatrix} \hat{\mathbf{V}}\,\hat{\mathbf{t}}_X & +\hat{\mathbf{V}}\,\hat{\mathbf{t}}_Z \end{bmatrix}^{-1} \right)' \\ \overline{} \\ \hat{\mathbf{C}}\,\hat{\mathbf{t}}_Y,\hat{\mathbf{t}}_X \left(\begin{bmatrix} \hat{\mathbf{V}}\,\hat{\mathbf{t}}_X & +\hat{\mathbf{V}}\,\hat{\mathbf{t}}_Z \end{bmatrix}^{-1} \right)' \end{bmatrix} \begin{bmatrix} \hat{\mathbf{t}}_Z - \hat{\mathbf{t}}_X \end{bmatrix} \qquad (16)$$

$$= \hat{\mathbf{t}}_Y + \begin{bmatrix} \hat{\mathbf{C}}\,\hat{\mathbf{t}}_Y,\hat{\mathbf{t}}_X \left(\begin{bmatrix} \hat{\mathbf{V}}\,\hat{\mathbf{t}}_X & +\hat{\mathbf{V}}\,\hat{\mathbf{t}}_Z \end{bmatrix}^{-1} \right)' \end{bmatrix} \begin{bmatrix} \hat{\mathbf{t}}_Z - \hat{\mathbf{t}}_X \end{bmatrix}$$

Like Eq. 16, the equations for the weighting matrix $\mathbf{K}$ and the covariance matrix estimator $\hat{\mathbf{V}}\!\left(\hat{\mathbf{t}}_{MvCE}\right)$ in Eq. 12 may be combined.

$$\hat{\mathbf{V}}\left(\hat{\mathbf{t}}_{RE}\right) = \hat{\mathbf{V}}\left(\hat{\mathbf{t}}_{XY}\right) - \begin{bmatrix} \hat{\mathbf{V}}\left(\hat{\mathbf{t}}_X\right)\left(\left[\hat{\mathbf{V}}\left(\hat{\mathbf{t}}_X\right)+\hat{\mathbf{V}}\left(\hat{\mathbf{t}}_Z\right)\right]^{-1}\right)' \\ \overline{} \\ \hat{\mathbf{C}}\left(\hat{\mathbf{t}}_Y,\hat{\mathbf{t}}_X\right)\left(\left[\hat{\mathbf{V}}\left(\hat{\mathbf{t}}_X\right)+\hat{\mathbf{V}}\left(\hat{\mathbf{t}}_Z\right)\right]^{-1}\right)' \end{bmatrix} \begin{bmatrix} \mathbf{I} & \mathbf{0} \end{bmatrix} \begin{bmatrix} \hat{\mathbf{V}}\left(\hat{\mathbf{t}}_X\right) & \vline & \hat{\mathbf{C}}\left(\hat{\mathbf{t}}_X,\hat{\mathbf{t}}_Y\right) \\ \overline{} & & \overline{} \\ \hat{\mathbf{C}}\left(\hat{\mathbf{t}}_X,\hat{\mathbf{t}}_Y\right)' & \vline & \hat{\mathbf{V}}\left(\hat{\mathbf{t}}_Y\right) \end{bmatrix}$$

$$= \begin{bmatrix} \hat{\mathbf{V}}\left(\hat{\mathbf{t}}_X\right) & \vline & \hat{\mathbf{C}}\left(\hat{\mathbf{t}}_X,\hat{\mathbf{t}}_Y\right) \\ \overline{} & & \overline{} \\ \hat{\mathbf{C}}\left(\hat{\mathbf{t}}_X,\hat{\mathbf{t}}_Y\right)' & \vline & \hat{\mathbf{V}}\left(\hat{\mathbf{t}}_Y\right) \end{bmatrix} - \begin{bmatrix} \hat{\mathbf{V}}\left(\hat{\mathbf{t}}_X\right)\left(\left[\hat{\mathbf{V}}\left(\hat{\mathbf{t}}_X\right)+\hat{\mathbf{V}}\left(\hat{\mathbf{t}}_Z\right)\right]^{-1}\right)' \\ \overline{} \\ \hat{\mathbf{C}}\left(\hat{\mathbf{t}}_Y,\hat{\mathbf{t}}_X\right)\left(\left[\hat{\mathbf{V}}\left(\hat{\mathbf{t}}_X\right)+\hat{\mathbf{V}}\left(\hat{\mathbf{t}}_Z\right)\right]^{-1}\right)' \end{bmatrix} \begin{bmatrix} \hat{\mathbf{V}}\left(\hat{\mathbf{t}}_X\right) & \vline & \hat{\mathbf{C}}\left(\hat{\mathbf{t}}_X,\hat{\mathbf{t}}_Y\right) \end{bmatrix}$$

$$(17)$$

$$= \begin{bmatrix} \begin{array}{c} \hat{\mathbf{V}}\left(\hat{\mathbf{t}}_X\right) \\[2mm] -\hat{\mathbf{V}}\left(\hat{\mathbf{t}}_X\right)\left(\left[\begin{array}{c}\hat{\mathbf{V}}\left(\hat{\mathbf{t}}_X\right) \\ +\hat{\mathbf{V}}\left(\hat{\mathbf{t}}_Z\right)\end{array}\right]^{-1}\right)'\hat{\mathbf{V}}\left(\hat{\mathbf{t}}_X\right) \end{array} & \vline & \begin{array}{c} \hat{\mathbf{C}}\left(\hat{\mathbf{t}}_X,\hat{\mathbf{t}}_Y\right) \\[2mm] -\hat{\mathbf{V}}\left(\hat{\mathbf{t}}_X\right)\left(\left[\begin{array}{c}\hat{\mathbf{V}}\left(\hat{\mathbf{t}}_X\right) \\ +\hat{\mathbf{V}}\left(\hat{\mathbf{t}}_Z\right)\end{array}\right]^{-1}\right)\hat{\mathbf{C}}\left(\hat{\mathbf{t}}_X,\hat{\mathbf{t}}_Y\right) \end{array} \\ \overline{} \\ \begin{array}{c} \hat{\mathbf{C}}\left(\hat{\mathbf{t}}_X,\hat{\mathbf{t}}_Y\right)' \\[2mm] -\hat{\mathbf{C}}\left(\hat{\mathbf{t}}_Y,\hat{\mathbf{t}}_X\right)\left(\left[\begin{array}{c}\hat{\mathbf{V}}\left(\hat{\mathbf{t}}_X\right) \\ +\hat{\mathbf{V}}\left(\hat{\mathbf{t}}_Z\right)\end{array}\right]^{-1}\right)\hat{\mathbf{V}}\left(\hat{\mathbf{t}}_X\right) \end{array} & \vline & \begin{array}{c} \hat{\mathbf{V}}\left(\hat{\mathbf{t}}_Y\right) \\[2mm] -\hat{\mathbf{C}}\left(\hat{\mathbf{t}}_Y,\hat{\mathbf{t}}_X\right)\left(\left[\begin{array}{c}\hat{\mathbf{V}}\left(\hat{\mathbf{t}}_X\right) \\ +\hat{\mathbf{V}}\left(\hat{\mathbf{t}}_Z\right)\end{array}\right]^{-1}\right)\hat{\mathbf{C}}\left(\hat{\mathbf{t}}_X,\hat{\mathbf{t}}_Y\right) \end{array} \end{bmatrix}$$

The partition of Eq. 17 that corresponds to the study variables is:

$$V\left(\hat{\mathbf{t}}_{RE}\right)_Y = \begin{bmatrix} \mathbf{0} & \mathbf{I} \end{bmatrix} V\left(\hat{\mathbf{t}}_{RE}\right) \begin{bmatrix} \mathbf{0} \\ \mathbf{I} \end{bmatrix}$$

(18)

$$= \hat{\mathbf{V}}\left(\hat{\mathbf{t}}_Y\right) - \left(\hat{\mathbf{C}}\left(\hat{\mathbf{t}}_Y, \hat{\mathbf{t}}_X\right)\left(\left[\hat{\mathbf{V}}\left(\hat{\mathbf{t}}_X\right) + \hat{\mathbf{V}}\left(\hat{\mathbf{t}}_Z\right)\right]^{-1}\right)\hat{\mathbf{C}}\left(\hat{\mathbf{t}}_X, \hat{\mathbf{t}}_Y\right)\right)$$

The expression of the RE covariance matrix for the study variables in Eq. 18, which is a special case of RE, is algebraically identical to the optimal calibration estimator. Because both estimators $\mathbf{t}_{XY}$ and $\mathbf{t}_Z$ in Eq. 8 are design-consistent, the weighted sum of those estimators with RRE in Eq. 10 is also design-consistent (Fuller 2009:117).

RRE for Complex Sampling Designs: The Basic Idea Revisited

The presentation above demonstrates the relative simplicity of RE as an optimal multivariate estimator. The next example is a Census Object produced with a spaceborne remote sensing protocol, a Phase 1 Object that features photo-interpretation of high-resolution sample imagery for a large sample, and a smaller Phase 2 sample of FIA field measurements. This example uses sequential application of the RE, which is termed the recursive RE (RRE). The following exposition is intended to explain this application further in simple, heuristic terms. Mathematical details follow in later sections.

Complex surveys can include two or more multiphase and/or multistage modules, among others (Magnussen 2003). An example of these modules in the forest health monitoring portion of FIA includes: (1) auxiliary census data from remote sensing and administrative records at Phase 1; (2) measurements of field plots at FIA Phase 2; and (3) more expensive measurements of forest health on a relatively small Phase 3 sub-sample of Phase 2 field plots.

RRE may be applied to multilevel sampling in a sequential recursive fashion (Bierman 1977) by combining two modules (e.g., **H** in Eq. 8) at a time until all modules are used in the final sample survey estimate. The sequential recursive character of RRE is analogous to object-oriented programming. RRE combines two, and only two, objects at a time. An object might be a vector constant from a population census, a population vector estimate from a single sample phase or stage, or the vector output from a previously executed object. RRE receives two input objects. In Kalman filter terms, one object is the full state-vector, and the other is the measurement vector. The vector dimensions of each module can vary, but every pair of modules in an object are related through a linear transformation with known constants (e.g., **H** in Eq. 8). In the following, the linear transformation is an indicator matrix composed of zeros and ones that maps the state-vector onto the measurement vector. RRE optimally combines these two vectors (Eq. 10) into a more precise estimate of the full population vector. The output vector is then available as one of the two input objects into the next RRE recursion.

The sequential recursive concept has precedence in more traditional approaches to estimation in complex sample surveys. (See Särndal and others (1992:148) for an example with three-stage sampling.) Again, using the FIA forest health monitoring example, RRE might start by combining the estimates from Phase 1 and 2 objects. The outcome is more efficient estimates of the variables measured at Phase 2. Then, the composite estimate for Phase 2 variables could be combined with the estimates based on the forest health monitoring variables that are measured with the small Phase 3 sample. The result is a second composite estimate that sequentially assimilates relevant information from all three phases.

If the correlations and associations are sufficiently strong among the field measurements from Phase 2 and Phase 3, then the relatively precise Phase 2 estimates will improve the precision from the sparse sample at Phase 3. Furthermore, if the correlations and associations are sufficiently strong between the remotely sensed measurements at Phase 1 and the field measurements at Phase 2, then the remotely sensed auxiliary data will improve the estimation precision for variables that use the Phase 2 protocols, which, in turn, will improve the estimation precision for the forest health monitoring variables collected at Phase 3. Because the RRE is a special case of the Kalman filter, the final composite estimate is optimal in the sense of minimum variance and EBLUE, and it would be the maximum likelihood estimate if all multivariate sampling errors are Gaussian (Jazwinski 1970; Maybeck 1977). The final composite estimates of forest health variables incorporate all gains in efficiency available from the remotely sensed data from Phase 1 and the field data from Phase 2.

Depending on how the estimation problem is formulated, RRE can constrain linear combinations of estimates to equal known constants from one or more auxiliary sources (Czaplewski in prep.[b]). Examples of such constants include a census of remotely sensed pixel values that completely cover the sampled population, including the prevalence of each category or the total of each remotely sensed, continuous variable in the population. Other examples include census statistics on population totals from official administrative records such as areal extent of geopolitical units (e.g., counties and National Forests) and large water bodies (e.g., "Census water"). This feature qualifies RRE as a calibration estimator (Estevao and Särndal 2004; Särndal 2007). Furthermore, RRE can directly apply inequality constraints (Doran 1997; Simon and Chia 2002) such as a population total that must be greater than or equal to zero, namely, non-negative. In addition, depending on how the estimation problem is formulated, RRE can combine auxiliary statistical estimates of unknown population constants from multiple phases and/or stages of probability sampling. If estimators for multivariate, multilevel sampling can be recast into the structure of a recursive Kalman filter, then the 50 years of theory and practice with the Kalman filter can be immediately transferred to estimation in complex sample survey designs.

Next, specific designs, which are not intended to be exhaustive, are considered in more detail. Table 1 is a short guide to the mathematical notation, which is somewhat deep in order to consistently cover diverse elements within a variety of complex sampling designs. These examples are followed by other applications that use the final results from RRE to make other types of estimates, such as small-area, synthetic estimators and model-based estimators for missing data. Some of these examples use non-linear transformations of population vector estimates, and multivariate Taylor series are used to estimate their covariance matrices. A recursive sequential object-oriented approach simplifies first- and second-order Taylor series approximations for transformations that use addition, subtraction, multiplication, and division operators.

Two-Phase Sampling for Continuous Variables with a Sample at Phase 1

This section recasts the generalized presentation of RRE (Eqs. 9 through 11) into an example that is more explicitly relevant to multilevel sample surveys, namely, a special case of two-phase sampling, in which: (1) a simple random sample of the Phase 1 object is measured with a multivariate, remotely sensed protocol (e.g., photo-interpretation of sample aerial photography, denoted M = 1); and (2) a second independent, simple random sub-sample of the Phase 1 object (i.e., Phase 2 sample) that is further measured with a multivariate field protocol, denoted M = 2, in addition to the multivariate photo-interpretation protocol (M = 1). Also, this section provides more specific details from the perspective of probability sampling (e.g., Särndal and others 1992; Knottnerus 2003; de Gruijter and others 2006).

Table 1. Abbreviated summary of notation.

Symbol	Matrix dimensions		Description
	Row	Column	
$\left[\mathbf{y}_{M=a}\right]_j$	1	$q_{M=a}$	Vector of $q_{M=a}$ variables measured with protocol M = a in PSU j
$\left[\dfrac{\mathbf{y}_{M=a}}{\mathbf{y}_{M=b}}\right]_j$	1	$q_{M=a}+$ $q_{M=b}$	Vector of $q_{M=a}$ variables measured with protocol M = a and $q_{M=b}$ variables measured with protocol M = b in PSU j
$\hat{\bar{\mathbf{y}}}_{M=bC} = \begin{bmatrix} \left[\mathbf{y}_{M=a}\right]_{i=1} \\ \hline \sum_{i=1}^{n_j}\left[\mathbf{y}_{M=b}\right]_{i,j}\big/n_j \\ \hline \left[\mathbf{y}_{M=b}\right]_{i=1} \\ \hline \left[\mathbf{y}_{M=c}\right]_{i=1} \end{bmatrix}_j$	1	$q_{M=a}+$ $2q_{M=b}+$ $q_{M=c}$	Vector of $q_{M=a}$ variables measured with protocol M = a at SSU = 1 in PSU = j, and the vector mean of $q_{M=b}$ variables measured with protocol M = b at all n_j SSUs in cluster plot PSU = j, and $q_{M=b}$ variables measured with protocol M=b at SSU = 1 in PSU = j, and $q_{M=c}$ variables measured with protocol M = c at SSU = 1 in PSU = j
$\left[\dfrac{\hat{\mathbf{t}}_{M=a}}{\hat{\mathbf{t}}_{M=b}}\right]_{s=d}$	1	$q_{M=a}+$ $q_{M=b}$	Design-based sample estimate for the vector of population totals for the $q_{M=a}$ variables measured with protocol M = a, and the $q_{M=b}$ variables measured with protocol M = b from sample $s = d$
$\hat{\mathbf{V}}\left[\dfrac{\hat{\mathbf{t}}_{M=a}}{\hat{\mathbf{t}}_{M=b}}\right]_{s=d} =$ $\left[\begin{array}{c:c} \hat{\mathbf{V}}\left[\hat{\mathbf{t}}_{M=a}\right]_{s=d} & \hat{\mathbf{C}}\left[\hat{\mathbf{t}}_{M=a},\hat{\mathbf{t}}_{M=b}\right]_{s=d} \\ \hdashline \hat{\mathbf{C}}\left[\hat{\mathbf{t}}_{M=b},\hat{\mathbf{t}}_{M=a}\right]_{s=d} & \hat{\mathbf{V}}\left[\hat{\mathbf{t}}_{M=b}\right]_{s=d} \end{array}\right]$	$q_{M=a}+$ $q_{M=b}$	$q_{M=a}+$ $q_{M=b}$	Design-based sample estimate for the covariance matrix for the vector of population totals for the $q_{M=a}$ variables measured with protocol M = a, and the $q_{M=b}$ variables measured with protocol M = b from sample $s = d$, where $\hat{\mathbf{C}}\left[\hat{\mathbf{t}}_{M=b},\hat{\mathbf{t}}_{M=a}\right]_{s=d}$ is the $q_{M=b}$-by-$q_{M=a}$ cross-covariance matrix between estimates for variables measured with the M = a and M = b protocols
$\left[\dfrac{\hat{\mathbf{t}}_{M=a}}{\hat{\mathbf{t}}_{M=b}}\right]_{s=\{d,e\}}$	1	$q_{M=a}+$ $q_{M=b}$	RRE estimate for the vector of population totals for the $q_{M=a}$ variables measured with protocol M = a, and the $q_{M=b}$ variables measured with protocol M = b from the combination of estimates from samples $s = d$ and $s = e$

Every i^{th} and j^{th} sampling unit from the Phase 1 or Phase 2 sample in this example is considered an infinitesimally small point, and both protocols (M = 1 and M = 2) measure each sample point from a small point support region in the immediate vicinity of that sample point. This uses the perspective of de Gruijter and others (2006:74-75) for sampling continuous populations in space, such as forests, in which the "target universe … (is) an infinitely large population of possible sampling locations, and the distinction between sampling with replacement and sampling without replacement is immaterial. … (Any) correlations between observations (caused by non-replacement) are negligible in this context, as are finite population corrections." The infinite-population perspective is simpler (Mandallaz 2008:61) and arguably more natural for continuous spatial populations. FIA shares this same perspective (Scott and others 2005). It is this independent and invariant perspective of de Gruijter and others that justifies treatment of the large Phase 1 sample as independent of the smaller Phase 2 sample. This differs from the perspective in finite population sampling, in which the Phase 2 sample is considered a probability sub-sample of the Phase 1 sample, which is not independent and not necessarily invariant (e.g., Särndal and others 1992:Chapter 9).

Phase 1

Phase 1 is a simple random point sample ($s = 1$) from a spatial population with an infinite number of points but of known area A. The sample size ($n_{s=1}$) is large relative to Phase 2 (below). A small support-region (de Gruijter and others 2006:74-75) for each sample point i is measured with the Phase 1 protocol (e.g., photo-interpretation), which is denoted with the M = 1 subscript. The multivariate sample survey estimates are denoted by the $q_{M=1}$-by-1 vectors and $q_{M=1}$-by-$q_{M=1}$ covariance matrix:

$$\left[\hat{\bar{\mathbf{y}}}_{M=1}\right]_{s=1} = \frac{1}{n_{s=1}} \sum_{j \in (s=1)} \left[\mathbf{y}_{M=1}\right]_j$$

$$\left[\hat{\mathbf{t}}_{M=1}\right]_{s=1} = A\left[\hat{\bar{\mathbf{y}}}_{M=1}\right]_{s=1}$$

$$\hat{\mathbf{V}}\left(\left[\hat{\mathbf{t}}_{M=1}\right]\right)_{s=1} = A^2 \left[\frac{\sum_{j \in (s=2)} \left(\left[\mathbf{y}_{M=1}\right]_j - \left[\hat{\bar{\mathbf{y}}}_{M=1}\right]_{s=1}\right)\left(\left[\mathbf{y}_{M=1}\right]_j - \left[\hat{\bar{\mathbf{y}}}_{M=1}\right]_{s=1}\right)'}{\left(n_{s=1}-1\right)n_{s=1}} \right]$$

(19)

where the constant A in Eq. 19 is the known size of the sampled population (e.g., 25 million acres), the $q_{M=1}$-by-1 vector [**y**] represents $q_{M=1}$ photo-interpreted variables, and the $q_{M=1}$-by-1 vector [**t**] represents the corresponding $q_{M=1}$ population totals.

For example, photo-interpreters inexpensively apply the M = 1 measurement protocol to a 1-acre support-region for each point in the large Phase 1 sample. The support-region covers an area approximately equivalent in size to one sub-plot in the four-point cluster plot used FIA field measurements (Bechtold and Scott 2005). The support-region is centered on the sample point. The number of photo-interpreted variables may be numerous (e.g., $5 < q_{M=1} < 1000$), and they may be a mixture of both binary and continuous measurements.

Different remotely sensed categorical variables need not be cross-classified into a single categorical variable as with stratification (see "Categorical Variables"). Polychotomous categorical variables with k categories ($k>2$) are converted into (k) binary variables (e.g., de Gruijter and others 2006:69). Furthermore, binary variables need not be mutually exclusive or exhaustive. In addition, if the support-region straddles multiple categorical conditions, then the corresponding 0-1 binary variables easily become continuous variables (bounded by 0 and 1) that represent the proportion of the support-region included in each binary category.

Phase 2

Phase 2 is an independent simple random sample (s = 2) that is measured with both the inexpensive M = 1 protocol (remote sensing) and the expensive M = 2 protocol (field measurements). The $q_{M=2}$-by-1 vector $[\mathbf{y}_{M=2}]_i$ in Eq. 20 represents these $q_{M=2}$ variables. The Phase 2 sample size ($n_{s=2}$) is small relative to the Phase 1 sample ($n_{s=2} << n_{s=1}$).

Let the Phase 2 estimates be the $(q_{M=1} + q_{M=2})$-by-1 vectors and covariance matrix $(q_{M=1} + q_{M=2})$-by-$(q_{M=1} + q_{M=2})$:

$$\left[\hat{\bar{\mathbf{y}}}_{M=(1,2)}\right]_{s=2} = \left[\begin{array}{c} \hat{\bar{\mathbf{y}}}_{M=1} \\ \hline \hat{\bar{\mathbf{y}}}_{M=2} \end{array}\right]_{s=2}$$

$$= \frac{1}{n_{s=2}} \sum_{j \in (s=2)} \left[\begin{array}{c} \mathbf{y}_{M=1} \\ \hline \mathbf{y}_{M=2} \end{array}\right]_{j}, \text{ where } \left(n_{s=2} \ll n_{s=1}\right)$$

$$\left[\begin{array}{c} \hat{\mathbf{t}}_{M=1} \\ \hline \hat{\mathbf{t}}_{M=2} \end{array}\right]_{s=2} = A \left[\begin{array}{c} \hat{\bar{\mathbf{y}}}_{M=1} \\ \hline \hat{\bar{\mathbf{y}}}_{M=2} \end{array}\right]_{s=2}$$

$$\hat{\mathbf{V}}\left(\left[\begin{array}{c} \hat{\mathbf{t}}_{M=1} \\ \hline \hat{\mathbf{t}}_{M=2} \end{array}\right]\right)_{s=2} = A^2 \left[\frac{\displaystyle\sum_{j \in (s=2)} \left\{ \left(\left[\begin{array}{c} \mathbf{y}_{M=1} \\ \hline \mathbf{y}_{M=2} \end{array}\right]_j - \left[\begin{array}{c} \hat{\bar{\mathbf{y}}}_{M=1} \\ \hline \hat{\bar{\mathbf{y}}}_{M=2} \end{array}\right]_{s=2} \right) \left[\left([\mathbf{y}_{M=1}]_j - \hat{\bar{\mathbf{y}}}_{M=1}\right)' \mid \left([\mathbf{y}_{M=2}]_j - \hat{\bar{\mathbf{y}}}_{M=2}\right)' \right] \right\}}{(n_{s=2}-1)\, n_{s=2}} \right]$$

$$= \left[\begin{array}{c|c} \hat{\mathbf{V}}\left([\hat{\mathbf{t}}_{M=1}]\right)_{s=2} & \hat{\mathbf{C}}\left([\hat{\mathbf{t}}_{M=1}], [\hat{\mathbf{t}}_{M=2}]\right)_{s=2} \\ \hline \hat{\mathbf{C}}\left([\hat{\mathbf{t}}_{M=2}], [\hat{\mathbf{t}}_{M=1}]\right)_{s=2} & \hat{\mathbf{V}}\left([\hat{\mathbf{t}}_{M=2}]\right)_{s=2} \end{array}\right]$$

(20)

The last term in Eq. 20 defines a partition of the sample covariance matrix. C in the partitioned covariance matrix denotes the $q_{M=2}$-by-$q_{M=1}$ cross-covariance sub-matrix between the $q_{M=2}$ estimated populations totals measured with the M = 2 protocol and the $q_{M=1}$ variables measured with the M = 1 protocol from the Phase 2 sample.

The M = 2 protocol represents the standard FIA Phase 2 field protocol, which results in standardized measurements of tree and stand characteristics within the 1/6-acre support-region. The support-region in the Phase 2 sample is centered on sub-plot 1 in the standard FIA field plot, and the support-region is composed of all four 1/24-acre FIA sub-plots (Bechtold and Scott 2005:29). The M = 1 protocol (i.e., photo-interpretation) used in the Phase 2 sample is exactly as described above under Phase 1, including the 1-acre support-region approximately centered on the same sample point used in the M = 2 protocol. As will be demonstrated, improvements in statistical efficiency with two-phase sampling depend upon the degree of covariance between variables measured with expensive and less-expensive protocols (e.g., field data and remote sensing). Therefore, it is important that the M = 1 protocol be applied to the same site as the M = 2 protocol, which requires minimization of registration errors between remotely sensed measurements and field measurements.

Recursive Restriction Estimator (RRE)

The Recursive Restriction Estimator (RRE) offers one means to combine the independent estimators from Phase 1 (Eq. 19) and Phase 2 (Eq. 20) into a more efficient estimator. This is accomplished by structuring the estimation problem in the context of the static multivariate Kalman filter. This is the key concept in simplifying the estimation problem in complex sample designs. Because the statistical properties of the Kalman filter are well understood, at least in certain disciplines, and because the filter is fully developed as an optimal linear estimator, the sample survey problem is largely solved by recasting it as a discrete multivariate stochastic process (Särndal 1992:21) using the Kalman filter as a static linear model (Maybeck 1979: Section 3.11) and then applying well-developed results for the Kalman filter to readily solve the problem. Much of that recasting has already been performed as an antecedent to Eqs. 9 through 12. The remaining steps follow.

First, the Phase 1 and Phase 2 samples are independent by definition; hence, $\mathbf{C}(1) = \mathbf{0}$, and the special case of the Kalman filter in Eq. 12 applies.

Second, consider state-vector in the Kalman filter. In the case of two-phase sampling, state-vector may be defined as the population totals for all variables of interest from both the $M = 1$ protocol (photo-interpretation) and the $M = 2$ protocol (FIA field data). In this case, n in Maybeck's definition of the state-vector equals $(q_{M=1} + q_{M=2})$. In the context of the current section, the state-vector $\mathbf{t}_{X(1)}$ in Eq. 12 is estimated from Phase 2 sample ($s = 2$) and the estimators in Eq. 20.

Third, define the measurement vector $\mathbf{t}_{Z(1)}$ in Eq. 12 as the estimated population totals for the remotely sensed variables from the Phase 1 sample ($s = 1$), with the corresponding estimators given in Eq. 19.

Fourth, a linear model must be defined that describes how the measurement vector $\mathbf{t}_{Z(1)}$ relates to the state-vector $\mathbf{t}_{X(1)}$ in Eq. 12. This model is given in Eq. 8 as $\mathbf{t}_{Z(1)} = \mathbf{H}\,\mathbf{t}_{X(1)}$, where $\mathbf{H}$ is a conformable matrix of known constants. In the current context, $\mathbf{H}$ is simply a matrix of ones and zeros that extracts the Phase 2 estimated totals of the photo-interrelated variables ($M = 1$ protocol) from the full state-vector and its corresponding partition from the covariance matrix for the full state-vector.

In summary, these steps yield a multivariate estimator for the special case of two-phase sampling considered here that is structured as the Kalman filter in Eq. 12:

$$
\begin{aligned}
&\hat{\mathbf{t}}_{X(1)} = \begin{bmatrix} \hat{\mathbf{t}}_{M=1} \\ \hline \hat{\mathbf{t}}_{M=2} \end{bmatrix}_{s=2}
&&\hat{\mathbf{V}}\left(\hat{\mathbf{t}}_{X(1)}\right) = \hat{\mathbf{V}}\left(\begin{bmatrix} \hat{\mathbf{t}}_{M=1} \\ \hline \hat{\mathbf{t}}_{M=2} \end{bmatrix}_{s=2}\right) \\[2em]
&\hat{\mathbf{t}}_{Z(1)} = \begin{bmatrix} \hat{\mathbf{t}}_{M=1} \end{bmatrix}_{s=1}
&&\hat{\mathbf{V}}\left(\hat{\mathbf{t}}_{Z(1)}\right) = \hat{\mathbf{V}}\left(\begin{bmatrix} \hat{\mathbf{t}}_{M=1} \end{bmatrix}_{s=1}\right) \\[2em]
&\mathbf{H} = \begin{bmatrix} \mathbf{I} \ \vdots \ \mathbf{0} \end{bmatrix}
&&\hat{\mathbf{C}}\left(\hat{\mathbf{t}}_{X(1)}, \hat{\mathbf{t}}_{Z(1)}\right) = \hat{\mathbf{C}}\left(\begin{bmatrix} \hat{\mathbf{t}}_{M=1} \\ \hline \hat{\mathbf{t}}_{M=2} \end{bmatrix}_{s=2}, \begin{bmatrix} \hat{\mathbf{t}}_{M=1} \end{bmatrix}_{s=1}\right) = \mathbf{0} \\[2em]
&\begin{bmatrix} \hat{\mathbf{t}}_{M=1} \end{bmatrix}_{s=2} = \mathbf{H}\begin{bmatrix} \hat{\mathbf{t}}_{M=1} \\ \hline \hat{\mathbf{t}}_{M=2} \end{bmatrix}_{s=2}
&&\hat{\mathbf{V}}\left(\begin{bmatrix} \hat{\mathbf{t}}_{M=1} \end{bmatrix}_{s=2}\right) = \mathbf{H}\,\hat{\mathbf{V}}\left(\begin{bmatrix} \hat{\mathbf{t}}_{M=1} \\ \hline \hat{\mathbf{t}}_{M=2} \end{bmatrix}_{s=2}\right)\mathbf{H}' \\[2em]
&\qquad = \begin{bmatrix} \mathbf{I} \ \vdots \ \mathbf{0} \end{bmatrix}\begin{bmatrix} \hat{\mathbf{t}}_{M=1} \\ \hline \hat{\mathbf{t}}_{M=2} \end{bmatrix}_{s=2}
&&\qquad = \begin{bmatrix} \mathbf{I} \ \vdots \ \mathbf{0} \end{bmatrix}\hat{\mathbf{V}}\left(\begin{bmatrix} \hat{\mathbf{t}}_{M=1} \\ \hline \hat{\mathbf{t}}_{M=2} \end{bmatrix}_{s=2}\right)\begin{bmatrix} \mathbf{I} \\ \hline \mathbf{0} \end{bmatrix}
\end{aligned} \tag{21}
$$

Here, the $\mathbf{H}$ matrix has dimensions $q_{M=1}$-by-$(q_{M=1} + q_{M=2})$. The cross-covariance matrix in Eq. 21 because the Phase 1 sample is, by design in this example, independent of the Phase 2 sample. From Eqs. 12, 19, 20, and 21, RRE (Kalman filter) that combines estimates from the Phase 1 ($s = 1$) and Phase 2 ($s = 2$) samples, denoted $s = \{1,2\}$, is:

$$
\begin{aligned}
\begin{bmatrix} \hat{\hat{\mathbf{t}}}_{M=1.} \\ \hat{\hat{\mathbf{t}}}_{M=2} \end{bmatrix}_{s=\{1,2\}} &= \begin{bmatrix} \hat{\hat{\mathbf{t}}}_{M=1.} \\ \hat{\hat{\mathbf{t}}}_{M=2} \end{bmatrix}_{s=2} + \mathbf{K}\left\{ \left[\hat{\mathbf{t}}_{M=1}\right]_{s=1} - \left(\mathbf{H}\begin{bmatrix} \hat{\hat{\mathbf{t}}}_{M=1.} \\ \hat{\hat{\mathbf{t}}}_{M=2} \end{bmatrix}_{s=2} \right) \right\} \\[2em]
&= \begin{bmatrix} \hat{\hat{\mathbf{t}}}_{M=1.} \\ \hat{\hat{\mathbf{t}}}_{M=2} \end{bmatrix}_{s=2} + \mathbf{K}\left\{ \left[\hat{\mathbf{t}}_{M=1}\right]_{s=1} - \left[\hat{\mathbf{t}}_{M=1}\right]_{s=2} \right\}
\end{aligned}
\tag{22}
$$

Equation 22 is a multivariate extension to the familiar univariate composite estimator in Eq. 2. In the current context, and using the partitions of the Phase 2 covariance matrix in Eq. 20, the $(q_{M=1} + q_{M=2})$-by-$q_{M=1}$ weighting matrix $\mathbf{K}$ (Eqs. 12 and 22) may be expressed as:

$$
\begin{aligned}
\mathbf{K} &= \left\{ \hat{\mathbf{V}}\left(\begin{bmatrix} \hat{\hat{\mathbf{t}}}_{M=1.} \\ \hat{\hat{\mathbf{t}}}_{M=2} \end{bmatrix}_{s=2} \right)\mathbf{H}' \right\} \left\{ \mathbf{H}\,\hat{\mathbf{V}}\left(\begin{bmatrix} \hat{\hat{\mathbf{t}}}_{M=1.} \\ \hat{\hat{\mathbf{t}}}_{M=2} \end{bmatrix}_{s=2} \right)\mathbf{H}' + \hat{\mathbf{V}}\left(\left[\hat{\mathbf{t}}_{M=1}\right]_{s=1} \right) \right\}^{-1} \\[2em]
&= \begin{bmatrix} \hat{\mathbf{V}}\left(\left[\hat{\mathbf{t}}_{M=1}\right]_{s=2} \right)\left\{ \hat{\mathbf{V}}\left(\left[\hat{\mathbf{t}}_{M=1}\right]_{s=2} \right) + \hat{\mathbf{V}}\left(\left[\hat{\mathbf{t}}_{M=1}\right]_{s=1} \right) \right\}^{-1} \\ \hline \hat{\mathbf{C}}\left(\left[\hat{\mathbf{t}}_{M=2}\right], \left[\hat{\mathbf{t}}_{M=1}\right] \right)_{s=2} \left\{ \hat{\mathbf{V}}\left(\left[\hat{\mathbf{t}}_{M=1}\right]_{s=2} \right) + \hat{\mathbf{V}}\left(\left[\hat{\mathbf{t}}_{M=1}\right]_{s=1} \right) \right\}^{-1} \end{bmatrix}
\end{aligned}
\tag{23}
$$

Equation 23 is the multivariate extension of the scalar weight in the univariate composite estimator (Eqs. 3 and 4). Equation 23 might not be numerically stable, and it is very important to use more numerically stable methods that are reviewed in the section "Robust Numerics."

The partition of the covariance matrix between the Phase 1 and Phase 2 estimators used in Eq. 23 is defined in Eq. 20. Combining Eqs. 22 and 23:

$$
\begin{bmatrix} \hat{\hat{\mathbf{t}}}_{M=1.} \\ \hat{\hat{\mathbf{t}}}_{M=2} \end{bmatrix}_{s=\{1,2\}} = \begin{bmatrix} \left[\hat{\mathbf{t}}_{M=1}\right]_{s=2} + \hat{\mathbf{V}}\left(\left[\hat{\mathbf{t}}_{M=1}\right]_{s=2}\right) \left\{ \begin{matrix} \hat{\mathbf{V}}\left(\left[\hat{\mathbf{t}}_{M=1}\right]_{s=2}\right) \\ + \hat{\mathbf{V}}\left(\left[\hat{\mathbf{t}}_{M=1}\right]_{s=1}\right) \end{matrix} \right\}^{-1} \left\{ \left[\hat{\mathbf{t}}_{M=1}\right]_{s=1} - \left[\hat{\mathbf{t}}_{M=1}\right]_{s=2} \right\} \\ \hline \left[\hat{\mathbf{t}}_{M=2}\right]_{s=2} + \hat{\mathbf{C}}\left(\left[\hat{\mathbf{t}}_{M=2}\right], \left[\hat{\mathbf{t}}_{M=1}\right]\right)_{s=2} \left\{ \begin{matrix} \hat{\mathbf{V}}\left(\left[\hat{\mathbf{t}}_{M=1}\right]_{s=2}\right) \\ + \hat{\mathbf{V}}\left(\left[\hat{\mathbf{t}}_{M=1}\right]_{s=1}\right) \end{matrix} \right\}^{-1} \left\{ \left[\hat{\mathbf{t}}_{M=1}\right]_{s=1} - \left[\hat{\mathbf{t}}_{M=1}\right]_{s=2} \right\} \end{bmatrix}
\tag{24}
$$

and the covariance matrix estimator for the vector estimate in Eq. 24 is:

$$\hat{\mathbf{V}}\left(\begin{bmatrix}\hat{\mathbf{t}}_{M=1}\\\hline \hat{\mathbf{t}}_{M=2}\end{bmatrix}_{s=\{1,2\}}\right)=\hat{\mathbf{V}}\left(\begin{bmatrix}\hat{\mathbf{t}}_{M=1}\\\hline \hat{\mathbf{t}}_{M=2}\end{bmatrix}_{s=2}\right)-\mathbf{K}\left[\begin{array}{c|c}\mathbf{I}_{q_{M=1}} & \mathbf{0}_{q_{M=1}\times q_{M=2}}\end{array}\right]\hat{\mathbf{V}}\left(\begin{bmatrix}\hat{\mathbf{t}}_{M=1}\\\hline \hat{\mathbf{t}}_{M=2}\end{bmatrix}_{s=2}\right)$$

$$=\hat{\mathbf{V}}\left(\begin{bmatrix}\hat{\mathbf{t}}_{M=1}\\\hline \hat{\mathbf{t}}_{M=2}\end{bmatrix}_{s=2}\right)-\mathbf{K}\left[\begin{array}{c|c}\hat{\mathbf{V}}\left(\left[\hat{\mathbf{t}}_{M=1}\right]_{s=2}\right) & \hat{\mathbf{C}}\end{array}\right]$$

$$=\left[\begin{array}{c|c}\hat{\mathbf{V}}\left(\left[\hat{\mathbf{t}}_{M=1}\right]_{s=2}\right)\left[\mathbf{I}-\left\{\begin{array}{c}\hat{\mathbf{V}}\left(\left[\hat{\mathbf{t}}_{M=1}\right]_{s=2}\right)\\+\hat{\mathbf{V}}\left(\left[\hat{\mathbf{t}}_{M=1}\right]_{s=1}\right)\end{array}\right\}^{-1}\hat{\mathbf{V}}\left(\left[\hat{\mathbf{t}}_{M=1}\right]_{s=2}\right)\right] & \left[\mathbf{I}-\hat{\mathbf{V}}\left(\left[\hat{\mathbf{t}}_{M=1}\right]_{s=2}\right)\left\{\begin{array}{c}\hat{\mathbf{V}}\left(\left[\hat{\mathbf{t}}_{M=1}\right]_{s=2}\right)\\+\hat{\mathbf{V}}\left(\left[\hat{\mathbf{t}}_{M=1}\right]_{s=1}\right)\end{array}\right\}^{-1}\right]\hat{\mathbf{C}}\\\hline \hat{\mathbf{C}}'\left[\mathbf{I}-\left\{\begin{array}{c}\hat{\mathbf{V}}\left(\left[\hat{\mathbf{t}}_{M=1}\right]_{s=2}\right)\\+\hat{\mathbf{V}}\left(\left[\hat{\mathbf{t}}_{M=1}\right]_{s=1}\right)\end{array}\right\}^{-1}\hat{\mathbf{V}}\left(\left[\hat{\mathbf{t}}_{M=1}\right]_{s=2}\right)\right] & \hat{\mathbf{V}}\left(\left[\hat{\mathbf{t}}_{M=2}\right]\right)_{s=2}-\hat{\mathbf{C}}'\left\{\begin{array}{c}\hat{\mathbf{V}}\left(\left[\hat{\mathbf{t}}_{M=1}\right]_{s=2}\right)\\+\hat{\mathbf{V}}\left(\left[\hat{\mathbf{t}}_{M=1}\right]_{s=1}\right)\end{array}\right\}^{-1}\hat{\mathbf{C}}\end{array}\right] \quad (25)$$

where $\hat{\mathbf{C}}=\hat{\mathbf{C}}\left(\left[\hat{\mathbf{t}}_{M=1}\right],\left[\hat{\mathbf{t}}_{M=2}\right]\right)_{s=2}$

RRE in Eqs. 22 to 25 improves estimates for remotely sensed variables (protocol M = 1) in addition to the variables measured in the field (protocol M = 2). However, the typical purpose of the Phase 1 sample is variance reduction for the population estimates from the Phase 2 sample and the M = 2 measurement protocol. The estimates of variables measured with the M = 1 protocol might not be relevant after their role in variance reduction is met. Only those sub-matrices in Eqs. 20 through 25 that apply to the Phase 2 protocol (M = 2) might be needed. Those $q_{M=2}$-dimensional partitions are readily extracted from the vector of estimated population totals and its estimated covariance matrix as follows:

$$\left[\hat{\mathbf{t}}_{M=2}\right]_{s=\{1,2\}}=\left[\begin{array}{c|c}\mathbf{0} & \mathbf{I}\end{array}\right]\begin{bmatrix}\hat{\mathbf{t}}_{M=1}\\\hline \hat{\mathbf{t}}_{M=2}\end{bmatrix}_{s=\{1,2\}}$$

$$=\left[\hat{\mathbf{t}}_{M=2}\right]_{s=2}+\left[\hat{\mathbf{C}}\left(\left[\hat{\mathbf{t}}_{M=2}\right],\left[\hat{\mathbf{t}}_{M=1}\right]\right)_{s=2}\left\{\begin{array}{c}\hat{\mathbf{V}}\left(\left[\hat{\mathbf{t}}_{M=1}\right]_{s=2}\right)\\+\hat{\mathbf{V}}\left(\left[\hat{\mathbf{t}}_{M=1}\right]_{s=1}\right)\end{array}\right\}^{-1}\left\{\left[\hat{\mathbf{t}}_{M=1}\right]_{s=1}-\left[\hat{\mathbf{t}}_{M=1}\right]_{s=2}\right\}\right]$$

$$(26)$$

$$\hat{\mathbf{V}}\left(\left[\hat{\mathbf{t}}_{M=2}\right]_{s=\{1,2\}}\right)=\left[\begin{array}{c|c}\mathbf{0} & \mathbf{I}\end{array}\right]\hat{\mathbf{V}}\left(\begin{bmatrix}\hat{\mathbf{t}}_{M=1}\\\hline \hat{\mathbf{t}}_{M=2}\end{bmatrix}_{s=\{1,2\}}\right)\begin{bmatrix}\mathbf{0}\\\mathbf{I}\end{bmatrix}$$

$$=\hat{\mathbf{V}}\left(\left[\hat{\mathbf{t}}_{M=2}\right]\right)_{s=2}-\left[\hat{\mathbf{C}}\left(\left[\hat{\mathbf{t}}_{M=2}\right],\left[\hat{\mathbf{t}}_{M=1}\right]\right)_{s=2}\left\{\begin{array}{c}\hat{\mathbf{V}}\left(\left[\hat{\mathbf{t}}_{M=1}\right]_{s=2}\right)\\+\hat{\mathbf{V}}\left(\left[\hat{\mathbf{t}}_{M=1}\right]_{s=1}\right)\end{array}\right\}^{-1}\hat{\mathbf{C}}\left(\left[\hat{\mathbf{t}}_{M=2}\right],\left[\hat{\mathbf{t}}_{M=1}\right]\right)'_{s=2}\right]$$

Because the regression estimator and RRE are both minimum variance linear predictors, it is no surprise that Eq. 26 has a multivariate structure somewhat analogous to the univariate regression estimator (e.g., Cochran 1977:Section 7.3). Knottnerus (2003:356) developed the same estimator from the perspective of the conditional restriction estimator.

The efficiency of two-phase sampling depends on the linear relationship between the variables measured with the M = 1 protocol (e.g., photo-interpretation) and the variables measured with the M = 2 protocol (e.g., FIA field data). The strength of this relationship is quantified from the Phase 2 sample estimate of the cross-covariance matrix $\mathbf{C}$ in Eq. 26. If there is little or no correlation between the M = 1 and M = 2 variables, then $\mathbf{C} \sim \mathbf{0}$, and the composite estimate of the M = 2 variables in Eq. 26 equals that of the Phase 2 sample ($s = 2$) alone (Eq. 20). This means that the Phase 1 sample of M = 1 variables would produce little or no gain in statistical efficiency for estimating the M = 2 variables. However, if the cross-covariance matrix $\mathbf{C}$ is relatively large, and the covariance matrix for population totals from the M = 1 measurements in Phase 1 ($s = 1$) are relatively small, then the composite variance in Eq. 24 can be substantially less than the covariance matrix for the Phase 2 sample alone (Eq. 20).

The next example is a minor modification of the above example. Rather than a sample of points at Phase 1, the next example uses a full-coverage census of remotely sensed pixels at Phase 1.

Two-Phase Sampling for Continuous Variables with a Census at Phase 1

Multivariate two-phase sampling with a **sample** at Phase 1 (previously discussed) is closely related to the two-phase sampling that uses a **census** at Phase 1, which is the subject of this section. The following example is an alternative to the situation in FIA, where remotely sensed Landsat data are used with a post-stratification estimator. Czaplewski (in prep.[b]) considers this example in substantially more detail and includes a discussion on the equivalence of RRE to direct design-based calibration estimators in sample surveys (Estevao and Särndal 2004) that are nearly design-unbiased (Särndal 2007).

In order to conform to notation in more complex examples that follow, let the census of pixels be denoted $s = U$, indicating that the sample is the complete set of pixels that completely cover the sampled population U. The remote sensing protocol used to measure each pixel is denoted by M = 0. If Phase 1 in the previous example was a census rather than a sample, then $[\hat{\mathbf{t}}_{M=1}]_{s=1}$ would exactly equal $\mathbf{t}_{M=1}$, and the covariance matrix for Phase 1 would be the $q_{M=1}$-by-$q_{M=1}$ zero matrix (i.e., $V([\hat{\mathbf{t}}_{M=1}]_{s=1}) = \mathbf{0}$). In the following example, the Phase 1 sample $s = 1$ is replaced by the $s = U$ census, and the M = 1 photo-interpretation protocol is replaced by the M = 0 spaceborne sensor protocol for all pixels in the sampled population. Therefore, $[\hat{\mathbf{t}}_{M=0}]_{s=U} = \mathbf{t}_{M=0}, V([\hat{\mathbf{t}}_{M=0}]_{s=U}) = \mathbf{0}$, and Eqs. 22 to 25 evolve into:

$$
\begin{bmatrix} \mathbf{t}_{M=0} \\ \hline \hat{\mathbf{t}}_{M=2} \end{bmatrix}_{s=\{U,2\}} = \begin{bmatrix} \hat{\mathbf{t}}_{M=0} \\ \hline \hat{\mathbf{t}}_{M=2} \end{bmatrix}_{s=2} + \mathbf{K}\left\{ \left[\mathbf{t}_{M=0}\right]_{s=U} - \left(\mathbf{H} \begin{bmatrix} \hat{\mathbf{t}}_{M=0} \\ \hline \hat{\mathbf{t}}_{M=2} \end{bmatrix}_{s=2} \right) \right\}
$$

$$
\hat{\mathbf{V}}\left(\begin{bmatrix} \mathbf{t}_{M=0} \\ \hline \hat{\mathbf{t}}_{M=2} \end{bmatrix}_{s=\{U,2\}} \right) = \hat{\mathbf{V}}\left(\begin{bmatrix} \hat{\mathbf{t}}_{M=0} \\ \hline \hat{\mathbf{t}}_{M=2} \end{bmatrix}_{s=2} \right) - \mathbf{K}\,\mathbf{H}\,\hat{\mathbf{V}}\left(\begin{bmatrix} \hat{\mathbf{t}}_{M=0} \\ \hline \hat{\mathbf{t}}_{M=2} \end{bmatrix}_{s=2} \right)
$$

(27)

where

$$\mathbf{H} = [\mathbf{I} \quad \mathbf{0}]$$

$$\mathbf{K} = \left\{ \hat{\mathbf{V}}\left(\begin{bmatrix} \hat{\mathbf{t}}_{M=0} \\ \hat{\mathbf{t}}_{M=2} \end{bmatrix}_{s=2} \right) \mathbf{H}' \right\} \left\{ \mathbf{H}\, \hat{\mathbf{V}}\left(\begin{bmatrix} \hat{\mathbf{t}}_{M=0} \\ \hat{\mathbf{t}}_{M=2} \end{bmatrix}_{s=2} \right) \mathbf{H}' \right\}^{-1}$$

$$= \left[\begin{array}{c} \hat{\mathbf{V}}\left([\hat{\mathbf{t}}_{M=0}]_{s=2} \right) \\ \hline \hat{\mathbf{C}}\left([\hat{\mathbf{t}}_{M=2}], [\hat{\mathbf{t}}_{M=0}] \right)_{s=2} \end{array} \right] \hat{\mathbf{V}}\left([\hat{\mathbf{t}}_{M=0}]_{s=2} \right)^{-1}$$

$$= \left[\begin{array}{c} \mathbf{I} \\ \hline \hat{\mathbf{C}}\left([\hat{\mathbf{t}}_{M=2}], [\hat{\mathbf{t}}_{M=0}] \right)_{s=2} \hat{\mathbf{V}}\left([\hat{\mathbf{t}}_{M=0}]_{s=2} \right)^{-1} \end{array} \right]$$

The Phase 1 census in Eq. 27 is denoted by $s = U$, and the measurement protocol used for the full-coverage satellite data is denoted by M = 0 rather than the Phase 1 protocol M = 1. This minor shift in nomenclature for the "M" protocol facilitates more complex estimators that follow. It is assumed that $V([\hat{\mathbf{t}}_{M=0}]_{s=2})$ is full rank, i.e., the matrix inverse is feasible for the partition of the sample covariance matrix that corresponds to the census variables. Knottnerus (2003:330, 333) uses this same approach, which is called a regression model with linear restrictions on the regression coefficients, in the Restriction Estimator.

The partition of RE corresponding to the auxiliary census will exactly equal the vector census constant $[\mathbf{t}_{M=0}]_{s=U}$:

$$\begin{bmatrix} \hat{\mathbf{t}}_{M=0} \\ \hat{\mathbf{t}}_{M=2} \end{bmatrix}_{s=\{U,2\}} = \begin{bmatrix} \hat{\mathbf{t}}_{M=0} \\ \hat{\mathbf{t}}_{M=2} \end{bmatrix}_{s=2} + \left[\begin{array}{c} \mathbf{I} \\ \hline \hat{\mathbf{C}}\left([\hat{\mathbf{t}}_{M=2}], [\hat{\mathbf{t}}_{M=0}] \right)_{s=2} \hat{\mathbf{V}}\left([\hat{\mathbf{t}}_{M=0}]_{s=2} \right)^{-1} \end{array} \right] \left\{ [\mathbf{t}_{M=0}]_{s=U} - \left(\mathbf{H} \begin{bmatrix} \hat{\mathbf{t}}_{M=0} \\ \hat{\mathbf{t}}_{M=2} \end{bmatrix}_{s=2} \right) \right\}$$

$$= \left[\begin{array}{c} [\hat{\mathbf{t}}_{M=0}]_{s=2} + [\mathbf{t}_{M=0}]_{s=U} - [\hat{\mathbf{t}}_{M=0}]_{s=2} \\ \hline [\hat{\mathbf{t}}_{M=2}]_{s=2} + [\hat{\mathbf{C}}\left([\hat{\mathbf{t}}_{M=2}], [\hat{\mathbf{t}}_{M=0}] \right)_{s=2} \hat{\mathbf{V}}\left([\hat{\mathbf{t}}_{M=0}]_{s=2} \right)^{-1} \left([\mathbf{t}_{M=0}]_{s=U} - [\hat{\mathbf{t}}_{M=0}]_{s=2} \right)] \end{array} \right] \qquad (28)$$

$$= \left[\begin{array}{c} [\mathbf{t}_{M=0}]_{s=U} \\ \hline [\hat{\mathbf{t}}_{M=2}]_{s=2} + [\hat{\mathbf{C}}\left([\hat{\mathbf{t}}_{M=2}], [\hat{\mathbf{t}}_{M=0}] \right)_{s=2} \hat{\mathbf{V}}\left([\hat{\mathbf{t}}_{M=0}]_{s=2} \right)^{-1} \left([\mathbf{t}_{M=0}]_{s=U} - [\hat{\mathbf{t}}_{M=0}]_{s=2} \right)] \end{array} \right]$$

Likewise, the corresponding partition of the RE covariance matrix equals zero, with zero cross-covariance for the off-diagonal partition.

$$\hat{\mathbf{V}}\left(\begin{bmatrix}\mathbf{t}_{M=0}\\\hat{\mathbf{t}}_{M=2}\end{bmatrix}_{s=\{U,2\}}\right) = \hat{\mathbf{V}}\left(\begin{bmatrix}\hat{\mathbf{t}}_{M=0}\\\hat{\mathbf{t}}_{M=2}\end{bmatrix}_{s=2}\right) - \begin{bmatrix}\mathbf{I}\\\hat{\mathbf{C}}\left([\hat{\mathbf{t}}_{M=2}],[\hat{\mathbf{t}}_{M=0}]\right)_{s=2}\hat{\mathbf{V}}\left([\hat{\mathbf{t}}_{M=0}]_{s=2}\right)^{-1}\end{bmatrix}\begin{bmatrix}\hat{\mathbf{V}}\left([\hat{\mathbf{t}}_{M=0}]_{s=2}\right)\\\hat{\mathbf{C}}\left([\hat{\mathbf{t}}_{M=2}],[\hat{\mathbf{t}}_{M=0}]\right)_{s=2}\end{bmatrix}$$

$$=\begin{bmatrix}\hat{\mathbf{V}}\left([\hat{\mathbf{t}}_{M=0}]_{s=2}\right) & \hat{\mathbf{C}}\left([\hat{\mathbf{t}}_{M=0}],[\hat{\mathbf{t}}_{M=2}]\right)_{s=2}\\ -\hat{\mathbf{V}}\left([\hat{\mathbf{t}}_{M=0}]_{s=2}\right)' & -\hat{\mathbf{C}}\left([\hat{\mathbf{t}}_{M=2}],[\hat{\mathbf{t}}_{M=0}]\right)'_{s=2}\\ \hat{\mathbf{C}}\left([\hat{\mathbf{t}}_{M=2}],[\hat{\mathbf{t}}_{M=0}]\right)_{s=2} & \hat{\mathbf{V}}\left([\hat{\mathbf{t}}_{M=2}]_{s=2}\right)\\ -\hat{\mathbf{C}}\left([\hat{\mathbf{t}}_{M=2}],[\hat{\mathbf{t}}_{M=0}]\right)_{s=2} & -\hat{\mathbf{C}}\left([\hat{\mathbf{t}}_{M=2}],[\hat{\mathbf{t}}_{M=0}]\right)_{s=2}\left(\hat{\mathbf{V}}\left([\hat{\mathbf{t}}_{M=0}]_{s=2}\right)^{-1}\right)\hat{\mathbf{C}}\left([\hat{\mathbf{t}}_{M=2}],[\hat{\mathbf{t}}_{M=0}]\right)'_{s=2}\end{bmatrix} \quad (29)$$

$$=\begin{bmatrix}\mathbf{0} & \mathbf{0}\\ \mathbf{0} & \hat{\mathbf{V}}\left([\hat{\mathbf{t}}_{M=2}]_{s=2}\right)-\hat{\mathbf{C}}\left([\hat{\mathbf{t}}_{M=2}],[\hat{\mathbf{t}}_{M=0}]\right)_{s=2}\left(\hat{\mathbf{V}}\left([\hat{\mathbf{t}}_{M=0}]_{s=2}\right)^{-1}\right)\hat{\mathbf{C}}\left([\hat{\mathbf{t}}_{M=2}],[\hat{\mathbf{t}}_{M=0}]\right)'_{s=2}\end{bmatrix}$$

Because it is the study variables that are of primary interest and not the auxiliary variables, the partitions of the RE for the study variables are extracted from Eqs. 28 and 29 as:

$$[\hat{\mathbf{t}}_{M=2}]_{s=\{U,2\}} = [\hat{\mathbf{t}}_{M=2}]_{s=2} + \left[\hat{\mathbf{C}}\left([\hat{\mathbf{t}}_{M=2}],[\hat{\mathbf{t}}_{M=0}]\right)_{s=2}\left(\hat{\mathbf{V}}\left([\hat{\mathbf{t}}_{M=0}]_{s=2}\right)^{-1}\right)\right]\left([\mathbf{t}_{M=0}]_{s=U} - [\hat{\mathbf{t}}_{M=0}]_{s=2}\right)$$

$$\hat{\mathbf{V}}\left([\hat{\mathbf{t}}_{M=2}]_{s=\{U,2\}}\right) = \hat{\mathbf{V}}\left([\hat{\mathbf{t}}_{M=2}]_{s=2}\right) - \hat{\mathbf{C}}\left([\hat{\mathbf{t}}_{M=2}],[\hat{\mathbf{t}}_{M=0}]\right)_{s=2}\left(\hat{\mathbf{V}}\left([\hat{\mathbf{t}}_{M=0}]_{s=2}\right)^{-1}\right)\hat{\mathbf{C}}\left([\hat{\mathbf{t}}_{M=2}],[\hat{\mathbf{t}}_{M=0}]\right)'_{s=2} \quad (30)$$

Simon and Chia (2002) prove that the RE in Eqs. 27, 28, and 30 satisfies the vector constraint $[\hat{\mathbf{t}}_{M=0}]_{s=\{U,2\}} = \mathbf{t}_{M=0} \neq [\hat{\mathbf{t}}_{M=0}]_{s=2}$; is unbiased (i.e., $E[\hat{\mathbf{t}}_{M=2}]_s = \{U,2\} = \mathbf{t}_{M=2}$); has a smaller error covariance than the unconstrained sample survey vector estimator (e.g., trace $(\hat{\mathbf{V}}[\hat{\mathbf{t}}_{M=2}]_{s=\{U,2\}}) \leq$ trace $(\hat{\mathbf{V}}[\hat{\mathbf{t}}_{M=2}]_{s=2})$; and is the BLUE. Czaplewski (in prep.[b]) further demonstrates that the diagonal partition of the covariance matrix for the variables in Eq. 16 is $\mathbf{R} = \mathbf{0}$, and the off-diagonal cross-correlation matrix partition between the study variables and the auxiliary census variables is exactly zero, i.e., $\hat{\mathbf{C}}([\hat{\mathbf{t}}_{M=2}],[\hat{\mathbf{t}}_{M=0}])_{s=(U,2)} = \mathbf{0}$. In effect, the auxiliary census vector acts as a constraint on RE. Exact agreement with the census vector is imposed by the RE without post-stratification. The estimated covariance matrix in Eq. 30 is unbiased (conditional upon the sample), and it is not an approximation, as with post-stratification (e.g., Cochran 1977:135; Särndal and others 1992:266; Scott and others 2005).

The RE partition in Eq. 30 contains all the relevant information available in the auxiliary census variables, and the information provided by those census variables is unnecessary for any subsequent recursions with the RRE. In other words, the RE has filtered out all relevant information in these census auxiliary variables. As discussed in the previous section, the efficiency of this sampling design and its estimator (Eq. 30) remains dependent upon the correlations and associations between the remotely sensed satellite measurements (M = 0) and the FIA field measurements (M = 2).

Recall that the covariance matrix $\hat{\mathbf{V}}([\hat{\mathbf{t}}_{M=0}]_{s=2})$ in Eq. 27 is assumed to be full rank. However, because the sum of all elements in vector estimate $\mathbf{1}[\hat{\mathbf{t}}_{M=0}]_{s=2} = A$, its covariance matrix is positive-semidefinite and not full rank. At least one of the census constraints is redundant.

Numerically Stable Algorithm

Equation 27 is infeasible because the inverse of the covariance matrix $\hat{V}([\hat{t}_{M=0}]_{s=2})$ is not full rank whenever the auxiliary vector contains proportions or totals for a dichotomous transformation of a polychotomous categorical variable. In more general terms, the Kalman filter is notoriously vulnerable to numerical round-off errors as the measurement error covariance matrix becomes small, especially as recursions accumulate. The challenges posed by numerical errors to optimal estimation, including RRE, and practical solutions are discussed in the section "Robust Numerics".

In the special case of a measurement vector of known census constants, as in this section, a slightly different algorithm applies a vector of equality constraints that is numerically robust, even with a positive-semidefinite covariance matrix (Simon and Chia 2002). Because the constraints are a vector of known census constants $t_{M=0}$, i.e., $V(t_{M=0}) = 0$, they are mutually independent, and each ith scalar census value $(t_{M=0})_i$ of the $q_{M=0}$-by-1 constraint vector $t_{M=0}$ may be applied separately in a sequential recursive procedure.

Let h_i be the 1-by-$(q_{M=0} + q_{M=2})$ vector containing row i of the $q_{M=0}$-by-$(q_{M=0} + q_{M=2})$ measurement matrix H in Eq. 27. The estimator that sequentially applies all $q_{M=0}$ constraints, $i = \{1, 2, \ldots, q_{M=0}\}$, is defined as:

$$\left(\begin{bmatrix} \hat{t}_{M=0} \\ \hat{t}_{M=2} \end{bmatrix}_{s=\{U,2\}}\right)_i = \left(\begin{bmatrix} \hat{t}_{M=0} \\ \hat{t}_{M=2} \end{bmatrix}_{s=\{U,2\}}\right)_{i-1} + k_i \left[(t_{M=0})_i - h_i \left(\begin{bmatrix} \hat{t}_{M=0} \\ \hat{t}_{M=2} \end{bmatrix}_{s=\{U,2\}}\right)_{i-1} \right] \qquad (31)$$

where

$$\left(\begin{bmatrix} \hat{t}_{M=0} \\ \hat{t}_{M=2} \end{bmatrix}_{s=\{U,2\}}\right)_0 = \begin{bmatrix} \hat{t}_{M=0} \\ \hat{t}_{M=2} \end{bmatrix}_{s=2} \qquad (32)$$

$$\hat{V}\left(\begin{bmatrix} \hat{t}_{M=0} \\ \hat{t}_{M=2} \end{bmatrix}_{s=\{U,2\}}\right)_i = (I - k_i h_i) \left[\hat{V}\left(\begin{bmatrix} \hat{t}_{M=0} \\ \hat{t}_{M=2} \end{bmatrix}_{s=\{U,2\}}\right)_{i-1}\right] (I - k_i h_i)'$$

where

$$k_i = \left(\frac{1}{h_i \hat{V}\left(\begin{bmatrix} \hat{t}_{M=0} \\ \hat{t}_{M=2} \end{bmatrix}_{s=\{U,2\}}\right)_{i-1} h_i'}\right) \hat{V}\left(\begin{bmatrix} \hat{t}_{M=0} \\ \hat{t}_{M=2} \end{bmatrix}_{s=\{U,2\}}\right)_{i-1} h_i' \qquad (33)$$

$$\hat{V}\left(\begin{bmatrix} \hat{t}_{M=0} \\ \hat{t}_{M=2} \end{bmatrix}_{s=\{U,2\}}\right)_0 = \hat{V}\left(\begin{bmatrix} \hat{t}_{M=0} \\ \hat{t}_{M=2} \end{bmatrix}_{s=2}\right)$$

k_i is the $(q_{M=0} + q_{M=2})$-by-1 column vector of optimal (EBLUE) weights, and $(t_{M=0})_i$ is the ith element of the census constraint vector $[t_{M=0}]$. The final RRE after $q_{M=0}$ recursions through Eqs. 31, 32, and 33 equals:

$$\left(\begin{bmatrix}\hat{\mathbf{t}}_{\mathrm{M=0}} \\ \hline \hat{\mathbf{t}}_{\mathrm{M=2}}\end{bmatrix}_{s=\{U,2\}}\right)_{q_{\mathrm{M=0}}} = \begin{bmatrix}\hat{\mathbf{t}}_{\mathrm{M=0}} \\ \hline \hat{\mathbf{t}}_{\mathrm{M=2}}\end{bmatrix}_{s=2} + \sum_{i=1}^{q_{\mathrm{M=0}}} \mathbf{k}_i \left[\left(t_{\mathrm{M=0}}\right)_i - \mathbf{h}_i\left(\begin{bmatrix}\hat{\mathbf{t}}_{\mathrm{M=0}} \\ \hline \hat{\mathbf{t}}_{\mathrm{M=2}}\end{bmatrix}_{s=\{U,2\}}\right)_{i-1}\right] \tag{34}$$

$$\hat{\mathbf{V}}\left(\begin{bmatrix}\hat{\mathbf{t}}_{\mathrm{M=0}} \\ \hline \hat{\mathbf{t}}_{\mathrm{M=2}}\end{bmatrix}_{s=\{U,2\}}\right)_{q_{\mathrm{M=0}}} = \left(\prod_{i=\{q_{\mathrm{M=0}},\cdots,2,1\}}\left(\mathbf{I} - \mathbf{k}_i\mathbf{h}_i\right)\right)\hat{\mathbf{V}}\left(\begin{bmatrix}\hat{\mathbf{t}}_{\mathrm{M=0}} \\ \hline \hat{\mathbf{t}}_{\mathrm{M=2}}\end{bmatrix}_{s=2}\right)\left(\prod_{i=\{1,2,\cdots,q_{\mathrm{M=0}}\}}\left(\mathbf{I} - \mathbf{k}_i\mathbf{h}_i\right)'\right) \tag{35}$$

The final RRE for the $q_{\mathrm{M=2}}$-by-1 vector of population estimates for the $q_{\mathrm{M=2}}$ study variables equals the linear transformations of Eqs. 34 and 35 with the $q_{\mathrm{M=2}}$-by-$(q_{\mathrm{M=0}} + q_{\mathrm{M=2}})$ indicator matrix $\mathbf{H}_y = [\mathbf{0}|\mathbf{I}]$:

$$\begin{bmatrix}\hat{\mathbf{t}}_{\mathrm{M=2}}\end{bmatrix}_{s=\{U,2\}} = \mathbf{H}_y \begin{bmatrix}\hat{\mathbf{t}}_{\mathrm{M=0}} \\ \hline \hat{\mathbf{t}}_{\mathrm{M=2}}\end{bmatrix}_{s=\{U,2\}} \tag{36}$$

$$\hat{\mathbf{V}}\left(\begin{bmatrix}\hat{\mathbf{t}}_{\mathrm{M=2}}\end{bmatrix}_{s=\{U,2\}}\right)_{q_{\mathrm{M=0}}} = \mathbf{H}_y\left[\hat{\mathbf{V}}\left(\begin{bmatrix}\hat{\mathbf{t}}_{\mathrm{M=0}} \\ \hline \hat{\mathbf{t}}_{\mathrm{M=2}}\end{bmatrix}_{s=\{U,2\}}\right)_{q_{\mathrm{M=0}}}\right]\mathbf{H}_y' \tag{37}$$

Each ith recursion (Eqs. 31 to 33) has an associated scalar residual difference between the auxiliary census total $(t_{\mathrm{M=0}})_I$ This residual may be standardized with its estimate variance:

$$r_i = \frac{\left(t_{\mathrm{M=0}}\right)_i - \mathbf{h}_i\left(\begin{bmatrix}\hat{\mathbf{t}}_{\mathrm{M=0}} \\ \hline \hat{\mathbf{t}}_{\mathrm{M=2}}\end{bmatrix}_{s=\{U,2\}}\right)_{i-1}}{\mathbf{h}_i\left[\hat{\mathbf{V}}\left(\begin{bmatrix}\hat{\mathbf{t}}_{\mathrm{M=0}} \\ \hline \hat{\mathbf{t}}_{\mathrm{M=2}}\end{bmatrix}_{s=\{U,2\}}\right)_{i-1}\right]\mathbf{h}_i'} \tag{38}$$

If all assumptions are correct, then r_i in Eq. 38 is expected to have a zero mean with unit variance. If its realized value is inconsistent with this expectation (e.g., r_i is larger than two standard deviation units [$r_i<$-2 or $r_i>$2]), then one or more assumptions are suspect. It is also possible that a rare extreme value for the sample estimate of the ith auxiliary variable was observed by chance. This may be most common for categorical auxiliary variables that are rare in the population. One ad hoc rule would be to omit the ith auxiliary variable with a relatively large residual (e.g., $|r_i|>$2) from the RRE. This rule would provide some insurance against over-zealous application of remotely sensed and other geospatial auxiliary data, which often can be cross-classified in numerous ways, especially when intersected with geopolitical boundaries (e.g., states, counties, and National Forests).

The final $(q_{\mathrm{M=0}})^{\mathrm{th}}$ recursion of the RRE in Eqs. 31 to 33 might be affected by the sequence $1 \le i \le q_{\mathrm{M=0}}$, in which the scalar census auxiliary variables are applied. This might be especially true if the ad hoc rule above is used to censor certain scalar auxiliary variables that have unexpectedly large residuals (Eq. 38). The first set of auxiliary variables might be geopolitical boundaries so that areal summaries of population estimates agree with the known area of each geopolitical entity. The next set might be common and important remotely sensed classifications, such as a binary forest/non-forest classification for each pixel. All pixels under this binary auxiliary variable might be cross-classified by geopolitical boundaries. The auxiliary variables with the largest extent might be applied first. Similar to methods used by Statistics Sweden (Särndal and Lundström 2008), some sort of stepwise approach might first apply those auxiliary variables that are most effective in increasing the precision of FIA study variables. Further research is warranted.

When census constants are imposed as constraints, the sequential algorithm in Eqs. 31 to 37 are numerically more efficient than the usual algorithm in Eq. 30 (Maybeck 1979:375; Grewal and Andrews 2001:226). At least as important, the sequential algorithm in Eqs. 31 to 37 is more easily implemented in database software because it replaces a single matrix inversion with a sequence of $q_{M=0}$ scalar inverses. Matrix algebra software is not required, which makes implementation more feasible within database software used by government programs like FIA. Regardless, all computations and data storage should use double precision numerics to reduce insidious round-off errors. The sequential algorithm does not eliminate redundant measurements; therefore, it adds no new information. Rather, it simply accommodates redundancies and avoids matrix inversion through a convenient and robust numerical solution.

RRE as the Optimal Linear Calibration Estimator

The seminal paper by Deville and Särndal (1992) signaled the emergence of calibration estimators in the sample survey literature as a means to improve efficiency with auxiliary data. The calibration estimator can achieve the same efficiency with a smaller sample size as the Horvitz-Thompson estimator. Therefore, the calibration estimator is relevant to small-area estimation where small sample sizes limit estimation precision. In their paper, titled *Borrowing Strength is Not the Best Technique Within a Wide Class of Design-Consistent Domain Estimators*, Estevao and Särndal (2004) consider direct estimators of small-domain parameters with fixed auxiliary census information. Other than their finite-population perspective, this is exactly the subject of this section.

If the number of PSUs in a domain is sufficiently large, then direct domain (or sub-population) estimators are feasible. Direct domain estimators make use of the study variable, that is, the variable of interest, and auxiliary variables that are solely within the domain (Rao 2005). (Indirect estimators, which borrow strength from outside the domain, are considered under "Non-Linear Pseudo-Estimators" below.) Estevao and Särndal (2004) conclude "for a fixed set of auxiliary information, the minimum asymptotic design-based variance is obtained with a direct estimator, derived by calibration rather than by regression fitting … and any estimator in the class that attempts to borrow strength is less precise."

This conclusion appears to include a different type of small-domain composite estimator, which combines an indirect synthetic model-based estimate with the direct design-based estimator for the small-domain. The objective is to reduce the inherent risk of bias with the model-based synthetic estimator. Examples of this approach include Lui and Cumberland (1991), Longford (1999), Fuller and Rao (2001), and Francisco (2003). However, based on the cited findings of Estevao and Särndal (2004), this type of composite estimator is not given further attention in the remainder of this report.

In the class of direct domain estimators considered by Estevao and Särndal (2004:657), the asymptotically optimal estimator of a scalar study variable y_{d+} from the sample s in domain d is given (with their notation) as:

$$\hat{y}_{d+} = \hat{y}_{d\oplus\pi} + \left(\mathbf{x}_{C+} - \hat{\mathbf{x}}_{d\oplus\pi}\right)\left(\sum_{k\in s}\sum_{l\in s}\left(a_k a_l - a_{kl}\right)\mathbf{x}_{Cl}\mathbf{x}_{Ck}'\right)^{-1}\left(\sum_{k\in s}\sum_{l\in s}\left(a_k a_l - a_{kl}\right)\mathbf{x}_{Cl}y_{dk}\right) \tag{39}$$

$U_d \subseteq U$	Domain d of the finite population $U = \{1,\ldots,k,\ldots,N\}$
$U_C \subseteq U$	Calibration group C within the finite population $U = \{1,\ldots,k,\ldots,N\}$
$y_{dk} = \delta_{dk} y_k : k \in s$	The observed scalar value of the study variable for PSU k in sample s in domain d ($\delta_{dk} = 1$ for k, a member of $U_d = 0$, otherwise)
$\hat{y}_{d\oplus\pi} = \sum_{k \in s} a_k y_{dk}$	Horvitz-Thompson (HT) estimator of the domain total for scalar study variable in domain d
$a_k = 1/\pi_k$	Sampling weight (i.e., expansion factor) for PSU k
$\mathbf{x}_{Ck}$	J-by-1 vector of auxiliary information for PSU k in calibration group C (i.e., population control group)
$\mathbf{x}_{C+}$	J-by-1 vector of auxiliary information in calibration group C
$\hat{\mathbf{x}}_{d\oplus\pi} = \sum_{k \in s} a_k \mathbf{x}_{dk}$	HT estimator of the domain total for the J-by-1 vector of auxiliary information in domain d, where $\mathrm{E}[\hat{\mathbf{x}}_{d\oplus\pi}] = \mathbf{x}_{C+}$

Equation 39 may be rewritten as:

$$\hat{y}_{d+} = \hat{y}_{d\oplus\pi} + \hat{\mathbf{C}}'_{Cdx}\left(\hat{\mathbf{V}}_{Cx}\right)^{-1}\left(\mathbf{x}_{C+} - \hat{\mathbf{x}}_{d\oplus\pi}\right)$$

where

$\hat{\mathbf{V}}_{Cx} = \left(\sum_{k \in s} \sum_{l \in s} (a_k a_l - a_{kl})\mathbf{x}_{Cl}\mathbf{x}'_{Ck}\right)$	HT estimator for the J-by-J non-singular covariance matrix for the vector of estimated totals for the auxiliary variables in calibration group C (Särndal and others 1992:43, 188) (40)
$\hat{\mathbf{C}}_{Cdxy} = \left(\sum_{k \in s} \sum_{l \in s} (a_k a_l - a_{kl})\mathbf{x}_{Cl} y_{dk}\right)$	HT estimator for the J-by-1 cross-covariance vector for the estimated totals for the vector of auxiliary variables $\mathbf{x}$ in calibration group C and the scalar study variable y in domain d (Särndal and others 1992:43, 188)

Equation 40 can be expressed in a different matrix expression, in which the dimensions are enlarged from J to $(J + 1)$ to form:

$$\begin{aligned}
\begin{bmatrix} \mathbf{x}_{d+} \\ \hline \hat{y}_{d+} \end{bmatrix} &= \begin{bmatrix} \hat{\mathbf{x}}_{d\oplus\pi} \\ \hline \hat{y}_{d\oplus\pi} \end{bmatrix} + \begin{bmatrix} \mathbf{I} \\ \hline \hat{\mathbf{C}}'_{Cdxy}\left(\hat{\mathbf{V}}_{Cx}\right)^{-1} \end{bmatrix}\left(\mathbf{x}_{C+} - \mathbf{H}\begin{bmatrix} \hat{\mathbf{x}}_{d\oplus\pi} \\ \hline \hat{y}_{d\oplus\pi} \end{bmatrix}\right) \\[2em]
&= \begin{bmatrix} \hat{\mathbf{x}}_{d\oplus\pi} \\ \hline \hat{y}_{d\oplus\pi} \end{bmatrix} + \begin{bmatrix} \hat{\mathbf{V}}_{Cx} \\ \hline \hat{\mathbf{C}}'_{Cdxy} \end{bmatrix}\left(\hat{\mathbf{V}}_{Cx}\right)^{-1}\left(\mathbf{x}_{C+} - \mathbf{H}\begin{bmatrix} \hat{\mathbf{x}}_{d\oplus\pi} \\ \hline \hat{y}_{d\oplus\pi} \end{bmatrix}\right)
\end{aligned}$$

(41)

where the J-by-$(J+1)$ indicator matrix $\mathbf{H} = [\mathbf{I}|\mathbf{0}]$. With further algebraic embellishment, Eq. 41 equals:

$$\left[\frac{\mathbf{x}_{d+}}{\hat{y}_{d+}}\right] = \left[\frac{\hat{\mathbf{x}}_{d\oplus\pi}}{\hat{y}_{d\oplus\pi}}\right] + \left[\frac{\hat{\mathbf{V}}_{Cx}}{\hat{\mathbf{C}}'_{Cdxy}}\right]\left(\mathbf{H}\left[\frac{\hat{\mathbf{V}}_{Cx}\ \vdots\ \hat{\mathbf{C}}_{Cdxy}}{\hat{\mathbf{C}}'_{Cdxy}\ \vdots\ \hat{v}(\hat{y}_{d\oplus\pi})}\right]\mathbf{H}'\right)^{-1}\left(\mathbf{x}_{C+} - \mathbf{H}\left[\frac{\hat{\mathbf{x}}_{d\oplus\pi}}{\hat{y}_{d\oplus\pi}}\right]\right)$$

$$= \left[\frac{\hat{\mathbf{x}}_{d\oplus\pi}}{\hat{y}_{d\oplus\pi}}\right] + \left[\left(\hat{\mathbf{V}}\left(\left[\frac{\hat{\mathbf{x}}_{d\oplus\pi}}{\hat{y}_{d\oplus\pi}}\right]_C\right)\mathbf{H}'\right)\left(\mathbf{H}\,\hat{\mathbf{V}}\left(\left[\frac{\hat{\mathbf{x}}_{d\oplus\pi}}{\hat{y}_{d\oplus\pi}}\right]_C\right)\mathbf{H}'\right)^{-1}\right]\left(\mathbf{x}_{C+} - \mathbf{H}\left[\frac{\hat{\mathbf{x}}_{d\oplus\pi}}{\hat{y}_{d\oplus\pi}}\right]\right)$$

$$= \left[\frac{\hat{\mathbf{x}}_{d\oplus\pi}}{\hat{y}_{d\oplus\pi}}\right] + \mathbf{K}\left(\mathbf{x}_{C+} - \mathbf{H}\left[\frac{\hat{\mathbf{x}}_{d\oplus\pi}}{\hat{y}_{d\oplus\pi}}\right]\right)$$

where

(42)

$$\hat{\mathbf{V}}\left(\left[\frac{\hat{\mathbf{x}}_{d\oplus\pi}}{\hat{y}_{d\oplus\pi}}\right]_C\right) = \left[\frac{\hat{\mathbf{V}}_{Cx}\ \vdots\ \hat{\mathbf{C}}_{Cdxy}}{\hat{\mathbf{C}}'_{Cdxy}\ \vdots\ \hat{v}(\hat{y}_{d\oplus\pi})}\right]$$

$$\hat{\mathbf{V}}\left(\left[\frac{\hat{\mathbf{x}}_{d\oplus\pi}}{\hat{y}_{d\oplus\pi}}\right]_C\right)\mathbf{H}' = \left[\frac{\hat{\mathbf{V}}_{Cx}\ \vdots\ \hat{\mathbf{C}}_{Cdxy}}{\hat{\mathbf{C}}'_{Cdxy}\ \vdots\ \hat{v}(\hat{y}_{d\oplus\pi})}\right]\left[\frac{\mathbf{I}}{\mathbf{0}}\right] = \left[\frac{\hat{\mathbf{V}}_{Cx}}{\hat{\mathbf{C}}'_{Cdxy}}\right]$$

$$\mathbf{K} = \left[\left(\hat{\mathbf{V}}\left(\left[\frac{\hat{\mathbf{x}}_{d\oplus\pi}}{\hat{y}_{d\oplus\pi}}\right]_C\right)\mathbf{H}'\right)\left(\mathbf{H}\,\hat{\mathbf{V}}\left(\left[\frac{\hat{\mathbf{x}}_{d\oplus\pi}}{\hat{y}_{d\oplus\pi}}\right]_C\right)\mathbf{H}'\right)^{-1}\right]$$

$$\hat{y}_{d+} = \left[0\ \vdots\ \cdots\ \vdots\ 0\ \vdots\ 1\right]\left[\frac{\mathbf{x}_{d+}}{\hat{y}_{d+}}\right]$$

Equation 42 is algebraically identical to the RE for the state-vector in Eq. 27, except the study variable is a scalar (y) rather than a vector ($\mathbf{t}_{M=2}$) and:

$$\hat{\mathbf{x}}_{d\oplus\pi} = \left[\hat{\mathbf{t}}_{M=0}\right]_{s=2}$$

Sample survey estimate of the domain totals for the vector of auxiliary variables

$$\mathbf{x}_{d+} = \left[\mathbf{t}_{M=0}\right]_{s=U}$$

Known census statistics for the domain totals for the vector of auxiliary variables

$$\hat{y}_{d\oplus\pi} = \left[\hat{\mathbf{t}}_{M=2}\right]_{s=2} = \left[\hat{t}_{M=2}\right]_{s=2}$$

Sample survey estimate of the scalar domain total for the study variable

$$\left[\frac{\hat{\mathbf{x}}_{d\oplus\pi}}{\hat{y}_{d\oplus\pi}}\right] = \left[\frac{\hat{\mathbf{t}}_{M=0}}{\hat{t}_{M=2}}\right]_{s=2}$$

The $[(J+1) = (q_{M=0} + q_{M=2})]$-by-1 column vector of sample survey estimates

$$\hat{y}_{d+} = \left[\hat{\mathbf{t}}_{M=2}\right]_{s=\{U,2\}}$$

The scalar calibration estimate of the study variable in domain d, which is exactly equal to the RRE estimate

Therefore, the RRE is algebraically identical to the optimal direct calibration estimator for domain d in which the domain total (e.g., a census) is known exactly without error for one or more auxiliary variables (e.g., $U_d = U$) for one or more calibration groups (Estevao and Särndal 2004:649), and the domain membership for each sampled unit is known without classification error. The domain census constants "must not be out-of-date, erroneous total" (Estevao and Särndal 2004:650).

With a univariate study variable (y) and a numerically stable inverse covariance matrix, the results from the RE in Eqs. 27 or 39 may be represented as a system of calibration weights, $w_k = a_k g_k$, for each sampled PSU = k (Estevao and Särndal 2004:651). Using the notation of (Estevao and Särndal 2004:651, 657),

$$w_k = a_k g_k = a_k + \left(\mathbf{x}_{C+} - \hat{\mathbf{x}}_{d\oplus\pi}\right)'\left(\hat{\mathbf{V}}_{C\mathbf{x}}\right)^{-1}\left(\sum_{l\in s}\left(a_k a_l - a_{kl}\right)\mathbf{x}_{Cl}y_{dk}\right) \tag{43}$$

These will be the optimal calibration weights for a single study variable, e.g., $(y_{dk})_a$, but they are sub-optimal for any other study variable, e.g., $(y_{dk})_b$, except in the rare case in which their cross-covariance matrices are identical, e.g., $(\hat{\mathbf{C}}_{Cdxy})_a = (\hat{\mathbf{C}}_{Cdxy})_b$. Otherwise, each study variable requires a different system of optimal scalar calibration weights from Eq. 43. The section "Optimal PSU Expansion Values" develops a vector system of expansion values that is optimal for each study variable in the RRE state vector [$\mathbf{y}$].

One simpler ad hoc method for a single scalar calibration weight w_k with a vector of L study variables [$\mathbf{y}$] is a linear transformation with a 1-by-L matrix for the first principal component from a Principal Component Analysis on all PSUs $k \in s$, yielding a scalar study variable $(y_{dk})_{PC=1}$ unique to each PSU. This scalar variable, which would contain much of the information available in a multivariate variable of interest, would be used solely to compute the calibration weight in Eq. 43.

There is a fundamental problem with the calibration estimator, regardless of the chosen study variable of interest. Estevao and Särndal (2004:657) make the following observation regarding the optimal calibration estimator: "In estimation for the whole population U, the asymptotically optimal estimator has been carefully examined in, for example, Casady and Valliant (1993), Montanari (1998, 2000), and Montanari and Ranalli (2002). It is known to be **unstable**, especially for designs more complex than SRS. Here we encounter the asymptotically optimal estimator in the context of domain estimation. The discussion in the cited references is relevant here too. … A prudent approach is to use … (a sub-optimal sampling weight) … in all cases."

As frequently recognized throughout this report, the RE, i.e., the static Kalman filter, is vulnerable to numerical errors, especially if the domain totals for the auxiliary variables (e.g., $\mathbf{x}_{d+} = [\mathbf{t}_{M=0}]_{s=U}$) are known with perfect or high precision. Similarly recognized are the numerical solutions that are well developed in the engineering literature on the Kalman filter. When the familiar calibration and regression estimators for complex sample surveys are seen from a different perspective, i.e., as special cases of the static Kalman filter, then numerical solutions instantly become available from 50 years of engineering experience. Equations 31 to 37 are examples.

In the current context, a census of vector constants for geopolitical domains, such as the areas of counties and public lands, are available from administrative records. Each sampled PSU is known to be a member of one of these domains. Such constraints not only assure summaries of statistical estimates are consistent with these widely known administrative records, but it is possible they can improve accuracy of sample survey estimates for other study variables (e.g., Van Deusen 2005). In addition, remotely sensed auxiliary census variables might further improve efficiency of the estimators for the study variables within a calibration group, which may be identical to a study domain. This might utilize multiple sets of overlapping or non-exhaustive domains, namely, complex auxiliary information (Estevao and Särndal 2006). Examples include domains based on polychotomous classifications of ecoregions, ecofloristic zones, climatic zones, land forms, landscape types, and land ownership maps. They may also include classifications of land cover and forest conditions with remotely sensed data. The recursive algorithm in Eqs. 31 to 37 can be sequentially applied to each set of independent census domains. This fortunate attribute of RRE further permits off-line optimization of prediction models for each individual dichotomous category of any polychotomous variable, which is familiar practice with remotely sensed predictor variables and software. Improvements through remote sensing techniques should, in principle, improve statistical accuracy of population and domain estimates. The various sets of independent calibration groups can be more broadly defined than domains of study, which can assure sufficient sample size within each group (Lehtonen and others 2003). They need not be cross-classified, which reduces the problem of very small-domains that contain too few PSUs for direct domain estimation. Additional research is needed to best use the very detailed auxiliary data possible with airborne and spaceborne sensors. For example, which auxiliary variables provide the most gain in statistical precision for FIA study variables without undo risks to numerical stability?

Three-Phase Sampling for Continuous Variables

Three-phase sampling "can be a very effective design for the estimation of regional and national forest cover type frequencies … with data gathered in each phase at a different resolution (scale)" (Magnussen 2003). Extension to three or more sampling phases is expedited by the sequential approach inherent to estimation within the RRE. For example, consider a three-phase design that starts with a census of satellite pixels ($s = U$) that is measured with M = 0 remote sensing protocol. The next phase is photo-interpretation of a large simple random sample of points that is measured with both the M = 1 photo-interpretation protocol and the M = 0 remote sensing protocol. The final phase is a small, simple random sample of points measured with the M = 2 FIA field protocol in addition to the M = 0 and M = 1 protocols. This example duplicates much of the previous section on "Two-Phase Sampling for Continuous Variables with a Census at Phase 1". However, the purpose of the current section is to demonstrate more fully the sequential application of the RRE to more complex sample survey designs.

The first step is a design-based estimate for population totals with the M = 0 remote sensing protocol and the M = 1 photo-interpretation protocol from the Phase 1 sample ($s = 1$). The ($q_{M=0} + q_{M=1}$)-by-1 vector estimate and its ($q_{M=0} + q_{M=1}$)-by-($q_{M=0} + q_{M=1}$) covariance matrix are:

$$\left[\begin{array}{c} \hat{\mathbf{t}}_{M=0} \\ \hline \hat{\mathbf{t}}_{M=1} \end{array}\right]_{s=1} = \frac{A}{n_{s=1}} \sum_{j \in (s=1)} \left[\begin{array}{c} \mathbf{y}_{M=0} \\ \hline \mathbf{y}_{M=1} \end{array}\right]_j$$

$$\hat{\mathbf{V}}\left(\left[\begin{array}{c} \hat{\mathbf{t}}_{M=0} \\ \hline \hat{\mathbf{t}}_{M=1} \end{array}\right]_{s=1}\right) = \frac{A^2}{(n_{s=1}-1)\,n_{s=1}} \left[\sum_{j \in (s=1)} \left\{ \left(\left[\begin{array}{c} \mathbf{y}_{M=0} \\ \hline \mathbf{y}_{M=1} \end{array}\right]_j - \left[\begin{array}{c} \left([\mathbf{t}_{M=0}]_{s=U}\right)\!/A \\ \hline \overline{\hat{\mathbf{y}}}_{M=1} \end{array}\right]_{s=1} \right) \left(\left[\begin{array}{c} \mathbf{y}_{M=0} \\ \hline \mathbf{y}_{M=1} \end{array}\right]_j - \left[\begin{array}{c} \left([\mathbf{t}_{M=0}]_{s=U}\right)\!/A \\ \hline \overline{\hat{\mathbf{y}}}_{M=1} \end{array}\right]_{s=1} \right)' \right\} \right] \qquad (44)$$

The sample covariance matrix in Eq. 44 uses the census values for the population means from the M = 0 remote sensing protocol (Eq. 48), rather than the corresponding estimates from the Phase 1 sample, to improve the estimated variances and covariances.

The second step is a design-based estimate for population totals with the M = 0 remote sensing protocol, the M = 1 photo-interpretation protocol, and the M = 2 FIA field data protocol from the small Phase 2 sample ($s = 2$). The ($q_{M=0} + q_{M=1} + q_{M=2}$)-by-1 vector estimate and its ($q_{M=0} + q_{M=1} + q_{M=2}$)-by-($q_{M=0} + q_{M=1} + q_{M=2}$) covariance matrix are:

$$\begin{bmatrix} \hat{\mathbf{t}}_{M=0} \\ \hat{\mathbf{t}}_{M=1} \\ \hat{\mathbf{t}}_{M=2} \end{bmatrix}_{s=2} = \frac{A}{n_{s=2}} \sum_{j \in (s=2)} \begin{bmatrix} \mathbf{y}_{M=0} \\ \mathbf{y}_{M=1} \\ \mathbf{y}_{M=2} \end{bmatrix}_j$$

$$\hat{\mathbf{V}} \left(\begin{bmatrix} \hat{\mathbf{t}}_{M=0} \\ \hat{\mathbf{t}}_{M=1} \\ \hat{\mathbf{t}}_{M=2} \end{bmatrix}_{s=2} \right) = \frac{A^2}{(n_{s=2}-1)\, n_{s=2}} \sum_{j \in (s=2)} \left(\begin{bmatrix} \mathbf{y}_{M=0} \\ \mathbf{y}_{M=1} \\ \mathbf{y}_{M=2} \end{bmatrix}_j - \begin{bmatrix} \left([\mathbf{t}_{M=0}]_{s=U} \right)/A \\ \dfrac{n_{s=2}}{n_{s=1}+n_{s=2}} [\hat{\overline{\mathbf{y}}}_{M=1}]_{s=1} + \dfrac{n_{s=1}}{n_{s=1}+n_{s=2}} [\hat{\overline{\mathbf{y}}}_{M=1}]_{s=2} \\ [\hat{\overline{\mathbf{y}}}_{M=2}]_{s=2} \end{bmatrix} \right) \left(\begin{bmatrix} \mathbf{y}_{M=0} \\ \mathbf{y}_{M=1} \\ \mathbf{y}_{M=2} \end{bmatrix}_j - \begin{bmatrix} \left([\mathbf{t}_{M=0}]_{s=U} \right)/A \\ \dfrac{n_{s=2}}{n_{s=1}+n_{s=2}} [\hat{\overline{\mathbf{y}}}_{M=1}]_{s=1} + \dfrac{n_{s=1}}{n_{s=1}+n_{s=2}} [\hat{\overline{\mathbf{y}}}_{M=1}]_{s=2} \\ [\hat{\overline{\mathbf{y}}}_{M=2}]_{s=2} \end{bmatrix} \right)'$$

$$\qquad (45)$$

$$= \begin{bmatrix} \hat{\mathbf{V}}\left(\begin{bmatrix} \hat{\mathbf{t}}_{M=0} \\ \hat{\mathbf{t}}_{M=1} \end{bmatrix} \right)_{s=2} & \hat{\mathbf{C}}\left(\begin{bmatrix} \hat{\mathbf{t}}_{M=0} \\ \hat{\mathbf{t}}_{M=1} \end{bmatrix}, [\hat{\mathbf{t}}_{M=2}] \right) \\ \hat{\mathbf{C}}\left([\hat{\mathbf{t}}_{M=2}], \begin{bmatrix} \hat{\mathbf{t}}_{M=0} \\ \hat{\mathbf{t}}_{M=1} \end{bmatrix} \right) & \hat{\mathbf{V}}\left([\hat{\mathbf{t}}_{M=2}] \right)_{s=2} \end{bmatrix}$$

The sample covariance matrix in Eq. 45 uses the census values for the population means from the M = 0 remote sensing protocol and a composite estimate of the M = 1 means from the Phase 1 and 2 samples, rather than the corresponding estimates from the Phase 2 sample alone, to improve the estimated variances and covariances. The final term in Eq. 45 defines a matrix partition of the sample covariance matrix.

The third step combines the $(q_{M=0} + q_{M=1})$-by-1 Phase 1 estimate (Eq. 44, $s = 1$) with the $(q_{M=0} + q_{M=1} + q_{M=2})$-by-1 Phase 2 estimate ($s = 2$, Eq. 45) with RRE, similar to Eq. 24. The notation corresponding to the Kalman filter in Eq. 12 is:

$\hat{\mathbf{t}}_{X(1)} = \begin{bmatrix} \hat{\mathbf{t}}_{M=0} \\ \hat{\mathbf{t}}_{M=1} \\ \hat{\mathbf{t}}_{M=2} \end{bmatrix}_{s=2}$	$\hat{\mathbf{V}}\left(\hat{\mathbf{t}}_{X(1)} \right) = \hat{\mathbf{V}}\left(\begin{bmatrix} \hat{\mathbf{t}}_{M=0} \\ \hat{\mathbf{t}}_{M=1} \\ \hat{\mathbf{t}}_{M=2} \end{bmatrix}_{s=2} \right)$
$\hat{\mathbf{t}}_{Z(1)} = \begin{bmatrix} \hat{\mathbf{t}}_{M=0} \\ \hat{\mathbf{t}}_{M=1} \end{bmatrix}_{s=1}$	$\hat{\mathbf{V}}\left(\hat{\mathbf{t}}_{Z(1)} \right) = \hat{\mathbf{V}}\left(\begin{bmatrix} \hat{\mathbf{t}}_{M=0} \\ \hat{\mathbf{t}}_{M=1} \end{bmatrix}_{s=1} \right)$
$\mathbf{H} = [\mathbf{I} \mid \mathbf{0}]$	$\hat{\mathbf{C}}\left(\hat{\mathbf{t}}_{X(1)}, \hat{\mathbf{t}}_{Z(1)} \right) = \mathbf{0}$

$$\qquad (46)$$

The **H** matrix has dimensions $(q_{M=0} + q_{M=1})$-by-$(q_{M=0} + q_{M=1} + q_{M=2})$. From Eqs. 12 and 46, the composite estimator is:

$$
\mathbf{K} = \hat{\mathbf{V}}\left(\begin{bmatrix} \hat{\mathbf{t}}_{M=0} \\ \hline \hat{\mathbf{t}}_{M=1} \\ \hline \hat{\mathbf{t}}_{M=2} \end{bmatrix}_{s=2}\right) \mathbf{H}' \left(\left[\mathbf{H}\,\hat{\mathbf{V}}\left(\begin{bmatrix} \hat{\mathbf{t}}_{M=0} \\ \hline \hat{\mathbf{t}}_{M=1} \\ \hline \hat{\mathbf{t}}_{M=2} \end{bmatrix}_{s=2}\right)\mathbf{H}' + \hat{\mathbf{V}}\left(\begin{bmatrix} \hat{\mathbf{t}}_{M=0} \\ \hline \hat{\mathbf{t}}_{M=1} \end{bmatrix}_{s=1}\right)\right]^{-1}\right)
$$

$$
\begin{bmatrix} \hat{\mathbf{t}}_{M=0} \\ \hline \hat{\mathbf{t}}_{M=1} \\ \hline \hat{\mathbf{t}}_{M=2} \end{bmatrix}_{s=\{1,2\}} = \begin{bmatrix} \hat{\mathbf{t}}_{M=0} \\ \hline \hat{\mathbf{t}}_{M=1} \\ \hline \hat{\mathbf{t}}_{M=2} \end{bmatrix}_{s=2} + \mathbf{K}\left(\begin{bmatrix} \hat{\mathbf{t}}_{M=0} \\ \hat{\mathbf{t}}_{M=1} \end{bmatrix}_{s=1} - \mathbf{H}\begin{bmatrix} \hat{\mathbf{t}}_{M=0} \\ \hline \hat{\mathbf{t}}_{M=1} \\ \hline \hat{\mathbf{t}}_{M=2} \end{bmatrix}_{s=2}\right) \tag{47}
$$

$$
\hat{\mathbf{V}}\left(\begin{bmatrix} \hat{\mathbf{t}}_{M=0} \\ \hline \hat{\mathbf{t}}_{M=1} \\ \hline \hat{\mathbf{t}}_{M=2} \end{bmatrix}_{s=\{1,2\}}\right) = \hat{\mathbf{V}}\left(\begin{bmatrix} \hat{\mathbf{t}}_{M=0} \\ \hline \hat{\mathbf{t}}_{M=1} \\ \hline \hat{\mathbf{t}}_{M=2} \end{bmatrix}_{s=2}\right) - \mathbf{K}\,\mathbf{H}\left[\hat{\mathbf{V}}\left(\begin{bmatrix} \hat{\mathbf{t}}_{M=0} \\ \hline \hat{\mathbf{t}}_{M=1} \\ \hline \hat{\mathbf{t}}_{M=2} \end{bmatrix}_{s=2}\right)\right]
$$

The composite estimator, denoted $s = (1,2)$ in Eq. 47, is the minimum variance estimate of population totals for variables measured with all three protocols (remotely sensed satellite data, photo-interpreted data and field data) given the large Phase 1 sample and the smaller Phase 2 sample but not the census of remotely sensed data. Equation 47 might not be numerically stable, and it is very important to use numerically more stable methods that are reviewed in the section "Robust Numerics." The first three steps are analogous to the sequential approach used by Magnussen (2003).

The fourth step is to enumerate the $q_{M=0}$-by-1 vector population totals for the variables measured with M = 0 (remote sensing) from the census of remotely sensed pixels in the full-coverage satellite imagery:

$$
\left[\hat{\mathbf{t}}_{M=0}\right]_{s=U} = \sum_{j\in U}\left[\mathbf{y}_{M=0}\right]_j
$$

$$
\hat{\mathbf{V}}\left(\left[\hat{\mathbf{t}}_{M=0}\right]\right)_{s=U} = \mathbf{0} \tag{48}
$$

The $q_{M=0}$-by-$q_{M=0}$ covariance matrix in Eq. 48 is the zero matrix because census totals are known exactly.

The fifth step is to combine the $(q_{M=0} + q_{M=1} + q_{M=2})$-by-1 composite estimate from the Phase 1 and Phase 2 samples, denoted $s = (1,2)$ in Eq. 47, with the $q_{M=0}$-by-1 census vector, denoted $s = U$ in Eq. 48, again, similar to Eq. 24. The notation corresponding to the Kalman filter in Eq. 12 is:

$\hat{\mathbf{t}}_{X(1)} = \begin{bmatrix} \hat{\mathbf{t}}_{M=0} \\ \hline \hat{\mathbf{t}}_{M=1} \\ \hline \hat{\mathbf{t}}_{M=2} \end{bmatrix}_{s=\{1,2\}}$	$\hat{\mathbf{V}}\left(\hat{\mathbf{t}}_{X(1)}\right) = \hat{\mathbf{V}}\left(\begin{bmatrix} \hat{\mathbf{t}}_{M=0} \\ \hline \hat{\mathbf{t}}_{M=1} \\ \hline \hat{\mathbf{t}}_{M=2} \end{bmatrix}_{s=\{1,2\}}\right)$
$\hat{\mathbf{t}}_{Z(1)} = \left[\hat{\mathbf{t}}_{M=0}\right]_{s=U}$	$\hat{\mathbf{V}}\left(\hat{\mathbf{t}}_{Z(1)}\right) = \mathbf{0}$
$\mathbf{H} = \begin{bmatrix} \mathbf{I} & \vdots & \mathbf{0} \end{bmatrix}$	$\hat{\mathbf{C}}\left(\hat{\mathbf{t}}_{X(1)}, \hat{\mathbf{t}}_{Z(1)}\right) = \mathbf{0}$

$$(49)$$

The $\mathbf{H}$ matrix has dimensions $q_{M=0}$-by-$(q_{M=0} + q_{M=1} + q_{M=2})$. From Eqs. 12 and 49, the composite estimator is:

$$\mathbf{K} = \hat{\mathbf{V}}\left(\begin{bmatrix} \hat{\mathbf{t}}_{M=0} \\ \hline \hat{\mathbf{t}}_{M=1} \\ \hline \hat{\mathbf{t}}_{M=2} \end{bmatrix}_{s=\{1,2\}}\right) \mathbf{H}' \left(\left[\mathbf{H}\,\hat{\mathbf{V}}\left(\begin{bmatrix} \hat{\mathbf{t}}_{M=0} \\ \hline \hat{\mathbf{t}}_{M=1} \\ \hline \hat{\mathbf{t}}_{M=2} \end{bmatrix}_{s=\{1,2\}}\right)\mathbf{H}' + \mathbf{0}\right]^{-1}\right)$$

$$= \hat{\mathbf{V}}\left(\begin{bmatrix} \hat{\mathbf{t}}_{M=0} \\ \hline \hat{\mathbf{t}}_{M=1} \\ \hline \hat{\mathbf{t}}_{M=2} \end{bmatrix}_{s=\{1,2\}}\right) \mathbf{H}' \left(\left[\hat{\mathbf{V}}\left(\left[\hat{\mathbf{t}}_{M=0}\right]_{s=\{1,2\}}\right)\right]^{-1}\right)$$

$$\begin{bmatrix} \hat{\mathbf{t}}_{M=0} \\ \hline \hat{\mathbf{t}}_{M=1} \\ \hline \hat{\mathbf{t}}_{M=2} \end{bmatrix}_{s=\{U,1,2\}} = \begin{bmatrix} \hat{\mathbf{t}}_{M=0} \\ \hline \hat{\mathbf{t}}_{M=1} \\ \hline \hat{\mathbf{t}}_{M=2} \end{bmatrix}_{s=\{1,2\}} + \mathbf{K}\left(\left[\hat{\mathbf{t}}_{M=0}\right]_{s=U} - \mathbf{H}\begin{bmatrix} \hat{\mathbf{t}}_{M=0} \\ \hline \hat{\mathbf{t}}_{M=1} \\ \hline \hat{\mathbf{t}}_{M=2} \end{bmatrix}_{s=\{1,2\}}\right)$$

$$(50)$$

$$= \begin{bmatrix} \hat{\mathbf{t}}_{M=0} \\ \hline \hat{\mathbf{t}}_{M=1} \\ \hline \hat{\mathbf{t}}_{M=2} \end{bmatrix}_{s=\{1,2\}} + \mathbf{K}\left(\left[\hat{\mathbf{t}}_{M=0}\right]_{s=U} - \left[\hat{\mathbf{t}}_{M=0}\right]_{s=\{1,2\}}\right)$$

$$\hat{\mathbf{V}}\left(\begin{bmatrix} \hat{\mathbf{t}}_{M=0} \\ \hline \hat{\mathbf{t}}_{M=1} \\ \hline \hat{\mathbf{t}}_{M=2} \end{bmatrix}_{s=\{U,1,2\}}\right) = \hat{\mathbf{V}}\left(\begin{bmatrix} \hat{\mathbf{t}}_{M=0} \\ \hline \hat{\mathbf{t}}_{M=1} \\ \hline \hat{\mathbf{t}}_{M=2} \end{bmatrix}_{s=\{1,2\}}\right) - \mathbf{K}\,\mathbf{H}\,\hat{\mathbf{V}}\left(\begin{bmatrix} \hat{\mathbf{t}}_{M=0} \\ \hline \hat{\mathbf{t}}_{M=1} \\ \hline \hat{\mathbf{t}}_{M=2} \end{bmatrix}_{s=\{1,2\}}\right)$$

The composite estimator in Eq. 47, denoted $s = (U,1,2)$, is the minimum variance estimator given the Phase 1 and Phase 2 samples and the census of remotely sensed pixel data. Equations 44 to 50 may be expanded, as in Eqs. 20 to 27, to reveal analogies between RRE and more traditional univariate regression estimators (e.g., Särndal and others 1992). Again, numerically stable, but algebraically equivalent methods must be used to apply Eq. 50. These methods are discussed in the section "Robust Numerics."

The final step is to extract the portions of the composite estimator in Eq. 47 that contain the estimated population totals for variables measured with the FIA field protocol (M = 2):

$$\left[\hat{\mathbf{t}}_{M=2}\right]_{s=\{U,1,2\}} = \begin{bmatrix} \mathbf{0} & \vdots & \mathbf{0} & \vdots & \mathbf{I} \end{bmatrix} \begin{bmatrix} \hat{\mathbf{t}}_{M=0} \\ \hline \hat{\mathbf{t}}_{M=1} \\ \hline \hat{\mathbf{t}}_{M=2} \end{bmatrix}_{s=\{U,1,2\}}$$

$$\hat{\mathbf{V}}\left(\left[\hat{\mathbf{t}}_{M=2}\right]\right)_{s=\{U,1,2\}} = \begin{bmatrix} \mathbf{0} & \vdots & \mathbf{0} & \vdots & \mathbf{I} \end{bmatrix} \left\{ \hat{\mathbf{V}}\left(\begin{bmatrix} \hat{\mathbf{t}}_{M=0} \\ \hline \hat{\mathbf{t}}_{M=1} \\ \hline \hat{\mathbf{t}}_{M=2} \end{bmatrix} \right)_{s=\{U,1,2\}} \right\} \begin{bmatrix} \mathbf{0} \\ \mathbf{0} \\ \mathbf{I} \end{bmatrix}$$

(51)

A similar sequential process (Eqs. 44 to 51) may be used with four or more phases. Knottnerus (2003:359) uses the same approach to complex designs. The dimensions of the vectors and covariance matrices will increase because the estimates for all protocols are required until the very last step in the estimation sequence. The sequential process may also be used with multiple sources of census data, such as areas by geopolitical categories (e.g., counties and land ownership types) or other full-coverage, remotely sensed data (e.g., classifications of pixel data from the MODIS satellite and stand management geospatial information system independently produced by a National Forest). Knottnerus (2003:364) and Czaplewski (in prep.[b]) give more details.

A Potentially More Robust but Less Efficient Estimator

A potentially more robust but less efficient estimator for a multiphase design is possible by reducing the matrix dimensions at each of the sequential steps described earlier in this section. Magnussen (2003) found that RRE, when applied to three-phase sampling of categorical variables, is not necessarily robust and consistent compared with a sub-optimal sequential estimator. Performance of RRE decreases as the multivariate dimensions become large relative to sample sizes. Dimensions may be decreased by sequentially considering only those variables shared by two levels at one time in the multilevel sampling design. For example, consider the three-phase estimator in Eqs. 44 to 51 that requires covariance matrices with dimensions of $(q_{M=0} + q_{M=1} + q_{M=2})$-by-$(q_{M=0} + q_{M=1} + q_{M=2})$. A description of the following recursions is offered in prose form above ("The Basic Idea").

The RRE that combines the first two sampling phases (Eqs. 44 to 47) can be modified to produce a $(q_{M=0} + q_{M=1})$-by-1 vector estimate of population totals for the $q_{M=1}$ photo-interpreted (M = 1) variables.

$\hat{\mathbf{t}}_{X(1)} = \begin{bmatrix} \hat{\mathbf{t}}_{M=0} \\ \hline \hat{\mathbf{t}}_{M=1} \end{bmatrix}_{s=1}$	$\hat{\mathbf{V}}\left(\hat{\mathbf{t}}_{X(1)}\right) = \hat{\mathbf{V}}\left(\begin{bmatrix} \hat{\mathbf{t}}_{M=0} \\ \hline \hat{\mathbf{t}}_{M=1} \end{bmatrix}_{s=1} \right)$
$\hat{\mathbf{t}}_{Z(1)} = \left[\hat{\mathbf{t}}_{M=0}\right]_{s=U}$	$\hat{\mathbf{V}}\left(\hat{\mathbf{t}}_{Z(1)}\right) = \mathbf{0}$
$\mathbf{H} = \begin{bmatrix} \mathbf{I} & \vdots & \mathbf{0} \end{bmatrix}$	$\hat{\mathbf{C}}\left(\hat{\mathbf{t}}_{X(1)}, \hat{\mathbf{t}}_{Z(1)}\right) = \mathbf{0}$

(52)

Incorporating the structure of Eq. 52 into RRE (Eq. 12) yields the first step in the alternative sequential approach:

$$\mathbf{K} = \hat{\mathbf{V}}\left(\begin{bmatrix} \hat{\mathbf{t}}_{M=0} \\ \hline \hat{\mathbf{t}}_{M=1} \end{bmatrix}_{s=1}\right) \mathbf{H}'\left(\ \left[\hat{\mathbf{V}}\left(\left[\hat{\mathbf{t}}_{M=0}\right]_{s=1}\right)\right]^{-1}\right)$$

$$\begin{bmatrix} \hat{\mathbf{t}}_{M=0} \\ \hline \hat{\mathbf{t}}_{M=1} \end{bmatrix}_{s=\{U,1\}} = \begin{bmatrix} \hat{\mathbf{t}}_{M=0} \\ \hline \hat{\mathbf{t}}_{M=1} \end{bmatrix}_{s=1} + \mathbf{K}\left(\left[\hat{\mathbf{t}}_{M=0}\right]_{s=U} - \left[\hat{\mathbf{t}}_{M=0}\right]_{s=1}\right) \qquad (53)$$

$$\hat{\mathbf{V}}\left(\begin{bmatrix} \hat{\mathbf{t}}_{M=0} \\ \hline \hat{\mathbf{t}}_{M=1} \end{bmatrix}_{s=\{U,1\}}\right) = \hat{\mathbf{V}}\left(\begin{bmatrix} \hat{\mathbf{t}}_{M=0} \\ \hline \hat{\mathbf{t}}_{M=1} \end{bmatrix}_{s=1}\right) - \mathbf{K}\,\mathbf{H}\,\hat{\mathbf{V}}\left(\begin{bmatrix} \hat{\mathbf{t}}_{M=0} \\ \hline \hat{\mathbf{t}}_{M=1} \end{bmatrix}_{s=1}\right)$$

Numerically reliable algorithms must be used to apply Eq. 53, and these methods are briefly covered in the section "Robust Numerics".

Since the population totals for the $q_{M=0}$ variables from the M = 0 census of satellite pixels are constants that are exactly known a priori by definition, they may be deleted from Eq. 53 in subsequent steps:

$$\left[\hat{\mathbf{t}}_{M=1}\right]_{s=\{U,1\}} = \begin{bmatrix} \mathbf{0} & \vdots & \mathbf{I} \end{bmatrix}\begin{bmatrix} \hat{\mathbf{t}}_{M=0} \\ \hline \hat{\mathbf{t}}_{M=1} \end{bmatrix}_{s=\{U,1\}}$$

$$\hat{\mathbf{V}}\left(\left[\hat{\mathbf{t}}_{M=1}\right]_{s=\{U,1\}}\right) = \begin{bmatrix} \mathbf{0} & \vdots & \mathbf{I} \end{bmatrix}\hat{\mathbf{V}}\left(\begin{bmatrix} \hat{\mathbf{t}}_{M=0} \\ \hline \hat{\mathbf{t}}_{M=1} \end{bmatrix}_{s=\{U,1\}}\right)\begin{bmatrix} \mathbf{0}' \\ \hline \mathbf{I} \end{bmatrix} \qquad (54)$$

Equation 54 is an estimate of population totals for variables measured with the M = 1 photo-interpretation protocol that is made more precise than the M = 0 census of classified satellite pixels. This first sequence involves covariance matrices with dimensions $(q_{M=0} + q_{M=1})$-by-$(q_{M=0} + q_{M=1})$ in Eq. 53 rather than $(q_{M=0} + q_{M=1} + q_{M=2})$-by-$(q_{M=0} + q_{M=1} + q_{M=2})$ in Eqs. 44 to 51.

The Phase 2 sample vector estimate, with dimension $(q_{M=1} + q_{M=2})$, and the sufficient $q_{M=1}$-dimensional statistics from Eq. 54 are inputs to the next sequential step:

$\hat{\mathbf{t}}_{X(1)} = \begin{bmatrix} \hat{\mathbf{t}}_{M=1} \\ \hline \hat{\mathbf{t}}_{M=2} \end{bmatrix}_{s=2}$	$\hat{\mathbf{V}}\left(\hat{\mathbf{t}}_{X(1)}\right) = \hat{\mathbf{V}}\left(\begin{bmatrix} \hat{\mathbf{t}}_{M=1} \\ \hline \hat{\mathbf{t}}_{M=2} \end{bmatrix}_{s=2}\right)$
$\hat{\mathbf{t}}_{Z(1)} = \left[\hat{\mathbf{t}}_{M=1}\right]_{s=\{U,1\}}$	$\hat{\mathbf{V}}\left(\hat{\mathbf{t}}_{Z(1)}\right) = \hat{\mathbf{V}}\left(\left[\hat{\mathbf{t}}_{M=1}\right]_{s=\{U,1\}}\right)$
$\mathbf{H} = \begin{bmatrix} \mathbf{I} & \vdots & \mathbf{0} \end{bmatrix}$	$\hat{\mathbf{C}}\left(\hat{\mathbf{t}}_{X(1)}, \hat{\mathbf{t}}_{Z(1)}\right) = \mathbf{0}$

(55)

Incorporating the structure of Eq. 55 into RRE (Eq. 12) yields the final step in the alternative sequential approach:

$$K = \left\{ \hat{V}\left(\begin{bmatrix} \hat{t}_{M=1} \\ \hat{t}_{M=2} \end{bmatrix}_{s=2} \right) H' \right\} \left\{ H\, \hat{V}\left(\begin{bmatrix} \hat{t}_{M=1} \\ \hat{t}_{M=2} \end{bmatrix}_{s=2} \right) H' + \hat{V}\left(\left[\hat{t}_{M=1} \right]_{s=\{U,1\}} \right) \right\}^{-1}$$

$$\begin{bmatrix} \hat{t}_{M=1} \\ \hat{t}_{M=2} \end{bmatrix}_{s=\{U,1,2\}} = \begin{bmatrix} \hat{t}_{M=1} \\ \hat{t}_{M=2} \end{bmatrix}_{s=2} + K\left\{ \left[\hat{t}_{M=1} \right]_{s=\{U,1\}} - \left[\hat{t}_{M=1} \right]_{s=2} \right\}$$

$$\left[\hat{t}_{M=2} \right]_{s=\{U,1,2\}} = \begin{bmatrix} 0 & \vdots & I \end{bmatrix} \begin{bmatrix} \hat{t}_{M=1} \\ \hat{t}_{M=2} \end{bmatrix}_{s=\{U,1,2\}} \tag{56}$$

$$\hat{V}\left(\begin{bmatrix} \hat{t}_{M=1} \\ \hat{t}_{M=2} \end{bmatrix}_{s=\{U,1,2\}} \right) = \hat{V}\left(\begin{bmatrix} \hat{t}_{M=1} \\ \hat{t}_{M=2} \end{bmatrix}_{s=2} \right) - K\, H\, \hat{V}\left(\begin{bmatrix} \hat{t}_{M=1} \\ \hat{t}_{M=2} \end{bmatrix}_{s=2} \right)$$

$$\hat{V}\left[\hat{t}_{M=2} \right]_{s=\{U,1,2\}} = \begin{bmatrix} 0 & \vdots & I \end{bmatrix} \hat{V}\left(\begin{bmatrix} \hat{t}_{M=1} \\ \hat{t}_{M=2} \end{bmatrix}_{s=\{U,1,2\}} \right) \begin{bmatrix} 0' \\ I \end{bmatrix}$$

Numerically stable methods, which are covered in the section "Robust Numerics," must be used with Eq. 56.

Equations 52 to 56 start with a combination of the Phase 1 census ($s = U$) and the Phase 2 photo-interpreted sample ($s = 1$) and then a combination of this multivariate result (denoted $s = U,1$) with the Phase 3 sample ($s = 2$) to produce the final estimate (denoted $s = U,1,2$). The sequence could be reversed, starting with a combination of Phase 2 ($s = 1$) and Phase 3 ($s = 2$) and then combining the composite vector estimate ($s = 1,2$) with the Phase 1 census of classified pixels ($s = U$). In the absence of numerical errors, the results should be identical, regardless of the particular sequence.

The three-phase estimator in Eq. 51 differs from the alternative estimator in Eq. 56, the latter of which uses matrices with smaller dimensions. Magnussen (2003) posited that smaller dimensions improve consistency and robustness of the three-phase estimator, although the estimator might be less efficient. Improvements to robustness require sacrificing sample data on variables measured with the satellite protocol ($M = 0$) with the third-phase sample ($s = 2$). The sample size at the third phase is typically small, and the sacrifice might have little practical significance, especially if it proves more robust. However, the concerns reported by Magnussen might be partially caused by numerical errors that are inherent to any digital computer with finite word length. This is a well-known hazard with the Kalman filter, especially when known constants (e.g., census of classified satellite pixels or administrative records that completely cover the sampled population) are incorporated. There is abundant engineering literature on more numerically robust solutions to the Kalman filter estimator and, hence, RRE. Solutions most often involve the matrix square roots of the covariance matrices and orthogonal transformations that substitute simultaneous multivariate solutions with sequential univariate solutions. Maybeck (1979:Chapter 7) provides a concise overview of these methods, and Bierman (1977) devotes an entire book to the subject. The hazard exists for any RRE applied to large, multilevel, multivariate sampling designs. This subject is briefly discussed in the section "Robust Numerics."

Single-Phase-Sampling for Continuous Variables with Cluster Plots

The multiphase designs considered until this point presuppose that the separate phases are composed of independent samples. However, this supposition is invalid for other feasible designs. One such case is the single-stage cluster design (Särndal 1992:125, 304), which is also termed trakt sampling (Mandallaz 2008:53). This special case of cluster sampling is considered from the perspectives of an infinite population, point sampling, and multiple collocated support-regions for each sample point. An example is modeled after the Nevada Photo-based Inventory Pilot (NPIP), which is an FIA initiative under its 2007 strategic plan (Frescino and others 2009a; Frescino and others 2009b) and is briefly described in the "Introduction".

Start with a simple random point-sample s of a continuous population in space. Each sample point j is centered on an FIA field plot. Each sample point is measured with a relatively inexpensive protocol ($M = 1$), namely photo-interpretation of high-resolution aerial photography, and the relatively expensive FIA field protocol ($M = 2$). The $M = 1$ protocol, and the support-region to which it is applied, are described as an example for Eq. 19. The $q_{M=1}$-by-1 vector $[\mathbf{y}_{M=1}]_{I,j}$ represents $q_{M=1}$ photo-interpreted variables at the sample point j. The $M = 2$ protocol and support-region are described as an example for Eq. 20. The $q_{M=2}$-by-1 vector $[\mathbf{y}_{M=2}]_j$ represents $q_{M=2}$ continuous variables measured by an FIA field crew at sample point j.

So far, this exactly describes the Phase 2 sample in the previous section on two-phase sampling. However, two-phase sampling assumes a large independent Phase 1 sample that is measured solely with the $M = 1$ protocol (e.g., photo-interpretation). In this section, the Phase 1 portion is omitted and is replaced with a related design based on a cluster plot. The primary motivation behind cluster plots is to increase the number of photo-interpreted measurements with little extra incremental cost.

For example, let each sample point j in sample s be circumscribed by a relatively large but proximate support-region. This large support-region supplements the much smaller support-region described in the previous paragraph. In the NPIP example, the large support-region is 50 acres, and it is measured with photo-interpretation ($M = 1$) of $n_j = 49$ points that are systematically distributed over the 50-acre support-region. The protocol used for each point (i, j), $i = \{1,2,\ldots,49\}$ in cluster plot j exactly matches the $M = 1$ protocol described in the previous paragraph. In fact, one of the 49 points, defined as $i = (1, j)$, is at the center of the 50-acre support-region, and it is identical to the jth sample point in the previous paragraph.

The $q_{M=2}$-by-1 vector mean of measurements from the $n_j = 49$ points in the large support-region is another quantitative descriptor of the sample point j. It is denoted as protocol $M = 1C$, which refers to application of the $M = 1$ protocol to a large support-region, which may be considered a cluster plot:

$$\left[\mathbf{y}_{M=1C}\right]_j = \sum_i^{n_j} \left[\mathbf{y}_{M=1}\right]_{i,j} \Big/ n_j \tag{57}$$

Had the problem been modeled as a finite population with two-stage sampling, then the points (i, j) would be considered "second-stage sampling units" (Särndal and others 1992:125).

The objective is to improve the estimated population totals for the $M = 2$ variables with the estimated population totals for the $M = 1$ variables. In fine-grained, heterogeneous landscapes at the scale of the large support-region, the estimated population totals for photo-interpreted variables measured with the

M = 1 protocol should be more precise with the large support-region (Eq. 57) compared to the single M = 1 measurement at the center of the support-region, namely, sample point $(1, j)$. The primary value of the M = 1 and M = 2 variables measured at sample point $(1, j)$ is estimation of $q_{M=2}$-by-$q_{M=1}$ sample cross-covariance matrix between the field (M = 2) and photo-interpreted (M = 1) variables. If the cross-covariances are relatively large and the $q_{M=1}$-by-1 vector estimate of the population totals for the photo-interpreted variables is relatively precise, then the $q_{M=2}$-by-1 vector estimate of the population totals for the FIA field variables will be more precise.

Start with the $(2 \times q_{M=1} + q_{M=2})$-by-1 design-based vector estimator for all variables measured at the point sample s and its $(2 \times q_{M=1} + q_{M=2})$-by-$(2 \times q_{M=1} + q_{M=2})$ sample covariance matrix:

$$
\begin{bmatrix} \hat{\mathbf{t}}_{M=1C} \\ \hat{\mathbf{t}}_{M=1} \\ \hat{\mathbf{t}}_{M=2} \end{bmatrix}_s = A \begin{bmatrix} \bar{\hat{\mathbf{y}}}_{M=1C} \\ \bar{\hat{\mathbf{y}}}_{M=1} \\ \bar{\hat{\mathbf{y}}}_{M=2} \end{bmatrix}_s = A \left(\frac{1}{n_s} \right) \sum_{j \in s} \begin{bmatrix} \mathbf{y}_{M=1C} = \sum_{i=1}^{n_j} [\mathbf{y}_{M=1}]_{i,j} \Big/ n_j \\ [\mathbf{y}_{M=1}]_{i=1} \\ [\mathbf{y}_{M=2}]_{i=1} \end{bmatrix}_j
$$

$$
\hat{\mathbf{V}} \left(\begin{bmatrix} \hat{\mathbf{t}}_{M=1C} \\ \hat{\mathbf{t}}_{M=1} \\ \hat{\mathbf{t}}_{M=2} \end{bmatrix}_s \right) = \frac{A^2}{(n_s - 1) n_s} \sum_{j \in s} \left(\begin{bmatrix} \mathbf{y}_{M=1C} \\ \mathbf{y}_{M=1} \\ \mathbf{y}_{M=2} \end{bmatrix}_j - \begin{bmatrix} \bar{\hat{\mathbf{y}}}_{M=1C} \\ \bar{\hat{\mathbf{y}}}_{M=1} \\ \bar{\hat{\mathbf{y}}}_{M=2} \end{bmatrix}_s \right) \left(\begin{bmatrix} \mathbf{y}_{M=1C} \\ \mathbf{y}_{M=1} \\ \mathbf{y}_{M=2} \end{bmatrix}_j - \begin{bmatrix} \bar{\hat{\mathbf{y}}}_{M=1C} \\ \bar{\hat{\mathbf{y}}}_{M=1} \\ \bar{\hat{\mathbf{y}}}_{M=2} \end{bmatrix}_s \right)'
$$

$$
= \begin{bmatrix} \hat{\mathbf{V}} \left([\hat{\mathbf{t}}_{M=1C}] \right) & \hat{\mathbf{C}} \left([\hat{\mathbf{t}}_{M=1C}] [\hat{\mathbf{t}}'_{M=1} \mid \hat{\mathbf{t}}'_{M=2}] \right) \\ \hat{\mathbf{C}} \left(\begin{bmatrix} \hat{\mathbf{t}}_{M=1} \\ \hat{\mathbf{t}}_{M=2} \end{bmatrix}, [\hat{\mathbf{t}}'_{M=1C}] \right) & \hat{\mathbf{V}} \left(\begin{bmatrix} \hat{\mathbf{t}}_{M=1} \\ \hat{\mathbf{t}}_{M=2} \end{bmatrix} \right) \end{bmatrix}
$$

$$
= \begin{bmatrix} \hat{\mathbf{V}} \left([\hat{\mathbf{t}}_{M=1C}] \right) & \hat{\mathbf{C}} \left([\hat{\mathbf{t}}_{M=1C}] [\hat{\mathbf{t}}'_{M=1}] \right) & \hat{\mathbf{C}} \left([\hat{\mathbf{t}}_{M=1C}] [\hat{\mathbf{t}}'_{M=2}] \right) \\ \hat{\mathbf{C}} \left([\hat{\mathbf{t}}_{M=1}] [\hat{\mathbf{t}}'_{M=1C}] \right) & \hat{\mathbf{V}} \left([\hat{\mathbf{t}}_{M=1}] \right) & \hat{\mathbf{C}} \left([\hat{\mathbf{t}}_{M=1}] [\hat{\mathbf{t}}'_{M=2}] \right) \\ \hat{\mathbf{C}} \left([\hat{\mathbf{t}}_{M=2}] [\hat{\mathbf{t}}'_{M=1C}] \right) & \hat{\mathbf{C}} \left([\hat{\mathbf{t}}_{M=2}] [\hat{\mathbf{t}}'_{M=1}] \right) & \hat{\mathbf{V}} \left([\hat{\mathbf{t}}_{M=2}] \right) \end{bmatrix}
$$

(58)

The last two terms in Eq. 58 define partitions of the sample covariance matrix. This estimator for the sample covariance matrix ignores heteroscedasticity among cluster plots, which simplifies variance estimates (e.g., Särndal 1992:153). This simplification is the norm with FIA estimators (Scott and others 2005).

Next, use the more complete version of the Kalman filter in Eqs. 9 through 11 that accommodates non-zero covariances between the state- and measurement-vectors. The following maps the correspondence among notation in Eq. 58 and Eqs. 9 through 11, and the remainder of this section.

$\hat{\mathbf{t}}_{X(1)} = \begin{bmatrix} \hat{\mathbf{t}}_{M=1} \\ \hline \hat{\mathbf{t}}_{M=2} \end{bmatrix}_s$	$\hat{\mathbf{V}}\left(\hat{\mathbf{t}}_{X(1)}\right) = \hat{\mathbf{V}}\left(\begin{bmatrix} \hat{\mathbf{t}}_{M=1} \\ \hline \hat{\mathbf{t}}_{M=2} \end{bmatrix}\right)_s$
$\hat{\mathbf{t}}_{Z(1)} = \left[\hat{\mathbf{t}}_{M=1C}\right]_s$	$\hat{\mathbf{V}}\left(\hat{\mathbf{t}}_{Z(1)}\right) = \hat{\mathbf{V}}\left(\left[\hat{\mathbf{t}}_{M=1C}\right]\right)_s$
$\mathbf{H} = \begin{bmatrix} \mathbf{I} & \vdots & \mathbf{0} \end{bmatrix}$	$\hat{\mathbf{C}}\left(\hat{\mathbf{t}}_{X(1)}, \hat{\mathbf{t}}_{Z(1)}\right) = \hat{\mathbf{C}}\left(\begin{bmatrix} \hat{\mathbf{t}}_{M=1} \\ \hline \hat{\mathbf{t}}_{M=2} \end{bmatrix}, \left[\hat{\mathbf{t}}'_{M=1C}\right]\right)_s$

$$(59)$$

The $\mathbf{H}$ matrix in Eq. 59 has dimensions $q_{M=1}$-by-$(q_{M=1} + q_{M=2})$. By substitution of the equalities in Eq. 59 into Eq. 9, the $(q_{M=1} + q_{M=2})$-by-$q_{M=1}$ Kalman gain matrix $\mathbf{K}$ equals:

$$
\mathbf{K} = \begin{bmatrix} \hat{\mathbf{V}}\left(\begin{bmatrix} \hat{\mathbf{t}}_{M=1} \\ \hline \hat{\mathbf{t}}_{M=2} \end{bmatrix}\right)_s \begin{bmatrix} \mathbf{I} \\ \mathbf{0} \end{bmatrix} \\ + \hat{\mathbf{C}}\left(\begin{bmatrix} \hat{\mathbf{t}}_{M=1} \\ \hline \hat{\mathbf{t}}_{M=2} \end{bmatrix}, \left[\hat{\mathbf{t}}'_{M=1C}\right]\right)_s \end{bmatrix} \left(\begin{bmatrix} \begin{bmatrix} \mathbf{I} & \vdots & \mathbf{0} \end{bmatrix} \hat{\mathbf{V}}\left(\begin{bmatrix} \hat{\mathbf{t}}_{M=1} \\ \hline \hat{\mathbf{t}}_{M=2} \end{bmatrix}\right)_s \begin{bmatrix} \mathbf{I} \\ \mathbf{0} \end{bmatrix} \\ + \hat{\mathbf{V}}\left(\left[\hat{\mathbf{t}}_{M=1C}\right]\right)_s \\ + \begin{bmatrix} \mathbf{I} & \vdots & \mathbf{0} \end{bmatrix} \hat{\mathbf{C}}\left(\begin{bmatrix} \hat{\mathbf{t}}_{M=1} \\ \hline \hat{\mathbf{t}}_{M=2} \end{bmatrix}, \left[\hat{\mathbf{t}}'_{M=1C}\right]\right)_s \\ + \hat{\mathbf{C}}\left(\left[\hat{\mathbf{t}}_{M=1C}\right], \left[\hat{\mathbf{t}}'_{M=1} \vdots \hat{\mathbf{t}}'_{M=2}\right]\right)_s \begin{bmatrix} \mathbf{I} \\ \mathbf{0} \end{bmatrix} \end{bmatrix} \right)^{-1}
$$

$$(60)$$

$$
= \begin{bmatrix} \hat{\mathbf{V}}\left(\left[\hat{\mathbf{t}}_{M=1}\right]\right)_s + \hat{\mathbf{C}}\left(\left[\hat{\mathbf{t}}_{M=1}\right], \left[\hat{\mathbf{t}}'_{M=1C}\right]\right)_s \\ \hline \hat{\mathbf{C}}\left(\left[\hat{\mathbf{t}}_{M=2}\right], \left[\hat{\mathbf{t}}'_{M=1}\right]\right)_s + \hat{\mathbf{C}}\left(\hat{\mathbf{t}}_{M=2}, \left[\hat{\mathbf{t}}'_{M=1C}\right]\right)_s \end{bmatrix} \left(\begin{array}{c} \left(\hat{\mathbf{V}}\left(\left[\hat{\mathbf{t}}_{M=1}\right]\right)\right)_s \\ + \hat{\mathbf{V}}\left(\left[\hat{\mathbf{t}}_{M=1C}\right]\right)_s \\ + \hat{\mathbf{C}}\left(\left[\hat{\mathbf{t}}_{M=1}\right], \left[\hat{\mathbf{t}}'_{M=1C}\right]\right)_s \\ + \hat{\mathbf{C}}\left(\left[\hat{\mathbf{t}}_{M=1C}\right], \left[\hat{\mathbf{t}}'_{M=1}\right]\right)_s \end{array} \right)^{-1}
$$

Numerically reliable algorithms must be used to apply Eq. 60, and these methods are briefly covered in the section "Robust Numerics".

From Eqs. 10, 59, and 60, the $(q_{M=1} + q_{M=2})$-by-1 vector estimate of population totals and its covariance matrix for all photo-interpreted (M = 1) and FIA field variables (M = 2), denoted M = (1,1C), is:

$$
\begin{bmatrix} \hat{\mathbf{t}}_{M=1} \\ \hline \hat{\mathbf{t}}_{M=2} \end{bmatrix}_{M=(1,1C)} = \begin{bmatrix} \hat{\mathbf{t}}_{M=1} \\ \hline \hat{\mathbf{t}}_{M=2} \end{bmatrix}_s + \mathbf{K}\left(\left[\hat{\mathbf{t}}_{M=1C}\right]_s - \left[\hat{\mathbf{t}}_{M=1}\right]_s\right)
$$

$$(61)$$

$$
\hat{\mathbf{V}}\left(\begin{bmatrix} \hat{\mathbf{t}}_{M=1} \\ \hline \hat{\mathbf{t}}_{M=2} \end{bmatrix}_{M=(1,1C)}\right)_s = \hat{\mathbf{V}}\left(\begin{bmatrix} \hat{\mathbf{t}}_{M=1} \\ \hline \hat{\mathbf{t}}_{M=2} \end{bmatrix}\right)_s + \mathbf{K}\left(\begin{bmatrix} \mathbf{I} & \vdots & \mathbf{0} \end{bmatrix}\hat{\mathbf{V}}\left(\begin{bmatrix} \hat{\mathbf{t}}_{M=1} \\ \hline \hat{\mathbf{t}}_{M=2} \end{bmatrix}\right)_s + \hat{\mathbf{C}}\left(\begin{bmatrix} \hat{\mathbf{t}}_{M=1} \\ \hline \hat{\mathbf{t}}_{M=2} \end{bmatrix}, \left[\hat{\mathbf{t}}'_{M=1C}\right]\right)_s\right)
$$

Equations 58 to 61 may be expanded, as in Eqs. 20 to 27, to reveal analogies between RRE and more traditional univariate regression estimators (e.g., Särndal and others 1992).

The example in Eq. 61 uses the M = 1C photo-interpretation protocol, which is identical to the M = 1 protocol applied to sample point $(1, j)$, except that the M = 1C protocol is the mean of the n_j point samples within the large support-region (i.e., cluster plot). In addition, other remote sensing protocols for measuring the large support-region are possible. Examples include MODIS satellite data (Frescino and others 2009b), with 15- to 60-acre pixels; earth-orbiting satellite Light Detection and Ranging (LiDAR) laser data; and airborne LiDAR data. If these supplemental measurements from other sensors are correlated with photo-interpretations, then they will improve the precision of estimated population totals for the photo-interpreted variables, which, in turn, will increase precision of the estimated population totals for the M = 2 FIA field variables.

Two-Phase Sampling for Continuous Variables with Cluster Plots

The final example considered here is relevant to the vision expressed in the FIA Strategic Plan (USDA Forest Service 2007). The following example uses full-coverage pixel data from a spaceborne sensor (protocol M = 0); a large sample of relatively inexpensive, 50-acre cluster plots measured with the M = 1 photo-interpretation protocol (in addition to the M = 0 protocol); and a small sample of 50-acre cluster plots that are fully measured with the M = 1 photo-interpretation protocol with a single 1/6-acre FIA plot within the 50-acre cluster plot measured with the M = 2 FIA field protocol. Spaceborne sensor data (M = 0 protocol) exists for the small sample of cluster plots that contain an FIA field plot; however, those M = 0 data are not used so as to reduce state-vector dimensions, avoid numerical problems, and avoid sampling zeros. This is similar to the non-optimal, but more robust, approach used in the example of "Three-Phase Sampling for Continuous Variables".

The following example is set in the Interior West and interior portions of Alaska in the United States where, in the absence of major disturbance events, ambient stand dynamics (tree growth, regeneration, and mortality) are relatively slow and predictable. These changes can only be reliably measured with field observations, such as the FIA field protocol, although photo-interpretation of time-series of high-resolution aerial photography can provide valuable auxiliary data. However, rapid and substantial changes in forest conditions over large areas of forest land are caused by land management treatments, changes in land use, and episodic tree mortality from insects, diseases, wildfires and other agents. These disturbance-related changes can be reliably, although not perfectly, measured with interpretation of multitemporal, high-resolution aerial photography that is accurately registered to a large permanent photo-plot (e.g., a 50-acre cluster plot). This situation is the motivation for NPIP (Frescino and others 2009a; Frescino and others 2009b), which is led by the Interior West Forest Inventory and Analysis program. The FIA study by Lister and others (2009) has some similarities. The following example uses inexpensive large photo-plots to improve statistical efficiency with Landsat auxiliary data and increase the sample size of 50-acre photo-plots in order to improve estimates of change. Accurate and efficient monitoring of changes in land cover and land use is a short-term priority for FIA research and development.

Assume each permanent, 1-acre FIA field plot, with sampling intensity of 1 plot per 6000 acres, is circumscribed by 50-acre cluster plot. Each cluster plot is measured through photo-interpretation (M = 1) of a systematic sample of 49 points. Every year, an interpenetrating, 15-percent sub-sample of these cluster plots is imaged with high-resolution aerial photography and measured with the M = 1 protocol. Each year, an independent, 5-percent sub-sample is measured with both the FIA field protocol (M = 2) and the M = 1 protocol with new, high-resolution aerial photography. This sums to 20 percent of all FIA plots measured each year, which fully complies with the authorities legislated in 1998 Farm Bill (USDA Forest Service 1998). In this hypothetical example, every FIA field plot, forested and otherwise, is measured once every five years with high-resolution aerial photography (M = 1 protocol), although every forested plot is measured only once every 20 years by FIA field crews (M = 2 protocol). For purposes of estimation with new data from a single year, the Phase 1 sample includes that 15 percent of all sample points that are imaged during the year with aerial photography alone and measured with the M = 1 protocol, and the Phase 2 sample includes that 5 percent of all sample points measured during that same year with both interpretation of aerial photography (M = 1 protocol) and FIA field crews (M = 2 protocol).

Each sample point j in the Phase 1 and Phase 2 samples is associated with a unique county and ownership category, and the resulting vector of binary indicator variables is denoted $[\mathbf{y}_{M=0}]_{i=1}$, where the $i = 1$ subscript signifies point 1 of the 49 points in the 50-acre cluster plot, which is located at the center-point of the 1/6-acre FIA field plot and the center of the 50-acre cluster plot. Finally, multispectral measurements from spaceborne sensors and other full-coverage geospatial census data are used to predict vegetation characteristics for each pixel that covers the sampled population (M = 0). These pixels may be registered to each of the 49 individual points in the 50-acre cluster plot, or summaries of the pixel values for that cluster plot.

The sample of large photo-plots in this example offers additional opportunities to improve empirical models that predict forest characteristics using full-coverage, remotely sensed data from earth-observing satellites. Compared to 1/6-acre FIA field plots, large photo-plots are more accurately registered to spaceborne sensors, such as those aboard the Landsat and Aqua earth-orbiting satellites. The spatial scales of 30-m (0.2-acre) or 250-m (16-acre) satellite pixels are more compatible with 50-acre photo-plots than the cluster of four 1/24-acre FIA subplots in the FIA field plot. Compatibility of scale affects success of prediction models that use remotely sensed data (Xu and others 2009). Accurate registration between satellite imagery and training data is important for fitting accurate prediction models (Pontius 2000; Verbyla and Boles 2000; Carmel and others 2001; Halme and Tomppo 2001; Czaplewski and Patterson 2003; Czaplewski 2005; Ashok and others 2007; McRoberts 2010). For example, Frescino and others (2009b) improved predictions of forest characteristics, at least to a modest degree, with 15-acre MODIS pixels by fitting models with photo-interpretation of 50-acre photo-plots in Nevada rather than measurements of FIA field plots. Registration accuracy also affects the strength of the cross-covariances among variables measured with different field and remote sensing protocols, hence, the gains in statistical efficiency that are possible with complex sampling designs. Therefore, a modified M = 1C protocol is defined as the aggregate sum of M = 1 photo-interpreted measurements for each of the 49 points in the 50-acre photo-plot.

Sequential application of RRE provides a suitable estimator for this complex example. First, compute the Phase 1 sample estimator as:

$$
\begin{bmatrix} \hat{\mathbf{t}}_{M=0} \\ \hline \hat{\mathbf{t}}_{M=1C} \end{bmatrix}_{s=1} = A \begin{bmatrix} \hat{\bar{\mathbf{y}}}_{M=0} \\ \hline \hat{\bar{\mathbf{y}}}_{M=1C} \end{bmatrix}_{s=1} = A \left(\frac{1}{n_{s=1}} \right) \sum_{j \in (s=1)} \begin{bmatrix} [\mathbf{y}_{M=0}]_{i=1} \\ \hline \mathbf{y}_{M=1C} = \sum_{i=1}^{n_j} [\mathbf{y}_{M=1}]_{i,j} \Big/ n_j \end{bmatrix}_j
$$

(62)

$$
\hat{\mathbf{v}} \left([\hat{\mathbf{t}}_{M=1C}] \right)_{s=1} = \frac{A^2}{(n_{s=1}-1)\, n_{s=1}} \sum_{j \in (s=1)} \left(\left(\begin{bmatrix} \mathbf{y}_{M=0} \\ \hline \mathbf{y}_{M=1C} \end{bmatrix}_j - \begin{bmatrix} \hat{\bar{\mathbf{y}}}_{M=0} \\ \hline \hat{\bar{\mathbf{y}}}_{M=1C} \end{bmatrix}_{s=1} \right) \left(\begin{bmatrix} \mathbf{y}_{M=0} \\ \hline \mathbf{y}_{M=1C} \end{bmatrix}_j - \begin{bmatrix} \hat{\bar{\mathbf{y}}}_{M=0} \\ \hline \hat{\bar{\mathbf{y}}}_{M=1C} \end{bmatrix}_{s=1} \right)' \right)
$$

This requires registration of 30-m Landsat pixels to the entire 50-acre photo-plot but not any of the 49 individual, photo-interpreted points. Measurements of the 250 Landsat pixels that cover the 50-acre photo-plot are summed into a single M = 0 measurement for each PSU. Likewise, photo-interpreted measurements for each of the 49 points in a 50-acre photo-plot are summed to a single measurement (M = 1C) of the entire photo-plot. Recall that this Phase 1 estimate uses the annual 15 percent interpenetrating sub-sample of all FIA plots.

Second, compute the Phase 2 sample estimator from the 5 percent annual sub-sample:

$$
\begin{bmatrix} \hat{\mathbf{t}}_{M=0} \\ \hline \hat{\mathbf{t}}_{M=1C} \\ \hline \hat{\mathbf{t}}_{M=1} \\ \hline \hat{\mathbf{t}}_{M=2} \end{bmatrix}_{s=2} = A \begin{bmatrix} \hat{\bar{\mathbf{y}}}_{M=0} \\ \hline \hat{\bar{\mathbf{y}}}_{M=1C} \\ \hline \hat{\bar{\mathbf{y}}}_{M=1} \\ \hline \hat{\bar{\mathbf{y}}}_{M=2} \end{bmatrix}_{s=2} = A \left(\frac{1}{n_{s=2}} \right) \sum_{j \in (s=2)} \begin{bmatrix} [\mathbf{y}_{M=0}]_{i=1} \\ \hline \hat{\bar{\mathbf{y}}}_{M=1C} = \sum_{i=1}^{n_j} [\mathbf{y}_{M=1}]_{i,j} \Big/ n_j \\ \hline [\mathbf{y}_{M=1}]_{i=1} \\ \hline [\mathbf{y}_{M=2}]_{i=1} \end{bmatrix}_j
$$

(63)

$$
\hat{\mathbf{v}} \left(\begin{bmatrix} \hat{\mathbf{t}}_{M=0} \\ \hline \hat{\mathbf{t}}_{M=1C} \\ \hline \hat{\mathbf{t}}_{M=1} \\ \hline \hat{\mathbf{t}}_{M=2} \end{bmatrix}_{s=2} \right) = \frac{A^2}{(n_{s=2}-1)\, n_{s=2}} \sum_{j \in (s=2)} \left(\left(\begin{bmatrix} [\mathbf{y}_{M=0}]_{i=1} \\ \hline [\mathbf{y}_{M=1C}] \\ \hline [\mathbf{y}_{M=1}]_{i=1} \\ \hline [\mathbf{y}_{M=2}]_{i=1} \end{bmatrix}_j - \begin{bmatrix} \hat{\bar{\mathbf{y}}}_{M=0} \\ \hline \hat{\bar{\mathbf{y}}}_{M=1C} \\ \hline \hat{\bar{\mathbf{y}}}_{M=1} \\ \hline \hat{\bar{\mathbf{y}}}_{M=2} \end{bmatrix}_{s=2} \right) \left(\begin{bmatrix} [\mathbf{y}_{M=0}]_{i=1} \\ \hline [\mathbf{y}_{M=1C}] \\ \hline [\mathbf{y}_{M=1}]_{i=1} \\ \hline [\mathbf{y}_{M=2}]_{i=1} \end{bmatrix}_j - \begin{bmatrix} \hat{\bar{\mathbf{y}}}_{M=0} \\ \hline \hat{\bar{\mathbf{y}}}_{M=1C} \\ \hline \hat{\bar{\mathbf{y}}}_{M=1} \\ \hline \hat{\bar{\mathbf{y}}}_{M=2} \end{bmatrix}_{s=2} \right)' \right)
$$

This estimate includes the M = 0 and M = 1C measurements for the entire 50-acre photo-plot, the M = 1 photo-interpretations for each of the 49 points in each 50-acre photo-plot, and the M = 2 measurement of the 1/6-acre FIA field plot at the center of the 50-acre photo-plot.

Third, apply the composite estimator that combines the vector estimates from the Phase 1 sample (Eq. 62) and the Phase 2 sample (Eq. 63). The primary purpose is to improve the estimated population totals for the photo-interpreted (M = 1) variables and the geopolitical areal variables (M = 0) by combining the Phase 1 and Phase 2 sample estimators, although this will also improve estimates of those FIA field variables (M = 2) that are correlated with remotely sensed and geopolitical variables. The notation corresponding to the Kalman filter in Eq. 12 is:

$$
\hat{\mathbf{t}}_{X(1)} = \begin{bmatrix} \hat{\mathbf{t}}_{M=0} \\ \hline \hat{\mathbf{t}}_{M=1C} \\ \hline \hat{\mathbf{t}}_{M=1} \\ \hline \hat{\mathbf{t}}_{M=2} \end{bmatrix}_{s=2}
\qquad
\hat{\mathbf{V}}\left(\hat{\mathbf{t}}_{X(1)}\right) = \hat{\mathbf{V}}\left(\begin{bmatrix} \hat{\mathbf{t}}_{M=0} \\ \hline \hat{\mathbf{t}}_{M=1C} \\ \hline \hat{\mathbf{t}}_{M=1} \\ \hline \hat{\mathbf{t}}_{M=2} \end{bmatrix}_{s=2}\right)
$$

$$
\hat{\mathbf{t}}_{Z(1)} = \begin{bmatrix} \hat{\mathbf{t}}_{M=0} \\ \hline \hat{\mathbf{t}}_{M=1C} \end{bmatrix}_{s=1}
\qquad
\hat{\mathbf{V}}\left(\hat{\mathbf{t}}_{Z(1)}\right) = \hat{\mathbf{V}}\left(\begin{bmatrix} \hat{\mathbf{t}}_{M=0} \\ \hline \hat{\mathbf{t}}_{M=1C} \end{bmatrix}_{s=1}\right) \tag{64}
$$

$$
\mathbf{H} = \begin{bmatrix} \mathbf{I} & | & \mathbf{0} \end{bmatrix}
\qquad
\hat{\mathbf{C}}\left(\hat{\mathbf{t}}_{X(1)}, \hat{\mathbf{t}}_{Z(1)}\right) = \mathbf{0}
$$

The **H** matrix has dimensions $(q_{M=0} + q_{M=1})$-by-$(q_{M=0} + 2 \times q_{M=1} + q_{M=2})$. From Eqs. 12 and 64, the composite estimator is:

$$
\begin{bmatrix} \hat{\mathbf{t}}_{M=0} \\ \hline \hat{\mathbf{t}}_{M=1C} \\ \hline \hat{\mathbf{t}}_{M=1} \\ \hline \hat{\mathbf{t}}_{M=2} \end{bmatrix}_{s=(1,2)} = \begin{bmatrix} \hat{\mathbf{t}}_{M=0} \\ \hline \hat{\mathbf{t}}_{M=1C} \\ \hline \hat{\mathbf{t}}_{M=1} \\ \hline \hat{\mathbf{t}}_{M=2} \end{bmatrix}_{s=2} + \mathbf{K}\left[\begin{bmatrix} \hat{\mathbf{t}}_{M=0} \\ \hline \hat{\mathbf{t}}_{M=1C} \end{bmatrix}_{s=1} - \begin{bmatrix} \mathbf{I} & | & \mathbf{0} \end{bmatrix} \begin{bmatrix} \hat{\mathbf{t}}_{M=0} \\ \hline \hat{\mathbf{t}}_{M=1C} \\ \hline \hat{\mathbf{t}}_{M=1} \\ \hline \hat{\mathbf{t}}_{M=2} \end{bmatrix}_{s=2} \right]
$$

$$
\hat{\mathbf{V}}\left(\begin{bmatrix} \hat{\mathbf{t}}_{M=0} \\ \hline \hat{\mathbf{t}}_{M=1C} \\ \hline \hat{\mathbf{t}}_{M=1} \\ \hline \hat{\mathbf{t}}_{M=2} \end{bmatrix}_{s=(1,2)}\right) = \hat{\mathbf{V}}\left(\begin{bmatrix} \hat{\mathbf{t}}_{M=0} \\ \hline \hat{\mathbf{t}}_{M=1C} \\ \hline \hat{\mathbf{t}}_{M=1} \\ \hline \hat{\mathbf{t}}_{M=2} \end{bmatrix}_{s=2}\right) - \mathbf{K}\begin{bmatrix} \mathbf{I} & | & \mathbf{0} \end{bmatrix} \hat{\mathbf{V}}\left(\begin{bmatrix} \hat{\mathbf{t}}_{M=0} \\ \hline \hat{\mathbf{t}}_{M=1C} \\ \hline \hat{\mathbf{t}}_{M=1} \\ \hline \hat{\mathbf{t}}_{M=2} \end{bmatrix}_{s=2}\right) \tag{65}
$$

$$
\mathbf{K} = \hat{\mathbf{V}}\left(\begin{bmatrix} \hat{\mathbf{t}}_{M=0} \\ \hline \hat{\mathbf{t}}_{M=1C} \\ \hline \hat{\mathbf{t}}_{M=1} \\ \hline \hat{\mathbf{t}}_{M=2} \end{bmatrix}_{s=2}\right) \begin{bmatrix} \mathbf{I} \\ \hline \mathbf{0} \end{bmatrix} \left(\begin{bmatrix} \mathbf{I} & | & \mathbf{0} \end{bmatrix} \hat{\mathbf{V}}\left(\begin{bmatrix} \hat{\mathbf{t}}_{M=0} \\ \hline \hat{\mathbf{t}}_{M=1C} \\ \hline \hat{\mathbf{t}}_{M=1} \\ \hline \hat{\mathbf{t}}_{M=2} \end{bmatrix}_{s=2}\right) \begin{bmatrix} \mathbf{I} \\ \hline \mathbf{0} \end{bmatrix} + \hat{\mathbf{V}}\left(\begin{bmatrix} \hat{\mathbf{t}}_{M=0} \\ \hline \hat{\mathbf{t}}_{M=1C} \end{bmatrix}_{s=1}\right) \right)^{-1}
$$

Fourth, apply the estimator for cluster plots, similar to Eq. 61, except use the composite estimate from equation Eq. 65 rather than the sample estimate of the same vector of population totals from Eq. 58. The purpose is to improve estimated population totals for photo-interpreted variables by combining the photo-interpreted measurements made at the sample point (M = 1, $i = 1$) and the mean of the photo-interpreted measurements made for the surrounding cluster plot (M = 1C, $i = 1,2,\ldots,n_j$), where $n_j = 49$ in this example. The notation corresponding to the Kalman filter in Eq. 12 is:

$$
\hat{\mathbf{t}}_{X(1)} = \begin{bmatrix} \hat{\mathbf{t}}_{M=0} \\ \hline \hat{\overline{\mathbf{t}}}_{M=1} \\ \hline \hat{\mathbf{t}}_{M=2} \end{bmatrix}_{s=(1,2)}
$$

$$
= \begin{bmatrix} \mathbf{I} & 0 & 0 & 0 \\ \hline 0 & 0 & \mathbf{I} & 0 \\ \hline 0 & 0 & 0 & \mathbf{I} \end{bmatrix} \begin{bmatrix} \hat{\mathbf{t}}_{M=0} \\ \hline \hat{\overline{\mathbf{t}}}_{M=1C} \\ \hline \hat{\overline{\mathbf{t}}}_{M=1} \\ \hline \hat{\mathbf{t}}_{M=2} \end{bmatrix}_{s=(1,2)}
$$

$$
\hat{\mathbf{V}}\left(\hat{\mathbf{t}}_{X(1)}\right) = \hat{\mathbf{V}}\left(\begin{bmatrix} \hat{\mathbf{t}}_{M=0} \\ \hline \hat{\overline{\mathbf{t}}}_{M=1} \\ \hline \hat{\mathbf{t}}_{M=2} \end{bmatrix}\right)_{s=(1,2)}
$$

$$
= \begin{bmatrix} \mathbf{I} & 0 & 0 & 0 \\ \hline 0 & 0 & \mathbf{I} & 0 \\ \hline 0 & 0 & 0 & \mathbf{I} \end{bmatrix} \hat{\mathbf{V}}\left(\begin{bmatrix} \hat{\mathbf{t}}_{M=0} \\ \hline \hat{\overline{\mathbf{t}}}_{M=1C} \\ \hline \hat{\mathbf{t}}_{M=1} \\ \hline \hat{\mathbf{t}}_{M=2} \end{bmatrix}\right)_{s=(1,2)} \begin{bmatrix} \mathbf{I} & 0 & 0 \\ \hline 0 & 0 & 0 \\ \hline 0 & \mathbf{I} & 0 \\ \hline 0 & 0 & \mathbf{I} \end{bmatrix}
$$

$$
\hat{\mathbf{t}}_{Z(1)} = \begin{bmatrix} \hat{\overline{\mathbf{t}}}_{M=1C} \end{bmatrix}_{s=(1,2)}
$$

$$
= \begin{bmatrix} 0 & \mathbf{I} & 0 & 0 \end{bmatrix} \begin{bmatrix} \hat{\mathbf{t}}_{M=0} \\ \hline \hat{\overline{\mathbf{t}}}_{M=1C} \\ \hline \hat{\overline{\mathbf{t}}}_{M=1} \\ \hline \hat{\mathbf{t}}_{M=2} \end{bmatrix}_{s=(1,2)}
$$

$$
\hat{\mathbf{V}}\left(\hat{\mathbf{t}}_{Z(1)}\right) = \hat{\mathbf{V}}\left(\begin{bmatrix} \hat{\overline{\mathbf{t}}}_{M=1C} \end{bmatrix}\right)_{s=(1,2)}
$$

$$
= \begin{bmatrix} 0 & \mathbf{I} & 0 & 0 \end{bmatrix} \hat{\mathbf{V}}\left(\begin{bmatrix} \hat{\mathbf{t}}_{M=0} \\ \hline \hat{\overline{\mathbf{t}}}_{M=1C} \\ \hline \hat{\mathbf{t}}_{M=1} \\ \hline \hat{\mathbf{t}}_{M=2} \end{bmatrix}\right)_{s=(1,2)} \begin{bmatrix} 0 \\ \hline \mathbf{I} \\ \hline 0 \\ \hline 0 \end{bmatrix}
$$

(66)

$$
\mathbf{H} = \begin{bmatrix} 0 & \mathbf{I} & 0 \end{bmatrix}
$$

$$
\hat{\mathbf{C}}\left(\hat{\mathbf{t}}_{X(1)}, \hat{\mathbf{t}}_{Z(1)}\right) = \hat{\mathbf{C}}\left(\begin{bmatrix} \hat{\mathbf{t}}_{M=0} \\ \hline \hat{\overline{\mathbf{t}}}_{M=1} \\ \hline \hat{\mathbf{t}}_{M=2} \end{bmatrix}, \begin{bmatrix} \hat{\mathbf{t}}'_{M=1C} \end{bmatrix}\right)_{s=(1,2)}
$$

$$
= \begin{bmatrix} \mathbf{I} & 0 & 0 & 0 \\ \hline 0 & 0 & \mathbf{I} & 0 \\ \hline 0 & 0 & 0 & \mathbf{I} \end{bmatrix} \hat{\mathbf{V}}\left(\begin{bmatrix} \hat{\mathbf{t}}_{M=0} \\ \hline \hat{\overline{\mathbf{t}}}_{M=1C} \\ \hline \hat{\mathbf{t}}_{M=1} \\ \hline \hat{\mathbf{t}}_{M=2} \end{bmatrix}\right)_{s=(1,2)} \begin{bmatrix} 0 \\ \hline \mathbf{I} \\ \hline 0 \\ \hline 0 \end{bmatrix}
$$

The $\mathbf{H}$ matrix in Eq. 66 has dimensions $q_{M=1}$-by-($q_{M=0} + q_{M=1} + q_{M=2}$). From Eqs. 9 through 11 and Eq. 66, the composite estimator is:

$$
\begin{bmatrix} \hat{\mathbf{t}}_{M=0} \\ \hat{\mathbf{t}}_{M=1} \\ \hat{\mathbf{t}}_{M=2} \end{bmatrix}_{\substack{s=(1,2) \\ M=(1,1C)}} = \begin{bmatrix} \hat{\mathbf{t}}_{M=0} \\ \hat{\mathbf{t}}_{M=1} \\ \hat{\mathbf{t}}_{M=2} \end{bmatrix}_{s=(1,2)} + \mathbf{K}\left[\left[\hat{\mathbf{t}}_{M=1C} \right]_{s=(1,2)} - \mathbf{H} \begin{bmatrix} \hat{\mathbf{t}}_{M=0} \\ \hat{\mathbf{t}}_{M=1} \\ \hat{\mathbf{t}}_{M=2} \end{bmatrix}_{s=(1,2)} \right]
$$

$$
\hat{\mathbf{V}}\left(\begin{bmatrix} \hat{\mathbf{t}}_{M=0} \\ \hat{\mathbf{t}}_{M=1} \\ \hat{\mathbf{t}}_{M=2} \end{bmatrix}_{\substack{s=(1,2) \\ M=(1,1C)}} \right) = \hat{\mathbf{V}}\left(\begin{bmatrix} \hat{\mathbf{t}}_{M=0} \\ \hat{\mathbf{t}}_{M=1} \\ \hat{\mathbf{t}}_{M=2} \end{bmatrix}_{s=(1,2)} \right) - \mathbf{K}\left[\mathbf{H}\,\hat{\mathbf{V}}\left(\begin{bmatrix} \hat{\mathbf{t}}_{M=0} \\ \hat{\mathbf{t}}_{M=1} \\ \hat{\mathbf{t}}_{M=2} \end{bmatrix} \right)_{s=(1,2)} + \hat{\mathbf{C}}\left(\begin{bmatrix} \hat{\mathbf{t}}_{M=0} \\ \hat{\mathbf{t}}_{M=1} \\ \hat{\mathbf{t}}_{M=2} \end{bmatrix}, \left[\hat{\mathbf{t}}'_{M=1C} \right] \right)_{s=(1,2)} \right]
$$

$$
\mathbf{K} = \begin{bmatrix} \hat{\mathbf{V}}\left(\begin{bmatrix} \hat{\mathbf{t}}_{M=0} \\ \hat{\mathbf{t}}_{M=1} \\ \hat{\mathbf{t}}_{M=2} \end{bmatrix} \right)_{s=(1,2)} \mathbf{H}' \\ + \hat{\mathbf{C}}\left(\begin{bmatrix} \hat{\mathbf{t}}_{M=0} \\ \hat{\mathbf{t}}_{M=1} \\ \hat{\mathbf{t}}_{M=2} \end{bmatrix}, \left[\hat{\mathbf{t}}'_{M=1C} \right] \right)_{s=(1,2)} \end{bmatrix} \left(\begin{bmatrix} \mathbf{H}\,\hat{\mathbf{V}}\left(\begin{bmatrix} \hat{\mathbf{t}}_{M=0} \\ \hat{\mathbf{t}}_{M=1} \\ \hat{\mathbf{t}}_{M=2} \end{bmatrix} \right)_{s=(1,2)} \mathbf{H}' \\ + \hat{\mathbf{V}}\left(\left[\hat{\mathbf{t}}_{M=1C} \right] \right)_{s=(1,2)} \\ + \mathbf{H}\,\hat{\mathbf{C}}\left(\begin{bmatrix} \hat{\mathbf{t}}_{M=0} \\ \hat{\mathbf{t}}_{M=1} \\ \hat{\mathbf{t}}_{M=2} \end{bmatrix}, \left[\hat{\mathbf{t}}'_{M=1C} \right] \right)_{s=(1,2)} \\ + \hat{\mathbf{C}}\left(\left[\hat{\mathbf{t}}_{M=1C} \right], \begin{bmatrix} \hat{\mathbf{t}}_{M=0} \\ \hat{\mathbf{t}}_{M=1} \\ \hat{\mathbf{t}}_{M=2} \end{bmatrix}' \right)_{s=(1,2)} \mathbf{H}' \end{bmatrix} \right)^{-1}
\tag{67}
$$

Numerically reliable algorithms must be used to apply Eq. 67. These methods are briefly covered in the section "Robust Numerics".

Fifth, use RRE to constrain the vector estimate of population totals for areal variables to exactly match the census totals for geopolitical variables (e.g., area by county and ownership type), which are exactly known from administrative records (Särndal and others 1992:230). The notation corresponding to the Kalman filter in Eq. 12 is:

$$
\hat{\mathbf{t}}_{X(1)} = \begin{bmatrix} \hat{\mathbf{t}}_{M=0} \\ \hline \hat{\mathbf{t}}_{M=1} \\ \hline \hat{\mathbf{t}}_{M=2} \end{bmatrix}_{\substack{s=(1,2) \\ M=[1,1C]}}
\qquad
\hat{\mathbf{V}}\left(\hat{\mathbf{t}}_{X(1)}\right) = \hat{\mathbf{V}}\left(\begin{bmatrix} \hat{\mathbf{t}}_{M=0} \\ \hline \hat{\mathbf{t}}_{M=1} \\ \hline \hat{\mathbf{t}}_{M=2} \end{bmatrix}_{\substack{s=(1,2) \\ M=[1,1C]}} \right)
$$

$$
\hat{\mathbf{t}}_{Z(1)} = \left[\mathbf{t}_{M=0} \right]_{s=U}
\qquad
\hat{\mathbf{V}}\left(\hat{\mathbf{t}}_{Z(1)}\right) = \mathbf{0}
\tag{68}
$$

$$
\mathbf{H} = \begin{bmatrix} \mathbf{I} & | & \mathbf{0} \end{bmatrix}
\qquad
\hat{\mathbf{C}}\left(\hat{\mathbf{t}}_{X(1)}, \hat{\mathbf{t}}_{Z(1)}\right) = \mathbf{0}
$$

The $\mathbf{H}$ matrix in Eq. 68 has dimensions $q_{M=0}$-by-$(q_{M=0} + q_{M=1} + q_{M=2})$. From Eqs. 12 and 68, the composite estimator is:

$$
\begin{bmatrix} \mathbf{t}_{M=0} \\ \hline \mathbf{t}_{M=1} \\ \hline \mathbf{t}_{M=2} \end{bmatrix}_{\substack{s=(U,1,2) \\ M=[1,1C]}} = \begin{bmatrix} \hat{\mathbf{t}}_{M=0} \\ \hline \hat{\mathbf{t}}_{M=1} \\ \hline \hat{\mathbf{t}}_{M=2} \end{bmatrix}_{\substack{s=(1,2) \\ M=[1,1C]}} + \mathbf{K}\left[\left[\mathbf{t}_{M=0} \right]_{s=U} - \mathbf{H} \begin{bmatrix} \hat{\mathbf{t}}_{M=0} \\ \hline \hat{\mathbf{t}}_{M=1} \\ \hline \hat{\mathbf{t}}_{M=2} \end{bmatrix}_{\substack{s=(1,2) \\ M=[1,1C]}} \right]
$$

$$
\hat{\mathbf{V}}\left(\begin{bmatrix} \hat{\mathbf{t}}_{M=0} \\ \hline \hat{\mathbf{t}}_{M=1} \\ \hline \mathbf{t}_{M=2} \end{bmatrix}_{\substack{s=(U,1,2) \\ M=[1,1C]}} \right) = \hat{\mathbf{V}}\left(\begin{bmatrix} \hat{\mathbf{t}}_{M=0} \\ \hline \hat{\mathbf{t}}_{M=1} \\ \hline \hat{\mathbf{t}}_{M=2} \end{bmatrix}_{\substack{s=(1,2) \\ M=[1,1C]}} \right) - \mathbf{K}\,\mathbf{H}\,\hat{\mathbf{V}}\left(\begin{bmatrix} \hat{\mathbf{t}}_{M=0} \\ \hline \hat{\mathbf{t}}_{M=1} \\ \hline \hat{\mathbf{t}}_{M=2} \end{bmatrix}_{\substack{s=(1,2) \\ M=[1,1C]}} \right)
\tag{69}
$$

$$
\mathbf{K} = \hat{\mathbf{V}}\left(\begin{bmatrix} \mathbf{t}_{M=0} \\ \hline \mathbf{t}_{M=1} \\ \hline \mathbf{t}_{M=2} \end{bmatrix}_{\substack{s=(1,2) \\ M=[1,1C]}} \right) \mathbf{H}' \left(\mathbf{H}\,\hat{\mathbf{V}}\left(\begin{bmatrix} \hat{\mathbf{t}}_{M=0} \\ \hline \hat{\mathbf{t}}_{M=1} \\ \hline \mathbf{t}_{M=2} \end{bmatrix}_{\substack{s=(1,2) \\ M=[1,1C]}} \right) \mathbf{H}' \right)^{-1}
$$

Equations 62 to 69 may be expanded, as in Eqs. 20 to 27, to reveal analogies between RRE and more traditional univariate regression estimators (e.g., Särndal and others 1992).

Numerically reliable algorithms must be used in these various steps. These methods are briefly covered in Eqs. 31 to 37 for a census of auxiliary data and, more generally, in the section "Robust Numerics".

Finally, extract the matrix partitions in Eq. 69 that represent the estimated population totals for the variables measured with the FIA field protocol M = 2.

$$\left[\hat{\mathbf{t}}_{M=2}\right]_{\substack{s=(U,1,2)\\M=[1,1C]}} = \begin{bmatrix} \mathbf{0} & \vdots & \mathbf{0} & \vdots & \mathbf{I} \end{bmatrix} \begin{bmatrix} \hat{\mathbf{t}}_{M=0} \\ \hline \hat{\mathbf{t}}_{M=1} \\ \hline \hat{\mathbf{t}}_{M=2} \end{bmatrix}_{\substack{s=(U,1,2)\\M=[1,1C]}}$$

$$\hat{\mathbf{V}}\left(\hat{\mathbf{t}}_{M=2}\right)_{\substack{s=(U,1,2)\\M=[1,1C]}} = \begin{bmatrix} \mathbf{0} & \vdots & \mathbf{0} & \vdots & \mathbf{I} \end{bmatrix} \hat{\mathbf{V}}\left(\begin{bmatrix} \hat{\mathbf{t}}_{M=0} \\ \hline \hat{\mathbf{t}}_{M=1} \\ \hline \hat{\mathbf{t}}_{M=2} \end{bmatrix}_{\substack{s=(U,1,2)\\M=[1,1C]}}\right) \begin{bmatrix} \mathbf{0}' \\ \hline \mathbf{0}' \\ \hline \mathbf{I} \end{bmatrix}$$

(70)

This example actually incorporates dual, two-phase sampling designs. One is the Phase 1 sample of cluster plots that are measured solely with photo-interpretation (M = 1C) and classified by county and ownership type (M = 0), which is given in Eq. 62. Phase 1 in the second two-phase design uses the administrative records for area by county and ownership type (M = 0), which is considered an exact census. Because of Eq. 69, the sum of all areal variables (e.g., area by land cover and forest type) in Eq. 70 within an ownership-type and within a county will exactly equal the administrative census statistics for that land area. Sequential application of RRE permits designs that use a variety of overlapping sampling phases and stages and different types of collocated support-regions that are treated as cluster plots.

The section titled "Multivariate Vector of Auxiliary Variables" describes the numerous types of remotely sensed auxiliary data that may be accommodated in this type of complex design with cluster plots, sub-sampling, and censuses of the sampled population. The next section covers some mathematical features of those auxiliary data that are part of a classification system of categorical discrete variables.

Categorical Variables

All estimators considered above assume the predictor variables are continuous, such as remotely sensed estimates of standing wood volume. However, remote sensing variables may be discrete, such as predictions of forest type and land cover type categories. In addition, many FIA variables are discrete, such as categories of various forest conditions. The units of measure on these discrete variables are generally "proportion of the population," which ranges between 0 and 1. Equivalently, the units might be hectares or acres, which range between 0 and the total area of the population.

The estimators above can directly accommodate any categorical variable as an auxiliary predictor variable, a population variable, or both. Any polychotomous categorical variable with c categories may be transformed into c binary dichotomous variables (e.g., de Gruijter and others 2006:69; Knottnerus 2003:130; Zhang 2000). Within the estimators already presented, these dichotomous variables may be included as sub-vectors, along with continuous variables in the $\mathbf{y}_{M=0}$ vector. Likewise, $C_{M=2'}$ categories in the FIA field protocol M = 2' may be converted into $C_{M=2'}$ dichotomous variables, and these may be inserted as sub-vectors in the $\mathbf{y}_{M=2'}$ measurement vector. The resulting RRE will retain their minimum variance property. However, the statistical efficiency of estimates might be improved by capturing the $C_{M=0'} \times C_{M=2'}$ cross-classification of categorical protocols M = 0' and M = 2'. Otherwise, the estimators above only include the $C_{M=0'} + C_{M=2'}$ margins of this cross-classification in $\mathbf{y}_{M=0'}$ and $\mathbf{y}_{M=2'}$. This enhancement is considered here.

For an FIA variable and a remotely sensed variable that are both polychotomous categorical variables, a contingency table can be built that includes statistics for the cross-classification by these two protocols. If both categorical variables have equivalent classification systems, then $C_{M=0'} = C_{M=2'}$, and the resulting square $C_{M=0'} \times C_{M=2'}$ contingency is directly related to an error matrix or confusion matrix in the remote sensing literature (Story and Congalton 1986).

In contrast, the classification systems for the M = 0' (e.g., spaceborne remote sensing) and M = 2' (e.g., FIA) protocols can differ in the number of categories and their definitions. The cross-classification with both protocols yields a $C_{M=0'} \times C_{M=2'}$ contingency table. Gallego and Bamps (2008) use the term "fine scale profiles" for the resulting rectangular contingency table to avoid misinterpretation as an error or confusion matrix in the remote sensing lexicon. Card (1982) and Czaplewski and Catts (1992) demonstrate that such a contingency table is the basis for multivariate inverse calibration (Tenenbein 1972; Brown 1982; Czaplewski and Catts 1992) or direct calibration (Dymond 1992; Gallego and Bamps 2008).

It is possible to imbed this contingency table within any of the above estimators for complex sampling designs. Joint classification probabilities are estimated by augmenting the M = 2' measurement vector with the cross-classification with both the remotely sensed (M = 0') and field (M = 2') protocols. This simply requires restructuring the $C_{M=0'} \times C_{M=2'}$ elements in the cross-classification contingency table as the $(C_{M=0'} \times C_{M=2'})$-by-1 sub-vector of $[\mathbf{y}_{M=2'}]_i$ for sample unit i in Eqs. 20, 45, 56, 58, or 63.

Czaplewski (in prep.[b]) provides a detailed example of this application, in which census statistics from full-coverage, remotely sensed data serve as constraints (Simon and Chia 2002). He offers solutions to numerical round-off errors that can cause unreliable results. There are also well-developed alternatives to numerical hazards, such as U-D factorization (Bierman 1977; Maybeck 1979:Chapter 7). Numerical problems are not always apparent from the final results, and numerical errors can exceed random estimation errors (Bierman 1977), which obviates the gains in statistical efficiency with the Kalman filter. It is strongly recommended that the numerically robust methods presented by Maybeck and Bierman be used as standard procedure.

The inclusion of the contingency table for all cross-classifications can create a large number of state variables. For example, if there are 12 categories in the field protocol and 17 categories in the remote sensing protocol, 204 variables must be estimated. However, only one margin of the contingency table might be required for FIA statistical reports, such as the estimated areas for each of the 12 categories classified with the field protocol. The remaining 192 variables are a nuisance in some sense. The Schmidt-Kalman filter is an alternative (Jazwinski 1970; Grewal and Andrews 2001). The Schmidt-Kalman filter does not specifically estimate the nuisance variables, thus reducing the dimensions of the vector estimates. However, this advantage is gained at a cost. The solution is not necessarily optimal, and estimates of the desired state variables might not be as efficient as a filter that directly estimates all nuisance variables. In the special case of multiphase sampling with a homogeneous PSU where each PSU can be classified into one and only one category in each classification system, the margins of the contingency table are sufficient statistics for constrained RRE (Czaplewski in prep.[b]).

There are well-developed alternatives available that apply constraints upon the Kalman filter solution (Doran 1997; Simon and Chia 2002). See the thorough and modern reviews by Gupta and Hauser (2007) and Gupta (2008) for linear equality constraints that might be imposed so that the estimated total for the remotely sensed categorical variables exactly equals the census totals. Also, it is possible with numerous rare categories that some estimated population totals will be negative. The likely cause is application of classification systems that are too detailed relative to the sample size. One pragmatic solution is to collapse the detail of a hierarchical classification system to be more realistic given limited sample sizes. Another alternative is application of inequality constraints that force relevant estimated state variables to be non-negative. Doran (1997), Simon and Chia (2002), Knottnerus (2003:352), Gupta and Hauser (2007) and Gupta (2008) provide a useful introduction to these estimators.

Robust Numerics

As repeatedly discussed above, numerical precision of the multivariate estimator merits special attention. Numerical precision is a function of the word length for a digital computer, and it is often referred to as round-off error. The subtraction operator, when applied to two large numbers or matrices, is especially prone to significant round-off error. The vector residual in Eq. 10 is an example. Also, matrix inversion is problematic for an ill-conditioned covariance matrix, as in Eq. 9 for the gain matrix **K**. The covariance matrix in Eq. 9 will be ill-conditioned whenever sub-sets of auxiliary variables are highly codependent. The dichotomous transformation of a polychotomous, remotely sensed categorical variable is a common example.

For example, Knottnerus (2003:236) found that small errors in decomposition of the Horvitz-Thompson estimator can invoke large errors in variance estimates. Estevao and Särndal (2004:657) warn that the calibration estimator is numerically unstable, especially for designs more complex than Simple Random Sampling. Magnussen (2003) found that RRE, when applied to three-phase sampling of categorical variables, is not necessarily robust and consistent compared with a sub-optimal sequential estimator. Magnussen posited that numerical stability can be improved if multivariate dimensions are decreased by sequentially considering only those variables shared by two levels at one time in the multilevel sampling design. For example, the three-phase estimator in Eqs. 44 to 51 requires covariance matrices with dimensions of $(q_{M=0} + q_{M=1} + q_{M=2})$-by-$(q_{M=0} + q_{M=1} + q_{M=2})$ at all sequential steps, where $q_{M=i}$ denotes the number of variables estimated with protocol $M = i$. The alternative three-phase estimator in Eqs. 52 to 56 involves dimensions of $(q_{M=0} + q_{M=1})$-by-$(q_{M=0} + q_{M=1})$ at one step and $(q_{M=1} + q_{M=2})$-by-$(q_{M=1} + q_{M=2})$ at another step. This requires modest sacrifice of statistical efficiency because it ignores the $M = 0$ measurements available for the small Phase 3 sub-sample, but the sacrifice is rewarded with improved robustness and consistency. This same strategy applies to any sampling design that employs three or more phases, stages, or measurement protocols within a cluster plot.

However, an additional solution is possible. Numerical issues with the multivariate Kalman filter are well known and extensively studied as components of the divergence problem. Bierman (1977) devotes an entire book to the subject. Maybeck's (1979) Chapter 7 is a succinct and thorough coverage of the subject. Comprehensive references on the applied Kalman filter all deal with this issue (e.g., Grewal and Andrews 2001; Bar-Shalom and others 2001; Chui and Chen 2009). The reliability of the Kalman filter is also vulnerable to spurious observations, outliers, or inaccurate models (Guttman and Lin 1995).

For example, inversion of a $q_{M=1}$-by-$q_{M=1}$ covariance matrix is required in Eq. 26. The dimensions of this covariance matrix may become large with three or more sampling phases or stages; detailed, remotely sensed census data; and areal constraints based on geopolitical domains. (Dimensions required in this matrix inversion are unaffected by the dimensions of the variables measured with the $M = 2$ protocol, i.e., FIA field data.) More seriously, the covariance matrix for auxiliary variables can be singular, making the matrix inversion infeasible (Särndal and others 1992:241). In especially pathological cases, the magnitude of numerical round-off errors can become large relative to the magnitude of random estimation errors (Bierman 1977:1).

Bierman (1977:22) cites one ad hoc method to detect significant numerical errors: solve the system of matrix equations with single-precision numerics (e.g., 32-bit), and then solve it again with double-precision (e.g., 64-bit). If the differences in the vector results are of pragmatic significance, then numerical errors are a problem that must be addressed.

In the early days of Kalman filtering, when 8-bit computers were state-of-the-art, numerous solutions to these numerical challenges were devised. The square root transformation of a covariance matrix has about twice the numerical precision compared to matrix operations with untransformed covariance matrices (Bierman 1977:91), which may be further improved with more numerically precise digital computers (e.g., double-precision with 64-bit processors versus 8-bit) and orthogonal transformations such as the Cholesky decomposition, the Householder orthogonal transformation, the Givens orthogonal transformation, and the Gram-Schmidt orthogonalization. One especially effective solution is the U-D factorization method, which is a modified Gram-Schmidt orthogonalization (Bierman 1977:148). Stengel (1986:357), Grewal and Andrews (2001) and Bar-Shalom and others (2001) also discuss U-D factorization and its derivation. The Square Root Information Filter (SRIF) is another alternative that surpasses the U-D factorization in some applications (Bierman 1977:69). Knottnerus (2003:281) shows the relationship between the numerically stable Gram-Schmidt orthogonalization and augmented regression (Blundell and Robin 1999) in recursive applications.

Most Kalman filtering algorithms based on these numerically robust methods orthogonalize the vector of auxiliary population totals with a linear transformation, such as the inverse square root of the corresponding covariance matrix. The resulting vector of transformed auxiliary statistics for the population is expected to have a unit covariance matrix, meaning each element of the transformed vector has zero covariance with all other elements of the transformed vector. Therefore, each element of the transformed auxiliary vector may be separately applied to improve precision of estimated population totals for the FIA study variables. The final vector estimate incorporates all elements of the transformed auxiliary vector after all elements are processed in this sequence of recursions.

> Boggs and others (1995) note that these types of algorithms are not very widely used, because of the erroneous perception that these factorization techniques are too complicated compared to the conventional (Kalman filter), use too much computer storage, and involve too much computation. This (incorrect) perception is due in large part: (1) to an incomplete understanding … of algorithms that are heavily dependent on advanced numerical analysis (Golub and Van Loan 1996, Lawson and Hanson 1974), and (2) on the use of inefficient computer … implementations (to process state-vectors with) … up to a few thousand variables (Jiang and Ghil 1993).

Boggs and others (1995) expect that Bierman's SRIF offers even further improvements. Furthermore, these methods are amenable to implementation in database software without the need for matrix algebra software. Implementation in corporate database software is convenient for a large production statistical program such as FIA (McRoberts and others 2004).

In unpublished Monte Carlo simulations by the author, the **U-D** factorization has been fast and very successful in the numerical sense, with covariance matrices having $q_{M=1} = 200$ remotely sensed and geopolitical census variables, even without specialized matrix algebra software. This confirms that even larger problems might be numerically feasible and robust. Czaplewski (in prep.[b]) presents other numerically robust yet simple methods with auxiliary census variables.

Czaplewski (in prep.[a]) applies the Kalman filter as a time-series estimator for FIA panel data (Patterson and Reams 2005). The multivariate innovation sequence is associated with a time-series of covariance matrices. These must be inverted to compute the multivariate weights (i.e., Kalman gain matrices) that combine the vector of expected observations with the realized observations. The covariance matrices are severely rank-deficient, and many full-rank covariance matrices remain ill conditioned.

Simon and Chia (2002) provide stable methods suitable for auxiliary constants such as a census of pixels from full-coverage "wall-to-wall" spaceborne sensors (e.g., Landsat, SPOT, IRS, and MODIS); these methods apply to both continuous and categorical predictions from remotely sensed data. Some variables are non-negative by definition (e.g., biomass must have a value greater than or equal to zero), but it is possible that the static Kalman filter can produce infeasible negative estimates, even with stable numerics. This problem is more common with rare attributes (e.g., forest clearings caused by small fires or clearcuts). Doran (1997), Simon and Chia (2002), and Knottnerus (2003:379) offer relevant inequality constaints that can eliminate infeasible results.

Czaplewski (in prep.[a]) successfully implements the dynamic Kalman filter under these adverse conditions. He uses the **LDL'** square root filter given by Bar-Shalom and others (2001:308-317). The **LDL'** factorization uses the Linear Algebra PACKage (LAPACK) routine for the **LU** decomposition (Anderson and others 1999), which is a freely available FORTRAN 90 routine applicable to singular covariance matrices. Results from the **LU** decomposition are further factored into the **LDL'** structure with methods given by Golub and Van Loan (1996: algorithm 4.1.2) for a symmetric nonsingular matrix. Any singular covariance matrix is pivoted so that the first diagonal partition is nonsingular and well conditioned. The remaining partition of the covariance matrix represents nearly redundant information that is simply omitted from the Kalman update estimator. The pivoting algorithm retains any portion of the innovation covariance matrix directly corresponding to state-variables that are associated with auxiliary observations. The remainder of the pivot priorites use LAPACK output. The **LDL'** square root filter requires orthogonalization of the observation matrix. This is done with the inverse square root of the covariance matrix for the auxiliary variables using Method 2 in Higham (2002:263).

The estimators given above, and many more related estimators that are envisioned for future research, are merely abstract matrix equations at this point. Important details such as numerical stability require further research and development before these methods can be confidentially incorporated into a government statistics program.

Optimal PSU Expansion Values for Each FIA Plot

Scott and others (2005:65) review the historical use of expansion factors in FIA.

> When periodic inventories and flat files were the FIA standards, it was convenient to calculate a small set of expansion factors by which individual plot-level or tree-level observations could be converted to their population level equivalents. This allowed population totals to be obtained via summation, which greatly simplified the estimation process. Expansion factors were popular with external FIA clients, many of whom used this concept to build their own processing systems. The tradeoff for such simplicity is that the use of expansion factors precludes the ability to calculate variances. At best, the variances of estimators derived from expanded values can only be approximated, and these approximations are known to be poor (Alegria and Scott 1991). Expansion factors are less practical with panelized inventory systems, which are designed to increase analytical flexibility by allowing panels to be combined in a variety of ways. Each different panel combination produces a unique set of expansion factors, rendering expansion factors associated with

panel systems less stable than those produced by periodic systems. The use of expansion factors is discouraged because they prohibit accurate variance estimation and they no longer have the advantage of simplicity. However, there is still a demand for them, and it may take a while to convert processing systems to the estimation procedures specified in this chapter. Therefore, FIA will continue to offer expansion factors until a demand is no longer apparent.

Calibration weights (Deville and Särndal 1992) are similar to FIA plot expansion factors. Calibration weights are a modification of the design weights (i.e., inverse of inclusion probability for each sampled PSU). The modification incorporates external information available from the auxiliary data, such as the population census of predictions for remotely sensed pixels. Estevao and Särndal (2006) discuss calibration weights as a convenient means to improve statistical efficiency with auxiliary information. FIA expansion factors serve the same role with post-stratification. FIA uses the temporally indifferent estimator (Patterson and Reams 2005), which facilitates the use of expansion factors in FIA databases.

The following demonstrates how the results from RRE for complex designs may be expressed as expansion values, much like the expansion factors traditionally used by FIA and calibration weights used in other surveys. Future research will investigate dependable methods that use dynamic expansion values with the Kalman filter.

Let the equal-probability, infinite-population, design-based, multivariate, single-phase estimator for the vector of auxiliary variables (**x**) and study variables (**y**) be the design-weighted sum of observations for each sampled unit k (i.e., FIA plot) in the equal-probability sample $s(XY)$ (i.e., the set of sampled FIA plots):

$$\begin{bmatrix} \hat{\bar{\mathbf{x}}} \\ \hat{\bar{\mathbf{y}}} \end{bmatrix}_{XY} = \sum\nolimits_{s(XY)} \frac{1}{n_{XY}} \begin{bmatrix} \mathbf{x} \\ \mathbf{y} \end{bmatrix}_k$$

$$\begin{bmatrix} \hat{\mathbf{t}}_X \\ \hat{\mathbf{t}}_Y \end{bmatrix}_{XY} = A_T \begin{bmatrix} \hat{\bar{\mathbf{x}}} \\ \hat{\bar{\mathbf{y}}} \end{bmatrix}_{XY} = \sum\nolimits_{s(XY)} \frac{A_T}{n_{XY}} \begin{bmatrix} \mathbf{x} \\ \mathbf{y} \end{bmatrix}_k \tag{71}$$

where $n_{(XY)}$ is the sample size of FIA plots in sample $s(XY)$, A is the total acres in the sampled population, and both $\mathbf{x}_k$ and $\mathbf{y}_k$ have units of measure such that the values per unit area are consistent with the units of A (e.g., 1 acre for a single-condition category in FIA plot k and volume per acre for wood volume measurements in plot k). The estimated covariance matrix for the population vector estimate in Eq. 71 is defined as:

$$\hat{\mathbf{V}} \begin{bmatrix} \hat{\mathbf{t}}_X \\ \hat{\mathbf{t}}_Y \end{bmatrix}_{XY} = \sum\nolimits_s \left[\frac{A_T^2}{n_{XY}(n_{XY}-1)} \left(\begin{bmatrix} \mathbf{x} \\ \mathbf{y} \end{bmatrix}_k - \begin{bmatrix} \hat{\bar{\mathbf{x}}} \\ \hat{\bar{\mathbf{y}}} \end{bmatrix}_{XY} \right) \left(\begin{bmatrix} \mathbf{x} \\ \mathbf{y} \end{bmatrix}_k - \begin{bmatrix} \hat{\bar{\mathbf{x}}} \\ \hat{\bar{\mathbf{y}}} \end{bmatrix}_{XY} \right)' \right] \tag{72}$$

Further, assume that comparable remotely sensed auxiliary data are available from a large independent probability sample $s(Z)$:

$$\hat{\mathbf{t}}_Z = \sum\nolimits_{s(Z)} \frac{A_T}{n_{(Z)}} \mathbf{x}_i \tag{73}$$

$$\hat{\mathbf{V}}(\hat{\mathbf{t}}_Z) = \sum\nolimits_{s(Z)} \left[\frac{A_T^2}{n_Z(n_Z-1)} (\mathbf{x}_i - \hat{\bar{\mathbf{x}}}_Z)(\mathbf{x}_i - \hat{\bar{\mathbf{x}}}_Z)' \right] \tag{74}$$

where X and Z share exactly the same measurement protocol, i.e., $\mathbf{x}_i = \mathbf{z}_i$. If the auxiliary data are available for a census of remotely sensed pixels for the entire sampled population, then the population totals for the vector of auxiliary data are known exactly as $\hat{\mathbf{t}}_Z = \sum_N [\mathbf{x}] = \mathbf{t}_Z$ without sampling or enumeration error, i.e., $\hat{V}[\hat{\mathbf{t}}_Z] = 0$.

Expansion Values for FIA Population Estimates

Based on Eq. 16, the optimal RRE given this vector of auxiliary variables has the general structure:

$$\left[\hat{\mathbf{t}}_{\text{RRE}}\right]_Y = \left[\hat{\mathbf{t}}_Y\right]_{XY} + \mathbf{W}\left(\hat{\mathbf{t}}_Z - \left[\hat{\mathbf{t}}_X\right]_{XY}\right) \tag{75}$$

where the matrix of RRE optimal weights in Eq. 75 is defined as the q_Y-by-q_X matrix $\mathbf{W}$:

$$\mathbf{W} = \begin{bmatrix} \mathbf{0} & \mathbf{I} \end{bmatrix} \mathbf{K}$$

$$= \left[\hat{\mathbf{C}}(\hat{\mathbf{t}}_Y, \hat{\mathbf{t}}_X)_{XY} \left(\left[\hat{\mathbf{V}}(\hat{\mathbf{t}}_X)_{XY} + \hat{\mathbf{V}}(\hat{\mathbf{t}}_Z)\right]^{-1} \right)' \right]$$

Substituting Eq. 71 into Eq. 75:

$$\left[\hat{\mathbf{t}}_{\text{RRE}}\right]_Y = \sum_{s(XY)} \frac{A_T}{n_{XY}} \mathbf{y}_k + \mathbf{W}\left(\hat{\mathbf{t}}_Z - \sum_{s(XY)} \frac{A_T}{n_{XY}} \mathbf{x}_k \right)$$

$$= \sum_{s(XY)} \mathbf{f}_k \tag{76}$$

where the q_Y-by-1 vector "expansion value" $\mathbf{f}_k$ for the kth PSU is:

$$\mathbf{f}_k = \frac{A_T}{n_{XY}}\left[\mathbf{y}_k + \mathbf{W}\left(\frac{\hat{\mathbf{t}}_Z}{A_T} - \mathbf{x}_k \right) \right]$$

By definition, the q_Y-by-1 vector sum of expansion values in Eq. 76 for all n_{XY} PSUs will exactly agree with the optimal RE vector estimate for the sampled population, thus allowing generic inference (Opsomer and others 2007). The vector of expansion values for the kth PSU is the sum of the design-weighted q_Y-by-1 vector measurement of the kth PSU $(A_T/n_{XY})\mathbf{y}_k$ plus the optimally weighted q_X-by-1 residual vector difference between the auxiliary data for the kth PSU and its corresponding population mean, namely $(A_T/n_{XY})\mathbf{W}[(\hat{\mathbf{t}}_Z/A_T) - \mathbf{x}_k]$. This is similar in structure to Knottnerus' (2003:395) minimum variance weighting procedure for univariate study variables.

The vector of optimal expansion values $\mathbf{f}_k$ for each sampling unit k in Eq. 76 has different numerical properties than the scalar expansion factor $(A_T/n)\mathbf{y}_k$ in Eq. 71. Unlike the traditional FIA expansion factor, optimal expansion values for a sampling unit can have negative elements, although this can be rare or nonexistent. Furthermore, expansion values for forest characteristics (e.g., wood volume and forest type) may be non-zero for an FIA plot that is classified as non-forest in the field. FIA uses a single multiplicative volume expansion factor for all measurements associated with wood volume, such as volume for different tree species, tree sizes, and tree conditions. This includes current volume and components of volume change (e.g., growth, regeneration, mortality, removals). However, the second term in Eq. 76 is an additive adjustment, not a multiplicative adjustment. To emulate fully the traditional use of expansion factors by FIA, ad hoc procedures might be necessary to apply these optimal expansion values from RRE. For example, merchantable wood volume measurements across all tally trees within PSU k might be summed into a single element in the $\mathbf{y}_k$ measurement vector for plot k. If so, then a single element of $\mathbf{f}_k$ is the expansion value that applies to volume measurements for all tally trees in sampling unit k, regardless of species, size, or condition. That value would need to be prorated to each category of wood volume measurement.

Expansion Values for FIA Variance Estimates

The previous section conveniently expressed RRE results as expansion vectors for each PSU. Likewise, the RRE covariance matrix for the population totals for both the auxiliary and study variables may be expressed as the sum of values for each FIA PSU (e.g., Knottnerus 2003:220, 236). This provides further conveniences in database procedures.

First, combine Eqs. 12 and 72. The resulting covariance matrix equals:

$$\hat{\mathbf{V}}\left(\hat{\mathbf{t}}_{\text{RRE}}\right) = \left(\mathbf{I} - \mathbf{KH}\right)\left[\mathbf{V}\left(\hat{\mathbf{t}}_{XY}\right)\right]\left(\mathbf{I} - \mathbf{KH}\right)'$$

$$= \sum_s \left[\frac{A_T^2}{n_{XY}\left(n_{XY} - 1\right)}\left(\mathbf{I} - \mathbf{KH}\right)\left(\begin{bmatrix}\mathbf{x}\\\mathbf{y}\end{bmatrix}_k - \begin{bmatrix}\hat{\bar{\mathbf{x}}}\\\hat{\bar{\mathbf{y}}}\end{bmatrix}_{XY}\right)\left(\begin{bmatrix}\mathbf{x}\\\mathbf{y}\end{bmatrix}_k - \begin{bmatrix}\hat{\bar{\mathbf{x}}}\\\hat{\bar{\mathbf{y}}}\end{bmatrix}_{XY}\right)'\left(\mathbf{I} - \mathbf{KH}\right)'\right] \quad (77)$$

Extracting the partitions in Eq. 77 specific to the study variables Y and defining a new vector $\mathbf{g}_k$ for the kth FIA field plot:

$$\hat{\mathbf{V}}\left(\hat{\mathbf{t}}_{\text{RRE}}\right)_Y = \begin{bmatrix}\mathbf{0} & \mathbf{I}\end{bmatrix}\hat{\mathbf{V}}\left(\hat{\mathbf{t}}_{\text{RRE}}\right)\begin{bmatrix}\mathbf{0}\\\mathbf{I}\end{bmatrix}$$

$$\approx \sum_s \mathbf{g}_k \mathbf{g}_k' \quad (78)$$

where

$$\mathbf{g}_k = \frac{A_T}{n_{XY}}\begin{bmatrix}\mathbf{0} & \mathbf{I}\end{bmatrix}\left(\mathbf{I} - \mathbf{KH}\right)\left(\begin{bmatrix}\mathbf{x}\\\mathbf{y}\end{bmatrix}_k - \begin{bmatrix}\hat{\bar{\mathbf{x}}}\\\hat{\bar{\mathbf{y}}}\end{bmatrix}_{XY}\right)$$

and the sample size of FIA field plots n_{XY} is sufficiently large such that $(n_{XY}-1) \approx n_{XY}$. The vector $\mathbf{g}_k$ for the kth FIA field plot in Eq. 78 may be rearranged such that:

$$\mathbf{g}_k = \frac{A_T}{n_{XY}}\left[\begin{bmatrix}\mathbf{0} & \mathbf{I}\end{bmatrix}\left(\begin{bmatrix}\mathbf{x}\\\mathbf{y}\end{bmatrix}_k - \begin{bmatrix}\hat{\bar{\mathbf{x}}}\\\hat{\bar{\mathbf{y}}}\end{bmatrix}_{XY}\right) - \begin{bmatrix}\mathbf{0} & \mathbf{I}\end{bmatrix}\mathbf{K}\begin{bmatrix}\mathbf{0} & \mathbf{I}\end{bmatrix}\left(\begin{bmatrix}\mathbf{x}\\\mathbf{y}\end{bmatrix}_k - \begin{bmatrix}\hat{\bar{\mathbf{x}}}\\\hat{\bar{\mathbf{y}}}\end{bmatrix}_{XY}\right)\right]$$

$$= \frac{A_T}{n_{XY}}\left[\left(\mathbf{y}_k - \hat{\bar{\mathbf{y}}}_{XY}\right) + \begin{bmatrix}\mathbf{0} & \mathbf{I}\end{bmatrix}\mathbf{K}\left(-\mathbf{x}_k + \hat{\bar{\mathbf{x}}}_{XY}\right)\right] \quad (79)$$

$$= \frac{A_T}{n_{XY}}\left[\mathbf{y}_k + \begin{bmatrix}\mathbf{0} & \mathbf{I}\end{bmatrix}\mathbf{K}\left(\hat{\bar{\mathbf{x}}}_{XY} - \mathbf{x}_k\right) - \hat{\bar{\mathbf{y}}}_{XY}\right]$$

Substituting Eqs. 14 and 75 into Eq. 79, using $\hat{\mathbf{t}}_Z / A_T$ as a more precise estimate of the population mean vector for the auxiliary variables than $\hat{\bar{\mathbf{x}}}_{XY}$, and then combing with Eq. 76:

$$\mathbf{g}_k = \frac{A_T}{n_{XY}}\left[\mathbf{y}_k + \mathbf{W}\left(\hat{\bar{\mathbf{x}}}_{XY} - \mathbf{x}_k\right) - \hat{\bar{\mathbf{y}}}_{XY}\right]$$

$$= \mathbf{f}_k - \frac{A_T}{n_{XY}}\hat{\bar{\mathbf{y}}}_{XY}$$

(80)

Replacing Eq. 80 into Eq. 78:

$$\hat{\mathbf{V}}\left(\hat{\mathbf{t}}_{\mathrm{RRE}}\right)_Y \approx \sum_s \left(\mathbf{f}_k - \frac{A_T}{n_{XY}}\hat{\bar{\mathbf{y}}}_{XY}\right)\left(\mathbf{f}_k - \frac{A_T}{n_{XY}}\hat{\bar{\mathbf{y}}}_{XY}\right)'$$

$$= \sum_s \left(\mathbf{f}_k - \frac{\left[\hat{\mathbf{t}}_Y\right]_{XY}}{n_{XY}}\right)\left(\mathbf{f}_k - \frac{\left[\hat{\mathbf{t}}_Y\right]_{XY}}{n_{XY}}\right)'$$

(81)

Thus, Eq. 81 expresses the RE covariance matrix for the vector of estimated population totals for the FIA study variables as the sum over all FIA PSUs of the cross-product of a vector specific to each PSU ($\mathbf{g}_k$). That vector equals the residual difference between the vector of expansion values for the RE for the kth PSU ($\mathbf{f}_k$) (Eq. 76) and the mean design-based vector of expansion values over all n_{XY} sampled PSUs.

Further Research

Equations 76 and 81 demonstrate that the optimal RRE population estimates and variances for FIA variables may be estimated with a vector of plot-level expansion values. Those expansion values use the design-based weights, the design-consistent approximately optimal RRE weights, the observed study variables ($\mathbf{y}_k$), and the auxiliary variables ($\mathbf{x}_k$) for each sampled PSU k. Unlike traditional FIA expansion factors, which cannot be used to estimate variances with post-stratification (Scott and others 2005:65), the RRE expansion values may be conveniently used in a database environment for FIA core tables *and* related variance estimation. Furthermore, the memoryless quality of the RRE produces expansion values that fully capture all information available in a prior set of ancillary remotely sensed data. Thereafter, those remotely sensed data may be (figuratively) discarded after they are processed by the RRE because they are no longer needed for subsequent estimates. This quality is expected to greatly simplify processing, application, and documentation of dynamic expansion values by FIA as new time-series of remotely sensed auxiliary data and FIA field data become available. However, these weights are based on heuristics, not formal theory. Knottnerus (2003:395) develops similar weights from the perspective of Pythagorean regression, which might be further simplified with the matrix inversion lemma. Further investigation is needed to gain confidence in the reliability, numerical stability, and processing simplicity of this approach to variance estimation.

Similarly, results from the numerically stable algorithm for use with auxiliary census data (Eqs. 34 and 35) may be captured as expansion values at the PSU level. However, these expansion values would need to be revised at each individual i^{th} recursion. Until the end of the recursive sequence, PSU-level expansion values would be necessary for the auxiliary variables in addition to the FIA study variables. The auxiliary variables may be removed from the state vector after all relevant information in those auxiliary variables is filtered out with the RRE. Future research will extend PSU-level expansion values for RE (Eqs. 76 and 81) to the more general case of RRE. The section "Robust Numerics" describes more general methods to assure numerical stability. It is not yet known how these results can be represented as expansion values at the PSU level.

These results are obtained by treating the sub-optimal matrix of weights $\mathbf{K}$ as fixed, which leads to a vector of expansion values for each PSU k that are additive shifts relative to the original direct estimators. This ad hoc approach is fully design-consistent when applied to the entire population, but its statistical properties are unknown when applied to small areas. Furthermore, it deviates from more traditional approaches (e.g., Särndal and others 1992) in which a single scalar regression or calibration weight is applied to all variables measured for a sampled PSU. An alternative might explicitly recognize that the optimal $\mathbf{K}$ is estimated. The estimator in Eq. 76 may be recast as a linear combination of the vector measurements for each sampled PSU k ($\mathbf{y}_k$) with the $\mathbf{y}_k$ appearing in the estimated covariance term in Eq. 77. If that is feasible, then the vector of expansion values for each PSU may be replaced by a scalar expansion weight. This would conform to traditional regression estimation. However, the resulting scalar weight is not necessarily optimal for all study variables, and, in extreme cases, it might be less efficient than the original direct estimator that does not use any auxiliary information (Lundström and Särndal 1999).

Multivariate Vector of FIA Study Variables

The M = 2 protocol produces accurate FIA field measurements (e.g., tree diameter and tree height) that are further transformed into other relevant FIA study variables (e.g., tree volume and tree biomass). These variables characterize forest structure and composition in terms of tree species, size, wood volume, and biomass; rates of tree volume growth, mortality, and removals; ownership of private lands and stewardship responsibilities for public lands; and other indicators of forest conditions, health, risks, and hazards (Gillespie 1999). Table 2 summarizes these variables in more detail. These variables are cross-classified in multiple ways to create detailed FIA core statistical tables (e.g., Reams and McCollum 2000; Smith 2002).

In all of the examples above, the $\mathbf{y}$ vector contains the FIA core variables that describe the current population totals $\mathbf{t}_y$, or state, of the population. The $\mathbf{y}$ vector also includes variables that describe the change over time in those same variables, i.e., the change in the state of the population. Thus, a dynamic Kalman filter can include efficient estimates of changes over time in the sampled population, while retaining its memoryless qualities to simplify data management.

Population sub-groups are defined by FIA as forest condition classes (e.g., aspen sawtimber stands) with detailed estimates of tree characteristics within each condition class (e.g., tree species by various categories of tree size). As a consequence, the number of parameters can increase 500-fold or more for populations at the scale of a state (e.g., Pennsylvania, which is approximately 28 million acres in size).

There may be literally thousands of such variables, depending on the degree of compartmentalization of continuous variables by discrete condition categories, the degree of cross-classification of nominal categorical variables, and the number of population groups. For numerical reasons, it is assumed that some simplification of the estimation problem reduces the dimension $q_{M=2}$ of the study variables in vector $\mathbf{y}$ such that $5 < q_{M=2} < 5000$. At the other extreme, the RRE may be structured as a univariate estimator, where each scalar study variable is separately estimated, one at a time, i.e., $q_{M=2} = 1$. This latter univariate approach is used in the vast majority of sample survey literature. It is also used by FIA (Scott and

Table 2. Summary of variables measured directly or indirectly with FIA field protocol (Czaplewski 1999).

Stand- or site-level conditions	Number of categories	Tree-level conditions[a]	Number of categories
Land use[b,c]	5	Tree species[d]	331
Broad forest types[b,d]	29	Tree size (DBH)	2-inch classes
Detailed forest types[d]	136	Tree damage	10
Stage of stand development[b]	4	Tree quality, value	5
Stand density[b,e]	5	Wood volume	continuous
Stand origin[b]	2	Growth in wood volume	continuous
Land ownership	10		
Stand age	9		
Stand productivity	7		
Number of trees per acre[b,f]	continuous		
Wood volume per acre[b,f]	continuous		
Volume growth per acre[f]	continuous		
Volume mortality per acre[b,f]	continuous		
Volume removals per acre[b,f]	continuous		

[a] FIA measures many other indicators that describe landscapes, habitats, non-tree vegetation, etc.
[b] Photo-interpretations and photogrammetric measurements with high-resolution imagery are well correlated with these field measurements (Aldrich 1979). The correlation is much lower with satellite data and high-altitude (low-resolution) aerial photography.
[c] Includes timberland, other forest land, protected forest, non-forest land, and water.
[d] Any single geographic region of the United States has only 20 to 40 percent of these national categories.
[e] Includes overstocked, fully stocked, understocked, and non-stocked.
[f] Totals are produced for thousands of permutations of different tree and forest categories.

others 2005). Future research will investigate the advantages and limitations of the multivariate approach, including accurate estimation of large covariance matrices with methods suitable to a production survey system.

Multivariate Vector of Auxiliary Variables

Särndal and others (1992:220, 304, 397) define auxiliary variables to "covary with the study variable and thus carry information about the study variable. Such covariation is used advantageously in the regression estimator ... (to explain the variable of interest, especially) … as a means of offsetting the scarcity of the sample data in small domains." The associations among auxiliary variables (e.g., remotely sensed data) and the study variables (e.g., FIA field measurements and transformations) need to be sufficiently strong. Särndal and others (1992:250) recommend correlations among continuous predictor and response variables be at least 0.5 or greater. For nominal categorical variables, Czaplewski and Patterson (2003) recommend agreements of at least 70 percent or greater.

The principle objective of this paper is to offer highly flexible statistical approaches capable of using multiple types of remotely sensed data (Czaplewski in prep.[b]) to improve statistical estimates and cost-effectiveness of FIA. These remote sensing technologies include:

- digital processing of multispectral optical Earth-observing satellite sensors, such as Landsat, with 30-m pixels;
- hyper-spectral optical Earth-observing satellite sensors, such as MODIS, with 250-m to 1000-m pixel resolution (e.g., Huete and others 2002; Tian and others 2002; Zhan and others 2002; Brown and others 2006; Achard and others 2007);
- LiDAR laser sensors, both airborne and spaceborne; and
- manual interpretation of aerial photography of various scales and resolutions.

All these technologies are briefly discussed here.

Digital Processing of Multispectral Landsat Data

Digital processing of multispectral Landsat data with 30-m pixel resolution has broad-scale applications in extensive monitoring of forest cover. The following is a partial list of the literature that assesses these applications: Horler and Ahern 1986; Bauer and others 1994; Cohen and others 1995, 2001; Trotter and others 1997; Wynne and Carter 1997; Holmgren and Thuresson 1998; Katila and Tomppo 2001; and Lefsky and others 2001. The relatively high spatial resolution of these data often permits registration to a support-region at the scale of a 1-acre FIA plot, although larger support-regions can also be useful.

The Landsat ($M = 0$) protocol may include continuous variables, such as remotely sensed estimates of biomass; discrete categorical variables, such as forest conditions classes; or model predictions of any measurement made by FIA field crews with the $M = 2$ protocol. The model might be parametric, such as with logistic regressions that predict probability of forest cover with optical satellite data as the predictors (e.g., McRoberts and Liknes 2005); might be non-parametric, such as with the classification and regression tree method (e.g., Breiman and others 1984; Block and others 2008) with a univariate response variable; or may have multivariate response variables, including k-nearest neighbor regression (e.g., Katila and Tomppo 2001).

Multispectral data for a Landsat scene, with an effective area of approximately 150 by 150 km, contains about 25 million Landsat pixels. They can be grouped into 4- by 4-pixel Landsat support-regions (3.6 acres or about 1.6 million pixel groups) that can be reasonably registered to the 1-acre support-region defined by the FIA field plot (Czaplewski 2005). The average state in the United States requires seven Landsat scenes to cover the state completely. Other geospatial data such as descriptors of biophysical and landscape features are merged with the multispectral Landsat data as potential predictor variables (Blackard and others 2008).

The average state has about 7000 FIA plots, of which about 2000 have forest cover. In the annual FIA panel system (Patterson and Reams 2005), 200 to 400 of these forested plots are grouped into a single panel that is measured during a single year. Data from these registered elements are used to train models that predict the FIA field measurements for each Landsat pixel. Remotely sensed and geospatial data are the predictor variables. The resulting predictions are designated as the $M = 0$ protocol.

Because RRE requires that polychotomous classification systems be transformed into multiple dichotomous variables, the classification categories do not necessarily need to be mutually exclusive. For example, classification of pixels into an aspen type can be independent from classification of pixels into a cottonwood type. The classifiers can be independently optimized for each category (Czaplewski and Patterson 2001, 2003). A single pixel might be classified into more than one category (both aspen and cottonwood) if spectral signatures for land cover types overlap to some degree. Also, the classification categories do not need to be complete. For example, some spectrally perplexing pixels might not be classified into any dichotomous category. One example is pixels obscured by clouds or cloud shadows. One limitation is that each category must cover a sufficient number of more accurately measured FIA field plots.

Landsat data currently support production of annual thematic maps that detect major changes in land cover. Such changes tend to be relatively rare at the landscape-scale, and the relatively sparse sample of FIA plots, by themselves, might not produce sufficiently accurate estimates of the attributes of the changed sub-population (Lister and others 2009). The wall-to-wall Landsat coverage can improve areal estimates for rare features. These changes in land cover are usually important in inventory and monitoring analyses. Therefore, incorporation of annual remotely sensed change detection information can be vital to the relevance of any monitoring system (Czaplewski 1999; Czaplewski and others 2005). However, the estimators might have to be applied to very large geographic areas, perhaps even to multiple states, in order to capture a sufficient sample size of FIA field plots.

Both RRE and post-stratification estimators assume the auxiliary variables are independent of the random errors from the sample of PSUs. However, those same PSUs are often used as training data to fit supervised classifiers or regression models that predict land characteristics (i.e., a thematic map) with remotely sensed and other geospatial data as predictor variables. This connection breaks the assumed independence. A different sample would produce a slightly different thematic map. It is commonly assumed that this dependence is small, and it can be ignored. Breidt and Opsomer (2008) provide weak support for this assumption. However, it is not necessary if these geospatial variables are directly used without fitting a prediction model. For example, unsupervised classification of multispectral data from Landsat does not require training data, and the results provide truly independent nominal auxiliary data. Other relevant geospatial variables may be combined with the Landsat data, such as terrain and climate maps. Independent continuous auxiliary variables are also available. The Normalized Difference Vegetation Index (NDVI) is an example (Tucker 1979). NDVI is defined as the difference of the red and infrared radiances divided by their sum. It partially normalizes for differences in solar zenith angle and atmospheric conditions. NDVI is correlated with green biomass density, which is further correlated with tree stocking and wood volume. No training data are necessary to define NDVI; therefore, NDVI is independent of FIA field plots. However, the census of pixel values for NDVI could directly serve as auxiliary data to improve population estimates for forest biomass and wood volume.

Geopolitical Domains of Study

FIA uses geopolitical domains of study (Särndal and others 1992:5) such as counties separated by major types of land ownership or stewardship. Administrative records are used to define the total area of each domain, and each area is defined as an exact constant that is known without error, i.e., a true census. FIA currently uses post-stratification to constrain its areal statistical estimates to agree exactly with certain administrative records. This often leads to numerous strata, many of which have small sample sizes, especially under the annual panel system employed by FIA. As an alternative, RRE may be configured to impose the same statistics as fixed constraints.

Domains of study may be represented in a linear model by "dummy variables" that have the value zero if the element is not a member of the intended population group (Särndal and others 1992:260), which, in the context of multivariate estimation, are represented in vector form (Särndal and others 1992:171). This is exactly analogous to a census of remotely sensed pixels in the previous section.

Photo-Interpretation and Photogrammetry

Photo-interpretation or photogrammetry is used to estimate continuous variables such as total wood volume in the point support-region by major groups of tree species and tree size classes, separated by living versus dead trees (e.g., Aldrich 1979; Lund and others 1997; Czaplewski in prep.[b]). Photo-interpretation has an important role in FIA (Catts and others 1987; Oswald 1988; Czaplewski and Catts 1992; Frayer and Furnival 1999; Coulston 2008; Frescino and others 2009a; Lister and others 2009). Photo-interpretation of high-resolution aerial photography can be accurate for broad characteristics of forest stands and individual trees. However, photo-interpretation and photogrammetry are too expensive for wall-to-wall full-coverage of the large populations. Likewise, full-coverage acquisition of high-resolution and current aerial photography is prohibitively expensive. Therefore, a sample of photo-plots is usually acquired and measured, typically with cluster plots in a multistage sampling design (e.g., Nusser and others 1998; Czaplewski 1999; Magnussen and others 2000; Gillis and others 2005; Lister and others 2009). Because the support-region (de Gruijter and others 2006:74-75) for each sample point is a well-defined area, measurements of all continuous variables can be expressed on a per unit area basis.

Other photo-interpreted variables may be nominal categories such as classification of each sampled support-region into one of 5 to 10 different types of land cover (e.g., forest, woodland, shrubland, grassland, cropland, barren lands, and water). Another type of photo-interpreted categorization might be predominant land use (e.g., timberland, grazing lands, reserves, parks and recreational areas, wildland-urban interface, urban lands, and transportation and utility corridors). Forest cover may be further classified through photo-interpretation by broad stand type (e.g., ponderosa pine, lodgepole pine, Douglas fir, spruce-fir, and cottonwood) and stage of stand development (e.g., seedling/sapling, poletimber, sawtimber, and over-mature sawtimber). The support-region for photo-interpretation of a nominal category might be the point itself (although a small surrounding area is necessary for context) where the measurement is binary; that is, point i is interpreted as belonging to category a, i.e., $y_{i,a} = 1$, or not, i.e., $y_{i,a} = 0$.

Photo-interpreted measurements need not necessarily have the same units as field measurements. For example, photo-interpretations of average tree height and crown density and their product in a 1-acre support-region can have a strong linear correlation with field measurements of wood volume from a collocated 1/6-acre FIA field plot. Such a correlation would produce gains in statistical efficiency, even though wood volume is not being directly photo-interpreted (see sub-matrix $\mathbf{C}$ in Eq. 26).

Photo-interpretation of high-resolution aerial photography can be used as preliminary reconnaissance to determine if a plot meets the definition of stocked forest (Frescino and others 2009b; Goeking and Liknes 2009). Field costs can be substantially reduced if field crews do not have to visit non-forest plots. However, errors in photo-interpretation can bias population estimates (Martinussen and others 2008). Methods similar to those in Eqs. 91 to 99 might be suitable to overcome this bias with a design-consistent approach; therefore, any photo-interpreted variables used as pre-field reconnaissance could be a component in the appropriate measurement vectors (Eq. 8).

A photo-interpreter might be very confident of an interpretation in some situations and less confident in other situations. Photo-interpreted variables that characterize the support-region might be separated into several variables based on the degree of certainty of the interpreter. For example, a 0-1 binary variable for a particular forest type can be cross-classified by a 0-1 binary "dummy" variable for confidence in an interpretation, which would produce four remotely sensed binary variables: Forest Type A with high confidence; Forest Type A with moderate confidence; not Forest Type A with high confidence; and not Forest Type A with moderate confidence. Likewise, accuracy can vary among different photo-interpreters, and dummy variables could separate remotely sensed data into categories of higher and lower quality.

The most severe effects of misregistration between support-regions for remotely sensed and field protocols can be at the boundaries between different forest conditions, or within fine-grained, spatially heterogeneous stands. Misregistration effects are fewer within interior of homogeneous stands. These different situations in measurement errors can be identified during the measurement processes (Zhu and others 2000) and made available in the estimation step. Even better, field crews can accurately locate the sample point on aerial photographs while in the field. If photo-interpreters subsequently apply the remote sensing protocol centered on the same point on the aerial photograph, then registration accuracy can be greatly improved, and the extra effort would be rewarded with increased statistical efficiency. The key principle is to avoid corrupting remotely sensed data that are accurate with a relatively small amount of remotely sensed data that are not accurate. The efficiency offered by remotely sensed data decreases rapidly as accuracy declines (Czaplewski and Patterson 2001, 2003).

Differences can be considerable in classification and measurement accuracy among photo-interpreters. If multiple interpreters with widely different skill levels produce the remotely sensed measurements, then there might be some advantages in treating the measurements by each interpreter as a separate variable. A randomization process of assigning photo-plots to individual interpreters might have some advantages worth consideration.

LiDAR Laser Technology

LiDAR laser technology provides measurements that can be well correlated with tree biomass and wood volume (e.g., Means and others 1999; Brandtberg and others 2003; Popescu and others 2003; Zimble and others 2003; Sun and others 2008; Nelson and others 2009b). A dimensionless index based on characteristics of LiDAR laser pulses and returns, which might not have the units of wood volume, might still be well correlated with field measurements of wood volume and biomass density. Gains in efficiency depend on strong linear correlations and associations between remote sensing and field data. These linear relationships are quantified by the sample cross-covariance matrix between the remotely sensed and field measurements (e.g., sub-matrix C in Eq. 26).

Synthetic Aperture Radar Technology (SAR)

Synthetic aperture radar technology (SAR) also offers promise in providing measurements that are reasonably correlated with forest inventory and monitoring field data, especially in geographic areas prone to chronic cloud cover that obscures remotely sensed data from optical sensors (Pope and others 1994), which includes many tropical and boreal forest ecosystems. Ranson and Sun (1994) found correlations of approximately 0.8 between biomass and airborne SAR sensor data for a boreal study area. Success often requires extensive ground-truth measurements to build empirical models between forest biomass and SAR backscatter, although there are alternatives (Ranson and Guoqing 1997). Ranson and Sun (1997) report similar results for spaceborne SAR data. However, RRE can directly use SAR metrics without an external biomass model. Accuracy will improve if the SAR metrics are sufficiently well correlated with field measurements of biomass and other similar variables.

Linear, Small-Area, Synthetic Estimator with Census Predictors

Matrix functions of multivariate estimates provide opportunities to construct model-based estimators for other applications. Estimation for small areas with known precision is an excellent example (e.g., Schreuder and others 1993:Chapter 8.1; Rao 2003:Chapter 1). Many analyses focus on small portions of a sampled population, also known as small domains (e.g., Särndal and others 1992:408) or small areas (e.g., Rao 2003). As with other large government statistical programs, FIA is constantly investigating methods to provide more reliable estimates for small geographic areas (e.g., USDA Forest Service 2007; Morin and others 2009; Magnussen and others 2009; Roesch 2009).

If the domain is a sufficiently sampled sub-population, then design-consistent methods, such as those presented above, are applicable. Inevitably, many areas are so small that they do not contain a sufficient number of samples to make reliable, design-consistent estimates. One solution available in forest inventory and monitoring is relying on full-coverage, remotely sensed pixel data from spaceborne sensors and other geospatial databases (Haslett and Jones 2005). Parametric and non-parametric regression models use such data to predict forest characteristics for each and every pixel in the satellite imagery (see "Digital Processing of Multispectral Landsat Data"). Statistical enumeration of all multivariate pixel predictions within the small area can provide useful predictor data. However, prediction models and the sum of all predictions within the small area can be biased, the degree and direction of the bias can be unknown, and the magnitude of the bias can be large (Bauer and others 1978; Card 1982; Chrisman 1983; Houston and Hall 1984; Hay 1988; Czaplewski 1992; Gallego 2004; Gallego and Bamps 2008; Iles 2010; Magnusen and others 2010; McRoberts 2010). Also, the statistical reliability of the predictions, which may be quantified with a covariance matrix, may be unknown.

If the small area includes a sufficient number of sample plots that are measured with sufficiently accurate protocols, then an unbiased difference or ratio estimator (e.g., Särndal and others 1992:Chapter 6) provides a direct estimator of the covariance matrix, which gauges statistical reliability. Baffetta and others (2009) apply this approach in the context of a National Forest inventory. Calibration estimates are also relevant (see p. 32).

If the sample size is insufficient within a small area, then indirect synthetic estimation, which is "simply the sum of predicted values," is an alternative (Särndal and others 1992:399). McRoberts and others (2007) and McRoberts (2008) provide examples relevant to forest inventories. Synthetic estimators are model-based by definition. Model-based estimators can be efficient, but they are biased if the model assumptions are inaccurate (Schreuder and others 1993:Chapter 6.3; Lehtonen and others 2003). The risk can be substantial because validation of model assumptions is rarely feasible (Estevao and Särndal 2004). For example, Blackard and others (2008) found that their non-parametric regression-tree model tended to underestimate biomass for test plots that had unusually high amounts of biomass and overestimate biomass for test plots that had unusually low amounts of biomass. Similar trends might be expected with k-nearest neighbor (kNN) non-parametric regression. This is evidence for conditional bias. If the distribution of pixel-level biomass within a small area differs from the population-level distribution, then the synthetic estimator will likely be biased for that small area.

The following example is a model-based, multivariate, synthetic estimator. It accomplishes the same objectives as those considered by McRoberts and others (2007), but it uses fewer assumptions and a much simpler model. The example uses a complex design of two-phase sampling with cluster plots: a census of full-coverage pixel data from spaceborne sensors and other geospatial datasets; a sample of high-resolution, remotely sensed data from airborne sensors for

50-acre cluster plots; and a sub-sample of 1-acre field plots that are collocated within the cluster plots (see Eqs. 62 to 70). This design is similar to that used in the FIA NPIP study (Frescino and others 2009a). However, the synthetic estimator in this example may be applied with any of the sampling designs and population estimators of the types covered on 21 through 53 pp.

Visualize an area that is very small with too few samples for a reliable, design-consistent estimate. One relevant case study is the 6000-acre hexagon used by FIA for its systematic sampling frame (Reams and others 2005). Each of the approximately 360,000 hexagons in this national sampling frame has a single FIA field plot, and only about 30 percent of those plots have forest cover. The same hexagons are also used for geospatial presentations and analyses (e.g., Wilson and Ibes 2005; Lowe and Cieszewski 2005).

In this example, multispectral measurements from the MODIS sensor (e.g., Cohen 2003) are predictors in geospatial models that estimate forest area and biomass for each 15-acre MODIS pixel in a full-coverage pixel database (e.g., Blackard and others 2008). The remotely sensed predictions for approximately 40 MODIS pixels are summarized for each collocated 6000-acre hexagon, and the resulting summary statistics are input into the hexagon database. Further, assume that the hexagons are grouped into ecoregions (Bailey 1995). Summary results for a 10,000,000-acre hypothetical ecoregion are given in Table 3.

Table 3. Population-level estimates of forest area and biomass from full-coverage, remotely sensed data from spaceborne sensors (protocol M = 0) and sample of field data (protocol M = 2).

	Population estimates with FIA protocol (M = 2)		
Spaceborne protocol (M = 0)	Forest cover	Non-forest cover	Population total
Forest cover (acres)	2,850,000	150,000	3,000,000
Non-forest cover (acres)	600,000	5,400,000	6,000,000
Boundary (edge) area (acres)	450,000	550,000	1,000,000
Total area	3,900,000	6,100,000	10,000,000

Area (acres) by joint classification with spaceborne (M = 0) and FIA (M = 2) protocols		Estimated calibration coefficient
Forest cover (M = 0)		
Forest cover (M = 2)	2,850,000	0.95
Non-forest cover (M = 2)	150,000	0.05
	3,000,000	
Non-forest cover (M = 0)		
Forest cover (M = 2)	600,000	0.10
Non-forest cover (M = 2)	5,400,000	0.90
	6,000,000	
Boundary (edge) area (M = 0)		
Forest cover (M = 2)	450,000	0.45
Non-forest cover (M = 2)	550,000	0.55
	1,000,000	
	10,000,000	

	FIA protocol (M = 2)	Spaceborne protocol (M = 0)	
Forest biomass (dry tons)	220,000,000	200,000,000	1.10

Because of misclassification bias and other systematic prediction errors, broad-scale predictions of forest area and biomass (e.g., ecoregion estimates) with the remotely sensed data will disagree with those from the unbiased sample survey estimator. Table 3 provides an example with a 10,000,000-acre hypothetical ecoregion. The remotely sensed data predicts 3,000,000 acres of forest cover plus an additional 1,000,000 acres of heterogeneous edge conditions. These are partially forested and non-forested, whereas the unbiased sample survey estimator predicts 3,900,000 acres of total forest cover.

The remotely sensed area estimates may be calibrated (e.g., Czaplewski and Catts 1992) with data from an unbiased estimator. Table 3 provides a simple example of the inverse multivariate calibration model (Brown 1982), which is also labeled direct calibration (Dymond 1992; Gallego and Bamps 2008). Of the 3,000,000 acres predicted with remotely sensed data to be forest cover, an estimated 95 percent is truly forest, and the remaining 5 percent is non-forest. Table 3 includes estimates of calibration coefficients for other cover conditions, in addition to biomass estimates. This may also be considered a form of multivariate synthetic estimation; see Särndal and others (1992:399) for a brief introduction to univariate synthetic estimation.

In matrix notation, the calibration coefficients ($\mathbf{b}$) and their estimated covariance matrix are computed as:

$$\hat{\mathbf{b}} = \mathbf{A} \left[\hat{\mathbf{t}}_{M=2} \right]_{M=[1,1C]}^{s=(U,1,2)}$$

$$\hat{\mathbf{V}}\left[\hat{\mathbf{b}}\right] = \mathbf{A}\, \hat{\mathbf{V}}\left[\hat{\mathbf{t}}_{M=2}\right]_{M=[1,1C]}^{s=(U,1,2)} \mathbf{A}'$$

$$\hat{\mathbf{b}} = \begin{bmatrix} 0.95 \\ \hline 0.05 \\ \hline 0.10 \\ \hline 0.90 \\ \hline 0.45 \\ \hline 0.55 \\ \hline 1.10 \end{bmatrix} \qquad \left[\hat{\mathbf{t}}_{M=2}\right]_{M=[1,1C]}^{s=(U,1,2)} = \begin{bmatrix} 2{,}850{,}000 \\ \hline 150{,}000 \\ \hline 600{,}000 \\ \hline 5{,}400{,}000 \\ \hline 450{,}000 \\ \hline 550{,}000 \\ \hline 200{,}000{,}000 \end{bmatrix}$$

$$\mathbf{A} = \begin{bmatrix} \frac{1}{3{,}000{,}000} & 0 & 0 & 0 & 0 & 0 & 0 \\ 0 & \frac{1}{3{,}000{,}000} & 0 & 0 & 0 & 0 & 0 \\ 0 & 0 & \frac{1}{6{,}000{,}000} & 0 & 0 & 0 & 0 \\ 0 & 0 & 0 & \frac{1}{6{,}000{,}000} & 0 & 0 & 0 \\ 0 & 0 & 0 & 0 & \frac{1}{1{,}000{,}000} & 0 & 0 \\ 0 & 0 & 0 & 0 & 0 & \frac{1}{1{,}000{,}000} & 0 \\ 0 & 0 & 0 & 0 & 0 & 0 & \frac{1}{220{,}000{,}000} \end{bmatrix}$$

(82)

The non-zero elements in matrix $\mathbf{A}$ in Eq. 82 are known constants because they are summary statistics from the full census of remotely sensed pixels within the ecoregion. Therefore, they are a straightforward linear function of the vector estimate $\mathbf{t}$ and its covariance matrix.

The following small-area estimator relies on the model that assumes the association between remotely sensed estimates and design-consistent sample survey estimates is linear and identical for all 1667 of the 6000-acre hexagons within the 10,000,000-acre ecoregion. Under this model, the calibration coefficients from Table 2 and Eq. 82 may be applied to the remotely sensed census statistics for any small area within the 10,000,000-acre ecoregion. Examples for two 6000-acre hexagons are given in Table 4. The model predictions and their joint covariance matrix for all 1667 hexagons within the ecoregion may be simultaneously expressed in matrix notation as:

$$\begin{bmatrix} \hat{\mathbf{t}}_{i=1} \\ \vdots \\ \hat{\mathbf{t}}_{i=1667} \end{bmatrix} = \begin{bmatrix} \mathbf{T}_{i=1} \\ \vdots \\ \mathbf{T}_{i=1667} \end{bmatrix} [\hat{\mathbf{b}}]_{s=\{U,1,2\}}$$

$$\hat{\mathbf{V}} \begin{bmatrix} \hat{\mathbf{t}}_{i=1} \\ \vdots \\ \hat{\mathbf{t}}_{i=1667} \end{bmatrix} = \begin{bmatrix} \mathbf{T}_{i=1} \\ \vdots \\ \mathbf{T}_{i=1667} \end{bmatrix} \hat{\mathbf{V}}[\hat{\mathbf{b}}]_{s=\{U,1,2\}} \begin{bmatrix} \mathbf{T}_{i=1} \\ \vdots \\ \mathbf{T}_{i=1667} \end{bmatrix}'$$

$$\begin{bmatrix} \hat{\mathbf{t}}_{i=1} \\ \vdots \\ \hat{\mathbf{t}}_{i=1667} \end{bmatrix} = \begin{bmatrix} 4{,}175 \\ 1{,}825 \\ 440{,}000 \\ \vdots \\ 1{,}630 \\ 4{,}370 \\ 22{,}000 \end{bmatrix} \qquad [\hat{\mathbf{b}}]_{s=\{U,1,2\}} = \begin{bmatrix} 0.95 \\ 0.05 \\ 0.10 \\ 0.90 \\ 0.45 \\ 0.55 \\ 1.10 \end{bmatrix} \qquad (83)$$

$$\begin{bmatrix} \mathbf{T}_{i=1} \\ \vdots \\ \mathbf{T}_{i=1667} \end{bmatrix} = \begin{bmatrix} 4{,}000 & 0 & 1{,}500 & 0 & 500 & 0 & 0 \\ 0 & 4{,}000 & 0 & 1{,}500 & 0 & 500 & 0 \\ 0 & 0 & 0 & 0 & 0 & 0 & 400{,}000 \\ \vdots & \vdots & \vdots & \vdots & \vdots & \vdots & \vdots \\ 800 & 0 & 4{,}200 & 0 & 1000 & 0 & 0 \\ 0 & 800 & 0 & 4{,}200 & 0 & 1000 & 0 \\ 0 & 0 & 0 & 0 & 0 & 0 & 20{,}000 \end{bmatrix}$$

The structure of Eq. 83 produces a covariance matrix for the propagated prediction errors for estimated parameters among all 1667 hexagons. In principle, this could directly produce covariance matrices for any linear function of statistics from multiple hexagons, such as the sum of estimates for all hexagons that meet certain selection criteria. This capability would further enhance the value of a hexagon database for rapid assessments with diverse, small-domain estimates.

Finally, this example may be expanded to be more relevant to FIA. Further, assume that a full-coverage geospatial database is composed of pixel data. It contains predictions of the forest composition of each pixel. The kNN model, which

Table 4. Example of inverse calibration model applied to two small-areas.

Small-area census with spaceborne protocol (M = 0)		Small-area estimates with FIA protocol (M = 2)			
		Forest cover		Non-forest cover	
Hexagon = 1					
Forest cover (acres)	4,000	0.95	3,800	0.05	200
Non-forest cover (acres)	1,500	0.10	150	0.90	1,350
Boundary (edge) area (acres)	500	0.45	225	0.55	275
	6,000		4,175		1,825
	M = 0	M = 2			
Forest biomass (dry tons)	400,000	1.10	440,000		
Hexagon = q					
Forest cover (acres)	800	0.95	760	0.05	40
Non-forest cover (acres)	4,200	0.10	420	0.90	3,780
Boundary (edge) area (acres)	1,000	0.45	450	0.55	550
	6,000		1,630		4,370
	M = 0	M = 2			
Forest biomass (dry tons)	20,000	1.10	22,000		

is a form of multivariate non-parametric regression (Härdle 1990), is used to predict all FIA plot-level variables for each and every pixel (Katila and Tomppo 2001; McRoberts and Tomppo 2007). When used as a model-based estimator for population totals, it is biased or, at least, the kNN estimator cannot be shown to be design-unbiased. However, there are design-based and model-assisted estimators of population totals that can be shown to be design-consistent. These estimators can include the same pixel census data within the multilevel sampling design.

Unlike categorical variables, the univariate, small-area estimator for a continuous variable can be based upon the simple ratio between the population estimate made with data from the field measurements (protocol M = 2) and population estimate made with the kNN model that uses spaceborne, remotely sensed data (protocol M = 0). The model in this estimator is simply this ratio multiplied by the total of pixel-level, remotely sensed predictions for a small area (e.g., Särndal and others 1992:399). The result is a synthetic estimate of the small-area total made with the M = 2 field protocol. This is a model-based estimator, in which it is assumed that the true ratio for every small area is identical to the ratio for the entire population. In the special case of the kNN non-parametric regression, the prediction with remotely sensed data protocol (M = 0) and the variable measured with the field protocol (M = 2) have identical definitions and units of measure. The ratio may be considered a calibration coefficient that proportionally scales the remotely sensed estimates to agree exactly with the unbiased design-consistent estimates at the population level. Univariate estimators for different continuous variables are readily assembled into a multivariate estimator, an example of which is illustrated with Eq. 83 and Table 3.

The multivariate synthetic estimator for a categorical variable is more complex, although it is related to the simpler case of continuous variables. The categorical model assumes that the misclassification error process is identical for all pixels or, at least, over all possible small areas. Rather than a single coefficient for calibrating a continuous variable, the sample survey estimator produces a contingency table of joint classification probabilities for each category, with one classifier based on remotely sensed data (M = 0) and the other based on field protocol (M = 2). The model transforms this contingency table into probabilities conditional on the remotely sensed classifier (e.g., Eq. 82), much like a probability transition matrix. Population estimates used to parameterize this model require observations with both the remotely sensed protocol (M = 0) and the field protocol (M = 2).

Joint classification probabilities are estimated by augmenting the $M = 2$ measurement vector containing the cross-classification with both the remotely sensed ($M = 0$) and field ($M = 2$) protocols. For example, assume there are 26 categories of land use and land cover types include: lodgepole pine, Engelmann spruce, Douglas-fir, ponderosa pine, western hardwoods, woodland, sagebrush, grassland, barren rock, alpine tundra, riparian areas, wetlands, standing water, urban zones, and transportation corridors. Also assume each type of forest cover is separated into large, medium, small, and non-stocked categories that describe stand size. In the special case of the current example, the kNN remote sensing protocol ($M = 0$) and the field protocol ($M = 2$) can classify every support-region based on this 26-category classification system. For each and every pixel, the $M = 0$ measurement vector (Eq. 8) contains a segment with 26 elements that represents the remotely sensed classification:

$$[\mathbf{y}_{M=0}]_j = \begin{bmatrix} \begin{bmatrix} \vdots \\ \hline \vdots \\ \hline y_A \\ \hline y_B \\ \hline \vdots \\ \hline y_Z \\ \hline \vdots \end{bmatrix}_{M=0} \end{bmatrix}_j \quad \text{where} \begin{cases} y_A = \begin{cases} = 1 \text{ if pixel classified with } M = 0 \text{ as category } A \\ = 0 \text{ otherwise} \end{cases} \\ \vdots \\ y_Z = \begin{cases} = 1 \text{ if pixel classified with } M = 0 \text{ as category } Z \\ = 0 \text{ otherwise} \end{cases} \end{cases} \tag{84}$$

In the current example, the $M = 0$ remotely sensed measurement vector (Eq. 8) segment in Eq. 84 is used in the sample survey steps (Eqs. 62 and 63) and in all sequential steps in the estimator for population totals (Eqs. 64 to 69).

The corresponding measurement vector for the $M = 2$ field protocol must include the joint classifications with both the remote sensing ($M = 0$) and field ($M = 2$) protocols.

$$[\mathbf{y}_{M=2}]_j = \begin{bmatrix} \begin{bmatrix} \vdots \\ \hline y_{A \cap A} \\ \hline y_{A \cap B} \\ \hline \vdots \\ \hline y_{A \cap Z} \\ \hline \vdots \\ \hline y_{Z \cap A} \\ \hline \vdots \\ \hline y_{Z \cap Z} \end{bmatrix}_{M=2} \end{bmatrix}_j \quad \text{where} \begin{cases} y_{A \cap A} = \begin{cases} = 1 \text{ if point classified with } M = 2 \text{ as category } A \\ \qquad \text{and with } M = 0 \text{ as category } A \\ = 0 \text{ otherwise} \end{cases} \\ y_{A \cap B} = \begin{cases} = 1 \text{ if point classified with } M = 2 \text{ as category } A \\ \qquad \text{and with } M = 0 \text{ as category } B \\ = 0 \text{ otherwise} \end{cases} \\ \vdots \\ y_{Z \cap Z} = \begin{cases} = 1 \text{ if point classified with } M = 2 \text{ as category } Z \\ \qquad \text{and with } M = 0 \text{ as category } Z \\ = 0 \text{ otherwise} \end{cases} \end{cases} \tag{85}$$

Because there are 26 categories of forest and land cover in this example, there will be $26 \times 26 = 676$ elements in the $M = 2$ measurement vector $[\mathbf{y}_{M=2}]_j$ (see Eq. 8) that estimate the 26-by-26 contingency table of joint classification probabilities. Equation 85 is used in the Phase 2 estimator (Eq. 63). The sequential estimators in Eqs. 64 to 69 are intended to improve the accuracy of the estimated joint classification with photo-interpretation of high-resolution aerial photography and cluster plots (M = 1 and M = 1C).

The final estimates of the joint classification probabilities are transformed into conditional transition probabilities, as in Eq. 82, for use in multivariate synthetic estimators for small areas (Eq. 83). However, the estimated population totals do not require small-area estimation or joint classification probabilities. In order to estimate the areas for each type of forest and land cover in the full population, the statistics used for joint probabilities are collapsed into the field protocol (M = 2) by summing over the joint probabilities cross-classified with the remotely sensed protocol (M = 0). Let **1** be a 1-by-26 row vector with all elements equal to 1. The estimated population totals for each of the 26 forest and land cover types with the FIA protocol (M = 2) is:

$$
\begin{bmatrix} \vdots \\ \hline \hat{\mathbf{y}}_{M=2} \\ \hline \vdots \end{bmatrix} = \begin{bmatrix} \mathbf{I} & \mathbf{0} & \mathbf{0} \\ & \begin{matrix} 1 & 0 & \cdots & 0 \\ 0 & 1 & \cdots & 0 \\ \vdots & \vdots & \ddots & \vdots \\ 0 & 0 & \cdots & 1 \end{matrix} & \\ \mathbf{0} & \mathbf{0} & \mathbf{I} \end{bmatrix} \begin{bmatrix} \vdots \\ \hline \hat{\mathbf{y}}_{M=2 \cap M=0} \\ \hline \vdots \end{bmatrix}
$$

(86)

$$
\hat{\mathbf{V}}[\hat{\mathbf{y}}_{M=2}] = \begin{bmatrix} \mathbf{I} & \mathbf{0} & \mathbf{0} \\ & \begin{matrix} 1 & 0 & \cdots & 0 \\ 0 & 1 & \cdots & 0 \\ \vdots & \vdots & \ddots & \vdots \\ 0 & 0 & \cdots & 1 \end{matrix} & \\ \mathbf{0} & \mathbf{0} & \mathbf{I} \end{bmatrix} \begin{bmatrix} \ddots & \vdots & \iddots \\ \hline \cdots & \hat{\mathbf{V}}[\hat{\mathbf{y}}_{M=2 \cap M=0}] & \cdots \\ \hline \iddots & \vdots & \ddots \end{bmatrix} \begin{bmatrix} \mathbf{I} & \mathbf{0} & \mathbf{0} \\ & \begin{matrix} 1 & 0 & \cdots & 0 \\ 0 & 1 & \cdots & 0 \\ \vdots & \vdots & \ddots & \vdots \\ 0 & 0 & \cdots & 1 \end{matrix} & \\ \mathbf{0} & \mathbf{0} & \mathbf{I} \end{bmatrix}^{'}
$$

In the current example, the inner partition of the indicator matrix in Eq. 86 would be a 26-by-676 matrix that collapses the M = 0 and M = 2 joint classification totals into the population totals for the 26 categories of land and forest cover types based on the field protocol (M = 2) alone.

To accommodate small-area estimation, the structure of the multivariate estimator remains unchanged for continuous variables (e.g., biomass variable in Eq. 82). However, the dimensions increase multiplicatively for categorical variables as the number of categories increases (e.g., Eq. 85). This increase can be large with detailed classification systems. In the current example, 26 categories of land use and land cover require 26×26 = 676 variables to estimate the conditional probabilities of a point being classified with the field protocol (M = 2) as one of the 26 categories, given that the remote sensing protocol (M = 0) classified it into one of the 26 categories. Even though most numerical problems with the Kalman filter are associated with the auxiliary measurement vector (Eq. 8), a large state-vector (Eq. 8) can introduce additional numerical problems. However, cells in an estimated contingency table whose estimated values equal zero, some of which are sampling zeros (e.g., Agresti 2007:54), can be removed from the multivariate estimators. The number of zero cells that need not be estimated depends on the detail classification system relative to the sample size of points classified with the FIA field protocol (M = 2). The number also depends on the accuracy of the M = 0 classifications relative to the M = 2 classifications. As classification accuracy increases, more observations are concentrated on the diagonal of the contingency table, which represent probabilities of correct classification. Figure 1 provides an

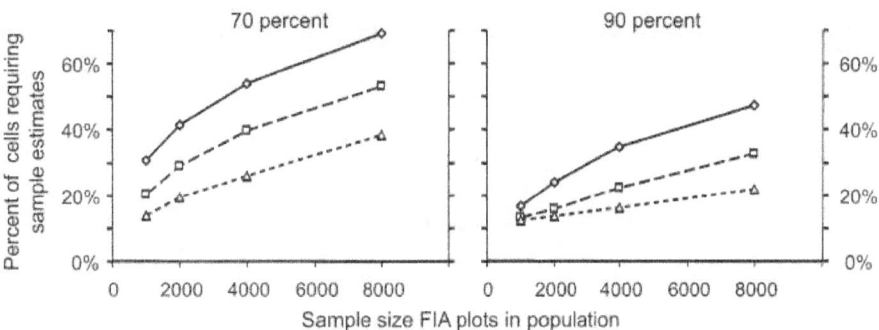

Figure 1. Example of reduction in dimensions of 26-by-26 contingency table after removing cells with values equal to zero and after grouping rare cells.

example. It uses the current example and realistic assumptions for the accuracies and misclassification probabilities for the 26 categories of land cover and land use. If the average classification accuracy is about 70 percent and there are 8000 FIA plots in the population, then about 70 percent ($676 \times 0.70 \sim 500$) of the cells are expected to have non-zero values that must be estimated from the sample. If cells that occur rarely are grouped together in a logical fashion, then the number of cells that must be estimated decreases to 30 to 50 percent of the total cells (i.e., estimates are required for about 200 to 350 of the 676 total cells). Using Figure 1 with 90 percent accuracy and 1000 FIA plots in the population, only about 15 percent of the cells ($676 \times 0.15 \sim 100$) would require sample estimates. Figure 1 is merely a realistic example that is intended to illustrate a specific case, and it does not necessarily apply to other cases. Any of these simplifications of the multivariate estimator would require restructuring the indicator matrix in Eq. 86.

Because of different management regimes, assume the M = 0 versus M = 2 classification probabilities are different within two different land ownerships, e.g., private versus public lands. The nominal number of categories would increase to $(26 \times 26) \times 2 = 1352$. However, many of these additional cells will have values of zero because the sample size of FIA plots would not change, and the sample size within each land ownership category would decrease. Therefore, the number of cells requiring sample estimates might not increase dramatically because the frequency of sampling zeros would also increase. The detail of the calibration model for categorical variables will be limited by the sample size of FIA field plots, even for geographically large populations with thousands of FIA plots. Furthermore, auxiliary categorical data might include certain cross-classifications that do not accurately distinguish among cells in a cross-classification contingency table. Those cells may be merged to reduce dimensions further. Research is needed to automate such a process.

RRE as a Synthetic Small-Area Estimator

Synthetic estimation in this section is primarily used as an example of a linear function of a vector estimate. For example, the RRE could be used to constrain a population-level vector estimate to agree with the auxiliary information for a small area. Again, using the complex RRE for the NPIP example, extract the partitions that include the full-coverage, spaceborne, remotely sensed variables (M = 0 protocol) and the FIA field measurements (M = 2 protocol) from Eq. 69.

$$\begin{bmatrix} \hat{\mathbf{t}}_{M=0} \\ \hat{\mathbf{t}}_{M=2} \end{bmatrix}_{\substack{s=(U,1,2) \\ M=[1,1C]}} = \begin{bmatrix} \mathbf{I} & 0 & 0 \\ 0 & 0 & \mathbf{I} \end{bmatrix} \begin{bmatrix} \hat{\mathbf{t}}_{M=0} \\ \hat{\mathbf{t}}_{M=1} \\ \hat{\mathbf{t}}_{M=2} \end{bmatrix}_{\substack{s=(U,1,2) \\ M=[1,1C]}}$$

(87)

$$\hat{\mathbf{V}}\left(\begin{bmatrix} \hat{\mathbf{t}}_{M=0} \\ \hat{\mathbf{t}}_{M=2} \end{bmatrix}\right)_{\substack{s=(U,1,2) \\ M=[1,1C]}} = \begin{bmatrix} \mathbf{I} & 0 & 0 \\ 0 & 0 & \mathbf{I} \end{bmatrix} \hat{\mathbf{V}}\left(\begin{bmatrix} \hat{\mathbf{t}}_{M=0} \\ \hat{\mathbf{t}}_{M=1} \\ \hat{\mathbf{t}}_{M=2} \end{bmatrix}\right)_{\substack{s=(U,1,2) \\ M=[1,1C]}} \begin{bmatrix} \mathbf{I} & 0' \\ 0' & 0' \\ 0' & \mathbf{I} \end{bmatrix}$$

Let $[\mathbf{t}_{M=0}]_k$ be the vector sum of all pixel values in small area k.

$$\begin{bmatrix} \mathbf{t}_{M=0} \\ \hat{\mathbf{t}}_{M=2} \end{bmatrix}_k = \begin{bmatrix} \hat{\mathbf{t}}_{M=0} \\ \hat{\mathbf{t}}_{M=2} \end{bmatrix}_{\substack{s=(1,2) \\ M=[1,1C]}} + \mathbf{K}\left[[\mathbf{t}_{M=0}]_k - \begin{bmatrix} \mathbf{I} & 0 \end{bmatrix} \begin{bmatrix} \hat{\mathbf{t}}_{M=0} \\ \hat{\mathbf{t}}_{M=2} \end{bmatrix}_{\substack{s=(1,2) \\ M=[1,1C]}} \right]$$

$$\hat{\mathbf{V}}\left(\begin{bmatrix} \mathbf{t}_{M=0} \\ \hat{\mathbf{t}}_{M=2} \end{bmatrix}\right)_k = \hat{\mathbf{V}}\left(\begin{bmatrix} \mathbf{t}_{M=0} \\ \hat{\mathbf{t}}_{M=2} \end{bmatrix}\right)_{\substack{s=(1,2) \\ M=[1,1C]}} - \mathbf{K}\begin{bmatrix} \mathbf{I} & 0 \end{bmatrix} \hat{\mathbf{V}}\left(\begin{bmatrix} \mathbf{t}_{M=0} \\ \hat{\mathbf{t}}_{M=2} \end{bmatrix}\right)_{\substack{s=(1,2) \\ M=[1,1C]}}$$

(88)

$$\mathbf{K} = \hat{\mathbf{V}}\left(\begin{bmatrix} \mathbf{t}_{M=0} \\ \hat{\mathbf{t}}_{M=2} \end{bmatrix}\right)_{\substack{s=(1,2) \\ M=[1,1C]}} \begin{bmatrix} \mathbf{I} \\ 0 \end{bmatrix} \left(\begin{bmatrix} \mathbf{I} & 0 \end{bmatrix} \hat{\mathbf{V}}\left(\begin{bmatrix} \mathbf{t}_{M=0} \\ \hat{\mathbf{t}}_{M=2} \end{bmatrix}\right)_{\substack{s=(1,2) \\ M=[1,1C]}} \begin{bmatrix} \mathbf{I} \\ 0 \end{bmatrix} \right)^{-1} \begin{bmatrix} \mathbf{I} \\ 0 \end{bmatrix}$$

Equation 88 is merely an algebraic operator that constrains a vector estimate. The vector difference between the known totals of the auxiliary data for the small area and the estimated population totals for the same auxiliary data

$$\left[[\mathbf{t}_{M=0}]_k - \begin{bmatrix} \mathbf{I} & 0 \end{bmatrix} \begin{bmatrix} \hat{\mathbf{t}}_{M=0} \\ \hat{\mathbf{t}}_{M=2} \end{bmatrix}_{\substack{s=(1,2) \\ M=[1,1C]}} \right]$$

will be large, which is uncommon in the intended application of RE. No claims are made regarding its statistical properties or numerical robustness. Alternative methods with the Generalized Restriction Estimator for consistent small-domain estimation exist (Sõstra and Traat 2009). The performance of the RE in this atypical context requires further investigation.

Non-Linear Pseudo-Estimators

Like the linear transformation covered in the previous section, non-linear transformations are often required. Such transformations are generally straightforward for estimation of population parameters or small-area statistics. However, they are not straightforward in variance estimation. An example is estimated wood volume per unit area of forest, where both total wood volume (t_1) and total forest area (t_2) are estimates, and their ratio is a non-linear transformation. The population estimate of a non-linear transformation is computed in the obvious, straightforward way, but the variance of the transformation typically requires a Taylor-series approximation with complex sampling designs (Tepping 1968; Woodruff 1971; Krewski and Rao 1981; Wolter 2007).

Särndal and others (1992:173-174, 205-207) term these sorts of non-linear transformations pseudo-estimators. Using their notation, define the non-linear function as $\theta = f(t_1, \ldots, t_q)$. Define the pseudo-estimator and its Taylor-series linear approximation as:

$$\hat{\theta} = f\left(\hat{t}_{1\pi}, \quad \cdots, \quad \hat{t}_{q\pi}\right)$$

$$= \theta + \sum_{j=1}^{q} a_j\left(\hat{t}_{j\pi} - t_j\right) + \frac{1}{2}\sum_{i}^{q}\sum_{j}^{q} a_{ij}\left(\hat{t}_{j\pi} - t_j\right)\left(\hat{t}_{j\pi} - t_j\right) + R \tag{89}$$

$$\approx \theta + \sum_{j=1}^{q} a_j\left(\hat{t}_{j\pi} - t_j\right)$$

where:

$$a_j = \frac{\partial f\left(t_1, \quad \cdots, \quad t_q\right)}{\partial t_j}\Bigg|_{\left(t_1, \quad \cdots, \quad t_q\right) = \left(\hat{t}_{1\pi}, \quad \cdots, \quad \hat{t}_{q\pi}\right)}$$

$$a_{ij} = \frac{\partial^2 f\left(t_1, \quad \cdots, \quad t_q\right)}{\partial t_i \partial t_j}\Bigg|_{\left(t_1, \quad \cdots, \quad t_q\right) = \left(\hat{t}_{1\pi}, \quad \cdots, \quad \hat{t}_{q\pi}\right)}$$

R = remainder term in the expansion

Cochran (1977:319) expounds on the value of this Taylor-series method for approximate variance estimators that use the vector estimate of population totals, which is denoted as the 1-by-q vector **t** in the following.

Using matrix calculus (Deutsch 1965:Chapter 6; Stengel 1986:33; Schott 2005:Chapter 9; Wolter 2007:Chapter 6), the first-order linear Taylor-series approximation of a pseudo-estimator has the following general form:

$$\hat{\theta} \approx \theta + \sum_{j=1}^{q} a_j\left(\hat{t}_{j\pi} - t_j\right)$$

$$\approx \theta + \begin{bmatrix} a_1 & \cdots, & a_q \end{bmatrix}\left(\begin{bmatrix} \hat{t}_{1\pi} \\ \vdots \\ \hat{t}_{q\pi} \end{bmatrix} - \begin{bmatrix} t_1 \\ \vdots \\ t_q \end{bmatrix}\right) \tag{90}$$

The values of the a_j terms depend on the application. Examples follow.

Product Estimator: Missing Data Imputation

The product estimator is a useful and simple non-linear transformation. A model-based pseudo-estimator that accommodates missing data is used here as an example of the product function of multivariate estimates for two random vectors. This example presupposes that a small portion of FIA field plots cannot be measured because they are on private lands for which the landowner denies access to FIA field crews. The study question in this example is "What is the estimated total biomass accretion rate on all private lands for which access was, or would be, denied by the landowner?" Research related to this application is a high priority in FIA short-term research and development.

Biomass accretion at a sample point is determined by re-measuring permanent plots in the field. These re-measurements are missing for "denied access" lands because the field crews are not permitted to measure the sample point. However, a model-based estimate of total biomass accretion can be made for all inaccessible lands.

The statistical model in this example assumes biomass accretion per unit area per year is the same for both accessible and inaccessible lands that are classified as "forest" with remote sensing. In the form of prose, the model estimates biomass accretion on inaccessible lands as the product of [total area of such lands] times the [accretion per unit area of similar accessible lands].

This example utilizes a complex design that combines spaceborne remote sensing technologies (protocol M = 0) and a census of pixels at Phase 1 ($s = U$) and the same remote sensing plus FIA field data (protocols M = 1 and M = 2, respectively) at Phase 2 ($s = 2$). The outcome is the two-phase vector estimate, similar to Eqs. 24 to 27, where the covariance matrix for Phase 1 exactly equals a $q_{M=1}$-by-$q_{M=1}$ zero matrix.

This example assumes all remotely sensed pixels are classified with the M = 1 protocol into likely "forest" and "non-forest" categories. The total areas of the population within each category (denoted A_f and A_{nf}, respectively) are constants that are known without error through census of all pixels that cover the population. The remotely sensed "forest" and "non-forest" classifications (M = 1) include some portion of pixel-level classification errors relative to field measurements with the M = 2 protocol, but the census of pixel classifications contain no sampling error.

It is further assumed that the Phase 2 measurements (M = 2) include cross-classification of landowner accessibility and remotely sensed classification of "forest" cover for each Phase 2 sampling unit. Therefore, a sample estimate is available for total area of inaccessible lands that are classified with remote sensing into the "forest" the category.

The exact area within the population that is classified as "forest" with the M = 1 remote sensing protocol from the Phase 1 census of pixels ($s = U$) is:

$$A_f = \begin{bmatrix} \mathbf{h}_A & | & \mathbf{0} \end{bmatrix} \begin{bmatrix} \hat{\mathbf{t}}_{M=1} \\ \hline \hat{\mathbf{t}}_{M=2} \end{bmatrix}_{s=\{U,2\}} \tag{91}$$

$$= \mathbf{h}_A \sum_U \begin{bmatrix} \mathbf{y}_{M=1} \end{bmatrix}_i$$

The estimated area of "denied access" in the entire population (t_1) is assumed to be a single element of the vector estimate. It is extracted by the linear transformation:

$$\left(\hat{t}_1 \right)_f = \begin{bmatrix} \mathbf{0} & | & \left(\mathbf{h}_1 \right)_f \end{bmatrix} \begin{bmatrix} \hat{\mathbf{t}}_{M=1} \\ \hline \hat{\mathbf{t}}_{M=2} \end{bmatrix}_{s=\{U,2\}} \tag{92}$$

where the 1-by-$q_{M=2}$ indicator matrix $(\mathbf{h}_1)_f$ is composed of zero elements, except the one element (equal to 1) for denied access conditions (M = 2) that are categorized as forest cover with the remote sensing protocol (M = 1).

The total biomass accretion for the "access granted" segment of the population, which is estimated from the "access granted" field plots, is assumed to be a single element of the vector estimate, and it is extracted from the vector estimate with the linear transformation:

$$\left(\hat{t}_2 \right)_f = \begin{bmatrix} \mathbf{0} & | & \left(\mathbf{h}_2 \right)_f \end{bmatrix} \begin{bmatrix} \hat{\mathbf{t}}_{M=1} \\ \hline \hat{\mathbf{t}}_{M=2} \end{bmatrix}_{s=\{U,2\}} \tag{93}$$

where the 1-by-$q_{M=2}$ indicator matrix $(\mathbf{h}_2)_f$ in Eq. 93 is composed of zero elements, except the one element (equal to 1) for "granted access" conditions (M = 2) that are categorized as forest cover with the remote sensing protocol (M = 1) for each sample plot in the Phase 2 sample ($s = 2$).

The desired population parameter is the total biomass accretion from lands that are expected to have "denied access" and that are classified as "forest" cover with the spaceborne sensor (M = 1). The presumed model is the product of the [area of "denied assess" in the population that is imperfectly classified as forest with remote sensing] times [the biomass accretion per unit area of "granted access" in "forest" cover as classified with the remote sensing]:

$$\theta_f = \left(t_1\right)_f \left[\left(t_2\right)_f \Big/ A_f \right] \tag{94}$$

The pseudo-estimator for the population parameter in Eq. 94 is a constant (Eq. 91) times the product of two population estimates:

$$\hat{\theta}_f = \left(\frac{1}{A_f} \right) \left(\hat{t}_1\right)_f \left(\hat{t}_2\right)_f \tag{95}$$

This model is similar to that of Martinussen and others (2008) for forest area estimates in presence of non-random missing observations.

The product of two estimates in Eq. 95 is a non-linear function for which the pseudo-estimator uses the first-order Taylor-series approximation for the variance estimator. The partial first derivatives of the non-linear function in Eq. 94 are:

$$a_1 \approx \left(\frac{\partial}{\partial t_1} \right) \frac{\left(t_1\right)_f \left(t_2\right)_f}{A_f} \Bigg|_{\left(t_1 = \hat{t}_1,\, t_2 = \hat{t}_2\right)_f} = \left(\frac{1}{A_f} \right) \left(\hat{t}_2\right)_f$$

$$a_2 \approx \left(\frac{\partial}{\partial t_2} \right) \frac{\left(t_1\right)_f \left(t_2\right)_f}{A_f} \Bigg|_{\left(t_1 = \hat{t}_1,\, t_2 = \hat{t}_2\right)_f} = \left(\frac{1}{A_f} \right) \left(\hat{t}_1\right)_f \tag{96}$$

From Eqs. 89, 90, and 96, the first-order Taylor-series approximation of the non-linear pseudo-estimator is:

$$
\begin{aligned}
\hat{\theta}_f &= \theta_f + a_1 \left[\left(\hat{t}_1\right)_f - \left(t_1\right)_f \right] + a_2 \left[\left(\hat{t}_2\right)_f - \left(t_2\right)_f \right] \\[6pt]
&= \theta_f + \left(\frac{\left(\hat{t}_2\right)_f}{A_f} \right) \left[\left(\hat{t}_1\right)_f - \left(t_1\right)_f \right] + \left(\frac{\left(\hat{t}_1\right)_f}{A_f} \right) \left[\left(\hat{t}_2\right)_f - \left(t_2\right)_f \right] \\[6pt]
&= \theta_f + \left[\left(\frac{\left(\hat{t}_2\right)_f}{A_f} \right) \; \Big| \; \left(\frac{\left(\hat{t}_1\right)_f}{A_f} \right) \right] \left[\begin{matrix} \left(\hat{t}_1\right)_f - \left(t_1\right)_f \\ \hline \left(\hat{t}_2\right)_f - \left(t_2\right)_f \end{matrix} \right] \\[6pt]
&= \theta_f + \frac{1}{A_f} \left[\left(\hat{t}_2\right)_f \; \Big| \; \left(\hat{t}_1\right)_f \right] \left[\begin{matrix} \left(\mathbf{h}_1\right)_f \\ \hline \left(\mathbf{h}_2\right)_f \end{matrix} \right] \left[\hat{\mathbf{t}}_{M=2} \right]_{s=\{U,2\}}
\end{aligned}
\tag{97}
$$

As in Eq. 102, the approximation in Eq. 97 yields an approximate variance estimator for the scalar pseudo-estimator:

$$
\hat{V}\!\left(\hat{\theta}_f\right) = \left[\left(\frac{(\hat{t}_2)_f}{A_f}\right) \;\middle|\; \left(\frac{(\hat{t}_1)_f}{A_f}\right)\right]\left[\begin{array}{c|c} \hat{V}(\hat{t}_1)_f & \hat{C}(\hat{t}_2,\hat{t}_1)_f \\ \hline \hat{C}(\hat{t}_1,\hat{t}_2)_f & \hat{V}(\hat{t}_2)_f \end{array}\right]\left[\begin{array}{c} \left(\dfrac{(\hat{t}_2)_f}{A_f}\right) \\ \left(\dfrac{(\hat{t}_1)_f}{A_f}\right) \end{array}\right]
$$

$$
= \left[\left(\frac{(\hat{t}_2)_f}{A_f}\right) \;\middle|\; \left(\frac{(\hat{t}_1)_f}{A_f}\right)\right]\left(\left[\begin{array}{c|c} \mathbf{0} & (\mathbf{h}_1)_f \\ \hline \mathbf{0} & \mathbf{h}_2 \end{array}\right]\left(\hat{\mathbf{V}}\left[\begin{bmatrix} \hat{\mathbf{t}}_{M=1} \\ \hat{\mathbf{t}}_{M=2} \end{bmatrix}_{s=\{U,2\}}\right]\right)\left[\begin{array}{c|c} \mathbf{0} & (\mathbf{h}_1')_f \\ \hline \mathbf{0} & (\mathbf{h}_2')_f \end{array}\right]\right)\left[\begin{array}{c} \left(\dfrac{(\hat{t}_2)_f}{A_f}\right) \\ \left(\dfrac{(\hat{t}_1)_f}{A_f}\right) \end{array}\right] \qquad (98)
$$

$$
= \left[\frac{(\hat{t}_2)_f}{A_f}(\mathbf{h}_1)_f + \frac{(\hat{t}_1)_f}{A_f}(\mathbf{h}_2)_f\right]\left(\hat{\mathbf{V}}\left[[\hat{\mathbf{t}}_{M=2}]_{s=\{U,2\}}\right]\right)\left[\frac{(\hat{t}_2)_f}{A_f}(\mathbf{h}_1)_f + \frac{(\hat{t}_1)_f}{A_f}(\mathbf{h}_2)_f\right]'
$$

Equation 98 is an unbiased variance estimator for the linear transformation in Eq. 97, which is accepted as reasonable for the desired non-linear transformation in Eq. 95. The second- and higher-order derivatives in Eq. 96 equal zero, i.e., $R = 0$ in Eq. 91. This is the case for all product functions. Therefore, the first-order Taylor-series for the product pseudo-estimator is exact in Eq. 98. It is not an approximation. However, in order to calculate the derivatives a_1 and a_2 in Eq. 96, the imperfect estimates in Eqs. 94 and 93 are required. Regardless, the pseudo-estimator for biomass accretion domain should not use the approximation in Eq. 97 but rather the direct product in Eq. 95.

The variance equation for the pseudo-estimator (Eq. 98) may be combined with linear transformations of the vector estimator. For example, "What is the estimated biomass accretion for the entire population, regardless of its accessibility condition and its remotely sensed land cover classification?" The answer (θ) is the sum of the total estimated accretion from the following four elements in the vector estimate: (1) two-phase, design-consistent estimate of accretion based on direct field re-measurements of "granted access" plots that have remotely sensed classification of "forest" (Eq. 93); (2) two-phase, design-consistent estimate of accretion based on direct field re-measurement of "granted access" plots that have remotely sensed classification of "non-forest" (similar to Eq. 93); (3) two-phase, model-based estimate of accretion from "denied access" plots that have remotely sensed classification of "forest" (Eqs. 95 and 98); and (4) two-phase, model-based estimate of accretion from "denied access" plots that have remotely sensed classification of "non-forest" (similar to Eqs. 95 and 98). The estimated scalar parameter and its variance are:

$$\hat{\theta} = \left(\hat{t}_2\right)_f + \left(\hat{t}_2\right)_{nf} + \left(\hat{\theta}\right)_f + \left(\hat{\theta}\right)_{nf}$$

$$= \begin{bmatrix} 1 & \vdots & 1 & \vdots & 1 & \vdots & 1 \end{bmatrix} \begin{bmatrix} (\mathbf{h}_2)_f \\ \hdashline (\mathbf{h}_2)_{nf} \\ \hdashline \left(\dfrac{(\hat{t}_2)_f}{A_f}(\mathbf{h}_1)_f + \dfrac{(\hat{t}_1)_f}{A_f}(\mathbf{h}_2)_f \right) \\ \hdashline \left(\dfrac{(\hat{t}_2)_{nf}}{A_{nf}}(\mathbf{h}_1)_{nf} + \dfrac{(\hat{t}_1)_{nf}}{A_{nf}}(\mathbf{h}_2)_{nf} \right) \end{bmatrix} \left[\hat{\mathbf{t}}_{M=2} \right]_{s=\{U,2\}} \tag{99}$$

$$= \mathbf{h}_\theta \left[\hat{\mathbf{t}}_{M=2} \right]_{s=\{U,2\}}$$

$$\hat{V}\left(\hat{\theta}\right) = \mathbf{h}_\theta \left(\hat{\mathbf{V}}\left[\hat{\mathbf{t}}_{M=2} \right]_{s=\{U,2\}} \right) \mathbf{h}'_\theta$$

where

$$\mathbf{h}_\theta = \left[\frac{(\hat{t}_2)_f}{A_f}(\mathbf{h}_1)_f + \frac{(\hat{t}_2)_{nf}}{A_{nf}}(\mathbf{h}_1)_{nf} + \left(1 + \frac{(\hat{t}_1)_f}{A_f}\right)(\mathbf{h}_2)_f + \left(1 + \frac{(\hat{t}_1)_{nf}}{A_{nf}}\right)(\mathbf{h}_2)_{nf} \right]$$

and the *nf* subscript in Eq. 99 denotes the sub-population identified as "non-forest" with the remotely sensed data, analogous to the *f* subscript in Eqs. 91 through 98.

Although not developed here, this approach to missing data may be enhanced with high-resolution aerial photography, which was previously identified as the M = 1 protocol. This could combine the model-based estimate (Eqs. 91 to 99) with a design-based estimate of photo-interpreted variables for the missing-data domain. Multivariate estimation facilitates full consideration of the dependencies between predictor and response variables. In addition, it would be convenient to express this estimator as expansion values (e.g., Lundström and Särndal 1999). These enhancements require future research and development.

Ratio Pseudo-Estimator: Volume per Estimated Unit Area of Forest Cover

The ratio is a common, non-linear transformation. For example, consider the ratio of two estimated population totals, such as the ratio of total wood volume (t_1) to total forest area (t_2), namely, the estimated wood volume per unit area of forest. From Eqs. 89 and 90:

$$\theta = \frac{t_1}{t_2}$$

$$\hat{\theta} = \frac{\hat{t}_{1\pi}}{\hat{t}_{2\pi}} \approx \theta + \sum_{j=1}^{2} a_j \left(\hat{t}_{j\pi} - t_j \right) \tag{100}$$

where , $\hat{t}_2 \neq 0, \hat{t}_2 \neq 0$ and

$$
\begin{array}{|c|c|}
\hline
a_1 \approx \left. \dfrac{\partial(t_1/t_2)}{\partial \hat{t}_{1\pi}} \right|_{\hat{t}_{1\pi}=t_1,\ \hat{t}_{2\pi}=t_2} = \dfrac{1}{\hat{t}_{2\pi}} & a_2 \approx \left. \dfrac{\partial(t_1/t_2)}{\partial \hat{t}_{2\pi}} \right|_{\hat{t}_{1\pi}=t_1,\ \hat{t}_{2\pi}=t_2} = -\dfrac{\hat{t}_{1\pi}}{\hat{t}_{2\pi}^2} \\
\hline
\end{array}
$$

The multivariate Taylor series linear approximation is simply:

$$
\begin{aligned}
\hat{\theta} &= \theta + a_1 \left(\hat{t}_{1\pi} - t_1 \right) + a_2 \left(\hat{t}_{2\pi} - t_2 \right) \\
&= \theta + \frac{1}{\hat{t}_{2\pi}} \left(\hat{t}_{1\pi} - t_1 \right) + \left(-\frac{\hat{t}_{1\pi}}{\hat{t}_{2\pi}^2} \right) \left(\hat{t}_{2\pi} - t_2 \right) \\
&= \theta + \frac{1}{\hat{t}_{2\pi}} \left(\hat{t}_{1\pi} - t_1 \right) + \left(-\frac{\hat{\theta}}{\hat{t}_{2\pi}} \right) \left(\hat{t}_{2\pi} - t_2 \right) \\
&= \theta + \left[\begin{array}{c|c} \dfrac{1}{\hat{t}_{2\pi}} & \left(-\dfrac{\hat{\theta}}{\hat{t}_{2\pi}} \right) \end{array} \right] \left[\begin{array}{c} \left(\hat{t}_{1\pi} - t_1 \right) \\ \hline \left(\hat{t}_{2\pi} - t_2 \right) \end{array} \right]
\end{aligned}
\tag{101}
$$

This simple calculus is easily applied to the variance estimator for the pseudo-estimator in Eq. 101:

$$
\hat{V}(\hat{\theta}) \approx \left[\begin{array}{c|c} \dfrac{1}{\hat{t}_{2\pi}} & \left(-\dfrac{\hat{\theta}}{\hat{t}_{2\pi}} \right) \end{array} \right] \left[\begin{array}{c|c} \hat{V}(\hat{t}_{1\pi}) & \hat{C}(\hat{t}_{1\pi}, \hat{t}_{2\pi}) \\ \hline \hat{C}(\hat{t}_{1\pi}, \hat{t}_{2\pi}) & \hat{V}(\hat{t}_{2\pi}) \end{array} \right] \left[\begin{array}{c} \dfrac{1}{\hat{t}_{2\pi}} \\ \hline -\dfrac{\hat{\theta}}{\hat{t}_{2\pi}} \end{array} \right] \tag{102}
$$

As a verification exercise, the Taylor-series approximation agrees with the results offered by Särndal and others (1992) in their Eq. 5.6.10. Algebraically manipulating Eq. 102:

$$\hat{V}(\hat{\theta}) = \left[\frac{1}{\hat{t}_{2\pi}} \,\middle|\, \left(-\frac{\hat{\theta}}{\hat{t}_{2\pi}} \right) \right] \left[\begin{array}{c} \frac{1}{\hat{t}_{2\pi}} \left[\hat{V}(\hat{t}_{1\pi}) - \hat{\theta}\,\hat{C}(\hat{t}_{1\pi},\hat{t}_{2\pi}) \right] \\ \hline \frac{1}{\hat{t}_{2\pi}} \left[\hat{C}(\hat{t}_{1\pi},\hat{t}_{2\pi}) - \hat{\theta}\hat{V}(\hat{t}_{2\pi}) \right] \end{array} \right]$$

$$= \frac{1}{\hat{t}_{2\pi}^2} \left[\hat{V}(\hat{t}_{1\pi}) - \hat{\theta}\,\hat{C}(\hat{t}_{1\pi},\hat{t}_{2\pi}) \right] + \left(-\frac{\hat{\theta}}{\hat{t}_{2\pi}^2} \right) \left[\hat{C}(\hat{t}_{1\pi},\hat{t}_{2\pi}) - \hat{\theta}\,\hat{V}(\hat{t}_{2\pi}) \right]$$

$$= \frac{1}{\hat{t}_{2\pi}^2} \left[\hat{V}(\hat{t}_{1\pi}) - \hat{\theta}\,\hat{C}(\hat{t}_{1\pi},\hat{t}_{2\pi}) - \hat{\theta}\,\hat{C}(\hat{t}_{1\pi},\hat{t}_{2\pi}) + \hat{\theta}^2\,\hat{V}(\hat{t}_{2\pi}) \right]$$

$$= \frac{1}{\hat{t}_{2\pi}^2} \left[\hat{V}(\hat{t}_{1\pi}) - 2\hat{\theta}\,\hat{C}(\hat{t}_{1\pi},\hat{t}_{2\pi}) + \hat{\theta}^2\hat{V}(\hat{t}_{2\pi}) \right]$$

In practice, the pseudo-estimator is computed directly from the non-linear transformation. For example, the pseudo-estimator for the ratio of total wood volume (t_1) to total forest area (t_2) from Eq. 100 should be:

$$\hat{\theta} = \frac{\hat{t}_{1\pi}}{\hat{t}_{2\pi}}, \hat{t}_{2\pi} \neq 0 \tag{103}$$

The variance estimator in Eq. 102 is actually a conditionally unbiased estimator of the linear transformation in Eq. 101. It is only an approximation when used as a variance estimator for the non-linear transformation in Eq. 100. Regardless, the pseudo-estimator for the desired population parameter should use the exact non-linear transformation in Eq. 100, with the Taylor-series approximation in Eqs. 101 and 102 used only for the associated variance and covariance estimates.

Recursive Object-Oriented Simplification of Taylor-Series Approximations

The methods given above for pseudo-estimators greatly facilitate construction of complex, multivariate, linear Taylor approximations. These can be daunting when dealing directly with the variance estimator, but are relatively easy when applied directly to the pseudo-estimator (e.g., Särndal and others 1992:205). In general, the method is object-oriented in that it disassembles a complex pseudo-estimator into small components that are recursively combined into the final Taylor series function.

For example, consider the product estimator for missing data on p. 77. Equation 94 defines the pseudo-estimator of the population total for biomass accretion on private lands that cannot be measured directly because of denied access, which is repeated here:

$$\theta_f = (t_1)_f \left[(t_2)_f \middle/ A_f \right] \tag{94}$$

The recursive process combines the objects in the complex Taylor series approximation in the following sequence:

1. The estimated area of "denied access" in the entire population (t_1) is estimated with the linear transformation in Eq. 92, resulting in an indicator vector of zeros and ones.

2. The total biomass accretion for the "access granted" segment of the population $(t_2)_f$ is estimated with the linear transformation in Eq. 93, resulting in an indicator vector of zeros and ones.

3. The census area imperfectly classified as "forest" cover (A_f) is computed with Eq. 57.

4. These two row vectors from steps 1 and 2 are stacked to form a 2-by-$(q_{M=1} + q_{M=2})$ indicator matrix.

5. This indicator matrix is multiplied by the 1-by-2 vector containing estimates of (t_1) and $(t_2)_f$ from steps 1 and 2.

6. The resulting 1-by-$(q_{M=1} + q_{M=2})$ vector is multiplied by the scalar inverse of the remotely sensed census of forest cover in the target population from step 3.

The final 1-by-$(q_{M=1} + q_{M=2})$ vector from step 6 is available for the linear Taylor series approximation for the variance of the pseudo-estimator in Eq. 94. This recursive process is continued in Eq. 99 to accommodate an even more complicated pseudo-estimator for the entire target population. Although not fully shown, the complex ratio pseudo-estimator in Eq. 101 is similarly developed as a recursive process. These procedures are readily applied to non-linear transformations of large numbers of elements in a vector of estimated population parameters and its estimated covariance matrix. The following is an example.

Returning to the example of total wood volume per unit forest area, assume that total wood volume in the vector estimate is distributed among multiple elements that segregate wood volume by tree species groups, and total forest area in the vector estimate is distributed among multiple elements that segregate forest area by forest type groups. Given a q-by-1 vector estimate of $\mathbf{t}$, the pseudo-estimator is simply the [sum of all estimated volume over all tree species groups = t_1] divided by the [sum of all area estimates for each forest type group = t_2]:

$$\hat{\theta} = \left(\mathbf{h}_1\left[\hat{\mathbf{t}}\right] \middle/ \mathbf{h}_2\left[\hat{\mathbf{t}}\right] \right)$$

$$\text{where} \begin{cases} i^{th} \text{ element of } \mathbf{h}_1 = \begin{cases} \mathbf{h}_1(i) = 1 \text{ if } i^{th} \text{ element of } \left[\hat{\mathbf{t}}\right] \text{ is an estimated volume} \\ \mathbf{h}_1(i) = 0 \text{ otherwise} \end{cases} \\ i^{th} \text{ element of } \mathbf{h}_2 = \begin{cases} \mathbf{h}_2(i) = 1 \text{ if } i^{th} \text{ element of } \left[\hat{\mathbf{t}}\right] \text{ is an estimated forest area} \\ \mathbf{h}_2(i) = 0 \text{ otherwise} \end{cases} \\ \mathbf{h}_2\left[\hat{\mathbf{t}}\right] \neq 0 \end{cases} \tag{104}$$

Both $\mathbf{h}_1$ and $\mathbf{h}_2$ in Eq. 104 are 1-by-q row vectors. The Taylor-series approximation of this pseudo-estimator is derived from Eq. 89 as:

$$\hat{V}(\hat{\theta}) \approx [a_1 \mid a_2 \mid \cdots \mid a_q]\hat{\mathbf{V}}([\hat{\mathbf{t}}]) \begin{bmatrix} a_1 \\ ---- \\ a_2 \\ --\vdots-- \\ ---- \\ a_{q_{M=2}} \end{bmatrix} = \mathbf{a}[\hat{\mathbf{V}}(\hat{\mathbf{t}})]\mathbf{a}' \tag{105}$$

where

$$a_i = \frac{\partial \theta}{\partial a_i} = \begin{cases} \left(a_i \Big/ \mathbf{h}_2[\hat{\mathbf{t}}] \right) \text{ if } \hat{\mathbf{t}}(i) \text{ is an estimated estimated volume} \\ \left(-a_i\hat{\theta} \Big/ \mathbf{h}_2[\hat{\mathbf{t}}] \right) \text{ if } \hat{\mathbf{t}}(i) \text{ is an estimated forest area} \\ 0 \text{ otherwise} \end{cases}$$

With modest algebra, the 1-by-q row vector **a** in Eq. 105 may be expressed as:

$$\mathbf{a} = \left(1 \Big/ \mathbf{h}_2[\hat{\mathbf{t}}] \right)\left(\mathbf{h}_1 - \hat{\theta}\,\mathbf{h}_2 \right) \tag{106}$$

The simple expression in Eq. 106 yields a valid Taylor-series variance approximation for any scalar statistic that is the ratio of two scalar linear transformations of **t**, i.e., ($\mathbf{h}_1\mathbf{t}$)/ ($\mathbf{h}_2\mathbf{t}$), where the elements of $\mathbf{h}_1$ and $\mathbf{h}_2$ may be any real number such that $\mathbf{h}_2\mathbf{t}\neq 0$, even if the same element of **t** has a non-zero coefficient in both the numerator and denominator of this ratio statistic.

The following derivation of Eq. 106 is offered as another example of a simplified approach to Taylor-series approximations. First, collapse the q-by-1 vector estimate of **t** into a 2-by-1 vector, where the first vector element is the sum of all elements in the **t** vector that are in the numerator of the pseudo-estimator, and the second vector element is the sum of all elements in the **t** vector that are in the denominator of the pseudo-estimator.

$$\theta = \left(t_1 \Big/ t_2 \right), \text{ where } \begin{bmatrix} \hat{t}_1 \\ -- \\ \hat{t}_2 \end{bmatrix} = \begin{bmatrix} \mathbf{h}_1 \\ -- \\ \mathbf{h}_2 \end{bmatrix} [\hat{\mathbf{t}}] \tag{107}$$

Then, treat the resulting 2-by-1 vector in Eq. 107 as the ratio of two scalar estimates in Eqs. 101 and 102 and Eq. 5.6.10 in Särndal and others (1992). The outcome is simply:

$$\mathbf{a} = \left[\left(\dfrac{1}{\mathbf{h}_2[\hat{\mathbf{t}}]}\right) \vdots \left(\dfrac{-\hat{\theta}}{\mathbf{h}_2[\hat{\mathbf{t}}]}\right)\right]\begin{bmatrix}\mathbf{h}_1 \\ \hline \mathbf{h}_2\end{bmatrix}$$

$$= \left(\dfrac{1}{\mathbf{h}_2[\hat{\mathbf{t}}]}\right)\begin{bmatrix}1 \vdots -\hat{\theta}\end{bmatrix}\begin{bmatrix}\mathbf{h}_1 \\ \hline \mathbf{h}_2\end{bmatrix} \tag{108}$$

$$= \left(\dfrac{1}{\mathbf{h}_2[\hat{\mathbf{t}}]}\right)\left(\mathbf{h}_1 - \hat{\theta}\,\mathbf{h}_2\right)$$

which validates Eq. 106.

The Taylor-series approximation may be stacked to recursively construct more complex pseudo-estimators (Wolter 2007:244). For example, the estimated difference between total volume per unit area of forest type A compared to forest type B is:

$$\hat{\theta} = \hat{\theta}_A - \hat{\theta}_B$$

$$= \left(\dfrac{\hat{t}_1}{\hat{t}_2}\right)_A - \left(\dfrac{\hat{t}_1}{\hat{t}_2}\right)_B \tag{109}$$

$$= \left(\dfrac{(\mathbf{h}_1)_A\,\hat{\mathbf{t}}}{(\mathbf{h}_2)_A\,\hat{\mathbf{t}}}\right) - \left(\dfrac{(\mathbf{h}_1)_B\,\hat{\mathbf{t}}}{(\mathbf{h}_2)_B\,\hat{\mathbf{t}}}\right)$$

The corresponding first-order Taylor-series linear approximation of the variance for the scalar difference in Eq. 109 is easily derived with the help of Eq. 106 from the q-by-1 vector estimate of $\mathbf{t}$ and its estimated q-by-q covariance matrix with the 1-by-q vector $\mathbf{a}$ as:

$$\hat{V}(\hat{\theta}) = \mathbf{a}\left[\mathbf{V}(\hat{\mathbf{t}})\right]\mathbf{a}' \tag{110}$$

where

$$\mathbf{a} = \begin{bmatrix}1 \vdots -1\end{bmatrix}\left[\begin{array}{cc:cc} \dfrac{1}{(\mathbf{h}_2)_A\hat{\mathbf{t}}} & \dfrac{-\hat{\theta}_A}{(\mathbf{h}_2)_A\hat{\mathbf{t}}} & 0 & 0 \\ \hline 0 & 0 & \dfrac{1}{(\mathbf{h}_2)_B\hat{\mathbf{t}}} & \dfrac{-\hat{\theta}_B}{(\mathbf{h}_2)_B\hat{\mathbf{t}}}\end{array}\right]\begin{bmatrix}(\mathbf{h}_1)_A \\ (\mathbf{h}_2)_A \\ \hline (\mathbf{h}_1)_B \\ (\mathbf{h}_2)_B\end{bmatrix}$$

$$= \left(\left[\dfrac{1}{(\mathbf{h}_2)_A\hat{\mathbf{t}}}\right]\left[(\mathbf{h}_1)_A - \hat{\theta}_A(\mathbf{h}_2)_A\right]\right) - \left(\left[\dfrac{1}{(\mathbf{h}_2)_B\hat{\mathbf{t}}}\right]\left[(\mathbf{h}_1)_B - \hat{\theta}_B(\mathbf{h}_2)_B\right]\right)$$

Equation 110 may be rewritten as:

$$\hat{V}\left(\hat{\theta}\right) = \mathbf{d}\left(\begin{bmatrix} \dfrac{(\mathbf{h}_1)_A}{(\mathbf{h}_2)_A} \\ \dfrac{(\mathbf{h}_1)_B}{(\mathbf{h}_2)_B} \end{bmatrix} \mathbf{V}\left(\hat{\mathbf{t}}\right) \begin{bmatrix} \dfrac{(\mathbf{h}_1)_A}{(\mathbf{h}_2)_A} \\ \dfrac{(\mathbf{h}_1)_B}{(\mathbf{h}_2)_B} \end{bmatrix}' \right)\mathbf{d}'$$

(111)

$$= \mathbf{d}\left(\mathbf{V}\begin{bmatrix} \dfrac{(\hat{t}_1)_A}{(\hat{t}_2)_A} \\ \dfrac{(\hat{t}_1)_B}{(\hat{t}_2)_B} \end{bmatrix}\right)\mathbf{d}'$$

where

$$\mathbf{d} = \left[\begin{array}{c|c|c|c} \dfrac{1}{(\mathbf{h}_2)_A\hat{\mathbf{t}}} & \dfrac{-\hat{\theta}_A}{(\mathbf{h}_2)_A\hat{\mathbf{t}}} & \dfrac{-1}{(\mathbf{h}_2)_B\hat{\mathbf{t}}} & \dfrac{\hat{\theta}_B}{(\mathbf{h}_2)_B\hat{\mathbf{t}}} \end{array}\right]$$

$$= \left[\begin{array}{c|c|c|c} \dfrac{1}{(\hat{t}_2)_A} & \dfrac{-1}{(\hat{t}_2)_A}\left(\hat{t}_1\big/\hat{t}_2\right)_A & \dfrac{-1}{(\hat{t}_2)_B} & \dfrac{1}{(\hat{t}_2)_B}\left(\hat{t}_1\big/\hat{t}_2\right)_B \end{array}\right]$$

Equation 111 agrees with Wolter's (2007:Eq. 6.9.3) results. Again, the covariance matrix may be the final results from the sequential application of RRE in any of the complex designs above. The estimators in Eqs. 109 and 110 might serve in a test-of-hypothesis regarding significant differences in volume per unit area of forest type A compared to forest type B.

While the procedures above require tedious application of simple matrix algebra, the tedium would be far more onerous with scalar algebra conducted on the full non-linear transformation, especially if applied directly to the covariance matrix with double summations. The scalar operators of addition, subtraction, multiplication, and inverse are considered above. Power functions are not, but these should not be too daunting in a recursive process. Furthermore, except for division, the second-order terms of the Taylor series are zero for these operators. Therefore, this recursive process could be used to generate more simply the second-order Taylor series approximation for any scalar pseudo-estimator that uses these four operators.

A Model-Based Estimator for Small-Domain Predictions

The next example uses a moderately intensive sample of relatively "less-expensive" field measurements of tree volume and a sparse sub-sample of "more-expensive" volume measurements. The "less-expensive" protocol includes systematically biased measurement errors, while the "more-expensive" protocol has unbiased measurement errors. Model-based predictions are applied to small domains, many of which do not have sufficient sample sizes for reliable direct estimates with the unbiased, "more-expensive" measurements of individual tree volumes.

Suppose a three-phase sampling design (e.g., Eqs. 44 to 51) employs inexpensive airborne photo-interpretation techniques (protocol M = 1), including photogrammetric estimates of stand volume; FIA field data (protocol M = 2), including relatively "less-expensive" measurements of tree diameter at breast height (DBH) and regional tree-volume equations, and a very precise "more-expensive" field protocol (M = 3), including upper stem diameter measurements made with ground-based laser instruments. Protocol M = 1 is applied to a very large Phase 1 sample ($s = 1$) of photo-interpreted sampling units. Protocols M = 1 and M = 2 are applied to all points in the moderate-intensity Phase 2 sample ($s = 2$). Protocols M = 1, M = 2, and M = 3 are applied to all points in the sparse Phase 3 sample ($s = 3$). The outcome is the three-phase vector estimate similar to Eq. 50.

The "more-expensive" M = 3 field protocol very accurately measures upper stem diameters and total tree heights of individual standing trees (e.g., Williams and others 1999). These physical measurements are inputs to a sophisticated stem profile model (e.g., Flewelling and others 2000) that provides accurate and un-biased estimates of wood volume for individual standing trees. Because these measurements are very expensive, they are only available for the sparse sample of Phase 3 ($s = 3$) plots, although correlations among variables measured at Phase 1 and Phase 2 improve overall precision in the three-phase sampling design.

As in Eq. 20, the vector of remotely sensed variables for each point i in the Phase 1 sample is composed of:

$$\left[\mathbf{y}_{M=1}\right]_i = \left[\begin{bmatrix} I_1\left(\mathbf{y}_{M=1}\right)_D \\ \vdots \\ I_i\left(\mathbf{y}_{M=1}\right)_D \\ \vdots \\ I_{q_D}\left(\mathbf{y}_{M=1}\right)_D \\ \hline \left(\mathbf{y}_{M=1}\right)_U \end{bmatrix}\right]_i \qquad \left[\hat{\mathbf{t}}_{M=(1)}\right]_{s=1} = \frac{A}{n_{s=1}} \sum_{j\in(s=1)} \left[\mathbf{y}_{M=1}\right]_i \qquad (112)$$

where

$$\left(\mathbf{y}_{M=1}\right)_D = \text{remotely sensed variables, for domain estimates}$$

$$I_i = \begin{cases} 1 \text{ if sample point is in domain } i \\ 0 \text{ otherwise} \end{cases}$$

$$\left(\mathbf{y}_{M=1}\right)_U = \text{other remotely sensed variables}$$

The vector of remotely sensed and field variables for each point i in the Phase 2 sample is defined in Eq. 113 as:

$$\begin{bmatrix} \mathbf{y}_{M=1} \\ \hline \mathbf{y}_{M=2} \end{bmatrix}_i = \left[\begin{bmatrix} \mathbf{y}_{M=1} \\ \hline I_1\left(\mathbf{y}_{M=2}\right)_D \\ \vdots \\ I_i\left(\mathbf{y}_{M=2}\right)_D \\ \vdots \\ I_{q_D}\left(\mathbf{y}_{M=2}\right)_D \\ \hline \left(\mathbf{y}_{M=2}\right)_U \end{bmatrix}\right]_i \qquad \left[\hat{\mathbf{t}}_{M=(1,2)}\right]_{s=2} = \frac{A}{n_{s=2}} \sum_{j\in(s=2)} \begin{bmatrix} \mathbf{y}_{M=1} \\ \hline \mathbf{y}_{M=2} \end{bmatrix}_i \qquad (113)$$

where

$$\left(\mathbf{y}_{M=2}\right)_D = \text{"less-expensive" field variables, for domain estimates}$$

$$I_i = \begin{cases} 1 \text{ if sample point is in domain } i \\ 0 \text{ otherwise} \end{cases}$$

$$\left(\mathbf{y}_{M=2}\right)_U = \text{other "less-expensive" field variables, for population estimates}$$

Finally, the vector of remotely sensed, "less-expensive" field variables, and "more-expensive" field variables for each point i in the Phase 3 sample is defined in Eq. 114 as:

$$
\begin{bmatrix} \mathbf{y}_{M=1} \\ \hline \mathbf{y}_{M=2} \\ \hline \mathbf{y}_{M=3} \end{bmatrix}_i = \begin{bmatrix} \mathbf{y}_{M=1} \\ \hline \mathbf{y}_{M=2} \\ \hline I_1(\mathbf{y}_{M=3})_D \\ \vdots \\ \hline I_i(\mathbf{y}_{M=3})_D \\ \vdots \\ \hline I_{q_D}(\mathbf{y}_{M=3})_D \\ \hline (\mathbf{y}_{M=3})_U \end{bmatrix}_i \qquad \left[\hat{\mathbf{t}}_{M=(1,2,3)}\right]_{s=3} = \frac{A}{n_{s=3}} \sum_{j\in(s=3)} \begin{bmatrix} \mathbf{y}_{M=1} \\ \hline \mathbf{y}_{M=2} \\ \hline \mathbf{y}_{M=3} \end{bmatrix}_i \qquad (114)
$$

where

$(\mathbf{y}_{M=3})_D = $ "more-expensive" field variables, for domains estimates

$I_i = \begin{cases} 1 \text{ if sample point is in domain } i \\ 0 \text{ otherwise} \end{cases}$

$(\mathbf{y}_{M=3})_U = $ other "more-expensive" field variables, for population estimates

RRE is sequentially used to combine the independent estimates from the three phases of sampling, as in Eqs. 44 to 51.

Define the scalar t_1 as the population total for tree volume measured with the M = 3 protocol, a scalar estimate for which is extracted from the final RRE vector estimate (e.g., Eq. 50) with the 1-by-$q_{M=3}$ indicator matrix $\mathbf{h}_1$ in Eq. 115:

$$
\hat{t}_1 = \begin{bmatrix} \mathbf{0} & \vdots & \mathbf{0} & \vdots & \mathbf{h}_1 \end{bmatrix} \begin{bmatrix} \hat{\mathbf{t}}_{M=1} \\ \hline \hat{\mathbf{t}}_{M=2} \\ \hline \hat{\mathbf{t}}_{M=3} \end{bmatrix}_{s=1,2,3} \qquad (115)
$$

The M = 2 field protocol includes "less-expensive" estimates of individual tree volumes that use measurements of DBH, ocular estimates of tree heights, and regional volume equations that were fit to off-frame convenience sample of historical data. Hypothetically, assume this M = 2 protocol produces biased estimates of individual tree volume at both the population and small-domain levels. In these situations, biases of 10 percent or more are possible, especially for domains that are small relative to the geographic scope of the database that was used to fit the regional volume equation. The vector estimate from the Phase 2 sample includes separate elements for the total volume in each of q_D domains, such as counties (Särndal and others 1992:220, 304, 397), as measured with the M = 2 protocol. The sampling error at Phase 2 is sufficiently small to make reliable tree volume estimates for each of q_D small domains. However, these estimates are biased because the "less-expensive" tree volume measurements (M = 2) are biased.

The vector partition with estimated total tree volumes for each of the q_D domains, which are measured with the M = 2 protocol, is isolated from the overall RRE vector estimate (Eq. 50) with the q_D-by-$q_{M=2}$ indicator matrix $\mathbf{H}_3$:

$$\hat{\mathbf{t}}_3 = \begin{bmatrix} \mathbf{0} & \vdots & \mathbf{H}_3 & \vdots & \mathbf{0} \end{bmatrix} \begin{bmatrix} \hat{\mathbf{t}}_{M=1} \\ \hline \hat{\mathbf{t}}_{M=2} \\ \hline \hat{\mathbf{t}}_{M=3} \end{bmatrix}_{s=1,2,3} \tag{116}$$

In this example, all elements in the conformable indicator matrix $\mathbf{H}_3$ equal zero except for each of the q_D elements that corresponds to the volume estimate made with the M = 2 protocol, in which case the element of $\mathbf{H}_3$ equals 1. Assume for notational convenience that these q_D elements are contiguous in the vector estimate; thus, the elements equal to 1 in indicator matrix $\mathbf{H}_3$ are an identity matrix partition ($\mathbf{I}$) in Eq. 116.

Define the sum of all elements in the $\mathbf{t}_3$ vector as the sum of all estimated domain volumes with the M = 2 protocol as t_2:

$$\hat{t}_2 = \begin{bmatrix} 1 & \vdots & \cdots & \vdots & 1 \end{bmatrix} \hat{\mathbf{t}}_3$$

$$= \begin{bmatrix} \mathbf{0} & \vdots & \mathbf{h}_2 & \vdots & \mathbf{0} \end{bmatrix} \begin{bmatrix} \hat{\mathbf{t}}_{M=1} \\ \hline \hat{\mathbf{t}}_{M=2} \\ \hline \hat{\mathbf{t}}_{M=3} \end{bmatrix}_{s=1,2,3} \tag{117}$$

$$= \sum_{d=1}^{q_D} \left([\hat{t}_{M=2}]_{s=1,2,3} \right)_d$$

The scalar t_2 in Eq. 117 equals the total tree volume in the entire population as measured with the biased M = 2 protocol. This scalar estimate is isolated from RRE vector estimate (Eq. 50) with the 1-by-$q_{M=3}$ indicator matrix $\mathbf{h}_2$. All elements of the conformable row vector $\mathbf{h}_2$ in Eq. 117 equal zero except for any of the q_D elements corresponding to estimated total tree volume made with the M = 2 protocol for a domain; each of these latter elements equals 1 in $\mathbf{h}_2$. For convenience of notation, these q_D elements are contiguous in RRE vector estimate (Eq. 50).

The objective is an unbiased, model-based prediction of the total volume for each of the q_D small domains using the biased estimates of total volume, which are based on the "less-expensive" M = 2 protocol. The model assumes that the bias of the M = 2 protocol relative to the M = 3 protocol, which is observed directly from the Phase 3 sample ($s = 3$), is constant for all domains. The resulting vector pseudo-estimator is defined for each of the q_D domains as:

$$\begin{bmatrix} \hat{\theta}_{d=1} \\ \hline \vdots \\ \hline \hat{\theta}_{d=q_D} \end{bmatrix} = \hat{\boldsymbol{\theta}} = \left[\left(\hat{t}_1 \Big/ \hat{t}_2 \right) \hat{\mathbf{t}}_3 \right] = \left(\hat{t}_1 \Big/ \hat{t}_2 \right) \begin{bmatrix} \hat{t}_{d=1} \\ \hline \vdots \\ \hline \hat{t}_{d=q_D} \end{bmatrix} \tag{118}$$

This model in Eq. 118 is similar to a synthetic estimator for small domains (Särndal and others 1992:410), which often provides exceptionally precise estimates, but it can induce considerable estimation bias if the model is inaccurate. The latter is a substantial risk because there is often no empirical evidence to judge the accuracy of the model.

The two scalar estimates (t_1 and t_2) and the q_D-by-1 column vector estimate ($\mathbf{t}_3$) in Eq. 118 equal the linear matrix function (Eqs. 115 to 117):

$$
\begin{bmatrix} \hat{t}_1 \\ -- \\ \hat{t}_2 \\ -- \\ \hat{\mathbf{t}}_3 \end{bmatrix}
=
\begin{bmatrix} \mathbf{0} & \vdots & \mathbf{0} & \vdots & \mathbf{h}_1 \\ --- & + & --- & + & --- \\ \mathbf{0} & \vdots & \mathbf{h}_2 & \vdots & \mathbf{0} \\ --- & + & --- & + & --- \\ \mathbf{0} & \vdots & \mathbf{H}_3 & \vdots & \mathbf{0} \end{bmatrix}
\begin{bmatrix} \hat{\mathbf{t}}_{M=1} \\ \cdots \\ \hat{\mathbf{t}}_{M=2} \\ \cdots \\ \hat{\mathbf{t}}_{M=3} \end{bmatrix}_{s=1,2,3}
$$

(119)

$$
\mathbf{V}\!\left(\begin{bmatrix} \hat{t}_1 \\ -- \\ \hat{t}_2 \\ -- \\ \hat{\mathbf{t}}_3 \end{bmatrix} \right)
=
\begin{bmatrix} \mathbf{0} & \vdots & \mathbf{h}_1 \\ --- & + & --- \\ \mathbf{h}_2 & \vdots & \mathbf{0} \\ --- & + & --- \\ \mathbf{H}_3 & \vdots & \mathbf{0} \end{bmatrix}
\left[\mathbf{V}\!\left(\begin{bmatrix} \hat{\mathbf{t}}_{M=2} \\ \cdots \\ \hat{\mathbf{t}}_{M=3} \end{bmatrix}_{s=1,2,3} \right) \right]
\begin{bmatrix} \mathbf{0} & \vdots & \mathbf{h}'_2 & \vdots & \mathbf{H}'_3 \\ --- & + & --- & + & --- \\ \mathbf{h}'_1 & \vdots & \mathbf{0} & \vdots & \mathbf{0} \end{bmatrix}
$$

The model in Eq. 118 is the basis for a non-linear pseudo-estimator of total volume in each of the q_D domains (i.e., elements of q_D-by-1 column vector $\boldsymbol{\theta}$) based on the "more-expensive" M = 3 tree measurement protocol.

Row i for the vector model in Eq. 118 is:

$$
\theta_{d=i} = t_1\!\left(\frac{t_{d=i}}{t_2} \right) = t_1\!\left(\frac{t_{d=i}}{t_{d=1} + \cdots + t_{d=i} + \cdots + t_{d=j} + \cdots + t_{d=q_D}} \right)
$$

(120)

The partial first derivatives for the function in Eq. 120, evaluated at the estimated values, are:

$$
\left. \left(\frac{\partial}{\partial t_1} \right) \theta_{d=i} \right|_{t_1 = \hat{t}_1} = \frac{\hat{t}_{d=i}}{\hat{t}_2}
$$

$$
\left. \left(\frac{\partial}{\partial t_{d=i}} \right) \theta_{d=i} \right|_{t_i = \hat{t}_i} = \frac{\hat{t}_1}{\hat{t}_2} - \frac{\hat{t}_1 \hat{t}_{d=i}}{\hat{t}_2^2}
$$

(121)

$$
\left. \left(\frac{\partial}{\partial t_{d=j}} \right) \theta_{d=i} \right|_{\substack{t_j = \hat{t}_j \\ j \neq i}} = \frac{-\hat{t}_1 t_{d=i}}{\hat{t}_2^2}
$$

From Eqs. 89, 90, and 121, the first-order Taylor-series approximation of the non-linear pseudo-estimator in Eq. 120 is:

$$\theta_{d=i} \approx \hat{\theta}_{d=i} + \left(\frac{\hat{t}_{d=i}}{\hat{t}_2}\right)\left(\hat{t}_1 - t_1\right) + \left(\frac{\hat{t}_1}{\hat{t}_2} - \frac{\hat{t}_1\,\hat{t}_{d=i}}{\hat{t}_2^2}\right)\left(\hat{t}_{d=i} - t_{d=i}\right) + \sum_{\substack{j=1 \\ j\neq i}}^{q_D}\left(-\frac{\hat{t}_1\,\hat{t}_{d=i}}{\hat{t}_2^2}\left(\hat{t}_{d=j} - t_{d=j}\right)\right)$$

$$\approx \hat{\theta}_{d=i} + \left(\frac{\hat{t}_{d=i}}{\hat{t}_2}\right)\left(\hat{t}_1 - t_1\right) - \left[\left(\frac{\hat{t}_1\,\hat{t}_{d=i}}{\hat{t}_2^2}\right)\sum_{j=1}^{q_D}\left(\hat{t}_{d=j} - t_{d=j}\right)\right] + \left(\frac{\hat{t}_1}{\hat{t}_2}\right)\left(\hat{t}_{d=i} - t_{d=i}\right)$$

$$\approx \hat{\theta}_{d=i} + \left(\frac{\hat{t}_{d=i}}{\hat{t}_2}\right)\left(\hat{t}_1 - t_1\right) - \left[\left(\frac{\hat{t}_1\,\hat{t}_{d=i}}{\hat{t}_2^2}\right)\left(\hat{t}_2 - t_2\right)\right] + \left(\frac{\hat{t}_1}{\hat{t}_2}\right)\left(\hat{t}_{d=i} - t_{d=i}\right)$$

$$\tag{122}$$

$$\approx \hat{\theta}_{d=i} + \left[\left(\frac{\hat{t}_{d=i}}{\hat{t}_2}\right) \;\middle|\; -\left(\frac{\hat{t}_1\,\hat{t}_{d=i}}{\hat{t}_2^2}\right) \;\middle|\; 0 \;\middle|\; \cdots \;\middle|\; \left(\frac{\hat{t}_1}{\hat{t}_2}\right) \;\middle|\; \cdots \;\middle|\; 0\right]\begin{bmatrix} \hat{t}_1 - t_1 \\ \hline \hat{t}_2 - t_2 \\ \hline \hat{t}_{d=1} - t_{d=1} \\ \vdots \\ \hline \hat{t}_{d=i} - t_{d=i} \\ \vdots \\ \hline \hat{t}_{d=q_D} - t_{d=q_D} \end{bmatrix}$$

Expanding Eqs. 118 to 122 for each domain into the 1-by-q_D vector of model-based estimates of total volume θ_D for each of the q_D domains:

$$\mathbf{\theta}_D \approx \hat{\mathbf{\theta}}_D + \mathbf{A}\begin{bmatrix} \hat{t}_1 - t_1 \\ \hline \hat{t}_2 - t_2 \\ \hline \hat{\mathbf{t}}_3 - \mathbf{t}_3 \end{bmatrix} \tag{123}$$

where $\mathbf{A}$ in Eq. 123 is the q_D-by-$(q_D + 2)$ matrix of coefficients from the Taylor-series approximation and the definitions in Eq. 119:

$$\mathbf{A} = \begin{bmatrix} \dfrac{\hat{t}_{d=1}}{\hat{t}_2} & \dfrac{-\hat{t}_1\hat{t}_{d=1}}{\hat{t}_2^2} & \dfrac{\hat{t}_1}{\hat{t}_2} & 0 & \cdots & 0 \\ \hline \dfrac{\hat{t}_{d=1}}{\hat{t}_2} & \dfrac{-\hat{t}_1\hat{t}_{d=1}}{\hat{t}_2^2} & 0 & \dfrac{\hat{t}_1}{\hat{t}_2} & \cdots & 0 \\ \hline \vdots & \vdots & \vdots & \vdots & \ddots & \vdots \\ \hline \dfrac{\hat{t}_{d=1}}{\hat{t}_2} & \dfrac{-\hat{t}_1\hat{t}_{d=1}}{\hat{t}_2^2} & 0 & 0 & \cdots & \dfrac{\hat{t}_1}{\hat{t}_2} \end{bmatrix} \tag{124}$$

$$= \left[\; \dfrac{1}{\hat{t}_2}\hat{\mathbf{t}}_3 \;\middle|\; \dfrac{-\hat{t}_1}{\hat{t}_2^2}\hat{\mathbf{t}}_3 \;\middle|\; \dfrac{\hat{t}_1}{\hat{t}_2}\,\mathbf{I} \;\right]$$

Equations 123 and 124 yield an approximate estimator (Eq. 125) of the covariance matrix for the vector pseudo-estimator of unbiased volume estimates for each domain (D = d) in the population:

$$\hat{\mathbf{V}}\left[\hat{\boldsymbol{\theta}}_D\right]_{s=1,2,3} \approx \mathbf{A}\left(\hat{\mathbf{V}}\left[\begin{array}{c}\hat{t}_1 \\ \hline \hat{t}_2 \\ \hline \hat{\mathbf{t}}_3\end{array}\right]_{s=1,2,3}\right)\mathbf{A}'$$

$$\approx \mathbf{A}\left(\left[\begin{array}{c|c}\mathbf{0} & \mathbf{h}_1 \\ \hline \mathbf{h}_2 & \mathbf{0} \\ \hline \mathbf{H}_3 & \mathbf{0}\end{array}\right]\hat{\mathbf{V}}\left[\begin{array}{c}\hat{\mathbf{t}}_{M=2} \\ \hline \hat{\mathbf{t}}_{M=3}\end{array}\right]_{s=1,2,3}\left[\begin{array}{c|c|c}\mathbf{0} & \mathbf{h}_2' & \mathbf{H}_3' \\ \hline \mathbf{h}_1' & \mathbf{0} & \mathbf{0}\end{array}\right]\right)\mathbf{A}' \qquad (125)$$

Straightforward, though tedious, matrix algebra demonstrates that the population estimate, and the sum of all elements in the Taylor-series approximation of its covariance matrix, for the sum of model-based predicted volumes over all domains estimates equals the direct estimate of the population volume with the M = 3 protocol:

$$\hat{t}_1 = \mathbf{1}\,\hat{\boldsymbol{\theta}}$$

$$\hat{V}\left(\hat{t}_1\right) = \mathbf{1}\mathbf{A}\left(\hat{\mathbf{V}}\left[\begin{array}{c}\hat{t}_1 \\ \hline \hat{t}_2 \\ \hline \hat{\mathbf{t}}_3\end{array}\right]_{s=1,2,3}\right)\mathbf{A}'\mathbf{1}'$$

Therefore, the vector of model-based volume estimates $\boldsymbol{\theta}_D$ for domain D, which uses the estimators in Eqs. 118 and 125, is consistent at the population level with the corresponding direct estimate (t_1), which uses the unbiased M = 3 measurement protocol. The biases in model-based, domain-level variance and covariance estimates, which are caused by the remainders from the first-order Taylor-series approximation, sum to zero when domain-level estimates are summed into population-level estimates. This supports generic inference (Opsomer and others 2007). However, this analysis does not demonstrate that the model-based estimator is unbiased at the domain level.

Finally, the covariance matrix for the model-based volume estimates, which is defined from Eqs. 124 and 125, and the population estimates for the remaining variables measured with the M = 2 protocol equal:

$$\hat{\mathbf{V}}\left[\begin{array}{c}\hat{\mathbf{t}}_{M=2} \\ \hline \hat{\boldsymbol{\theta}}_D\end{array}\right]_{s=1,2,3} = \left[\begin{array}{c|c}\mathbf{I} & \mathbf{0} \\ \hline -\frac{\hat{t}_1}{\hat{t}_2^2}\hat{\mathbf{t}}_3\mathbf{h}_2 + \frac{\hat{t}_1}{\hat{t}_2}\mathbf{H}_3 & \frac{1}{\hat{t}_2}\hat{\mathbf{t}}_3\mathbf{h}_1\end{array}\right]\hat{\mathbf{V}}\left[\begin{array}{c}\hat{\mathbf{t}}_{M=2} \\ \hline \hat{\mathbf{t}}_{M=3}\end{array}\right]_{s=1,2,3}\left[\begin{array}{c|c}\mathbf{I} & \frac{-\hat{t}_1}{\hat{t}_2^2}\mathbf{h}_2'\hat{\mathbf{t}}_3' + \frac{\hat{t}_1}{\hat{t}_2}\mathbf{H}_3' \\ \hline \mathbf{0} & \frac{1}{\hat{t}_2}\mathbf{h}_1'\hat{\mathbf{t}}_3'\end{array}\right] \qquad (126)$$

In this way, the model-based domain estimates ($\boldsymbol{\theta}_D$) may be merged with the direct estimates ($\mathbf{t}_{M=2}$) for subsequent analyses and further application of other linear or non-linear pseudo-estimators (e.g., volume per forested acre with the M = 3 protocol for each domain).

This approach might be useful in other FIA applications. For example, estimates of wood volume cull are needed. Cull is defined by Helms (1998) as "parts of logs deducted ... from gross timber volume because of defects. ... in a standing (live) tree, the cull expressed as a percent of the tree's gross volume is termed the cull factor." Direct measurement of the cull factor often requires destructive sampling, which is not conducted on a permanent FIA sample plot. Rather, estimates of the cull factor are made external to the FIA sampling frame, and prediction equations are constructed to estimate the cull factor for on-frame sample trees based on the standard FIA non-destructive field protocol. If the destructive measurements come from a probability sample, then the methods in this section are relevant. These methods do not produce a PSU weight for individual sample trees from the Phase 2 FIA sample. This is an advantage because it avoids the curious situation where the exact same cull factor is used for a large number of sample trees. This does not necessarily produce more accurate population estimates, but it does avoid anomalous results in the FIA database.

Second-Order Taylor-Series Approximation to Assess Bias

The covariance matrix for non-linear pseudo-estimators can be biased by the first-order Taylor-series approximation because the second-order and higher terms in the expansion are treated as zeros (Ahmed and Al-Khasawneh 2005). In other words, the remainder R in Eq. 91 is assumed to be negligibly small, even though this assumption is rarely tested. The reason for ignoring the second-order terms is that the derivation of the covariance matrix estimator is perceived as too daunting, and the magnitude of the Taylor-series remainder beyond the first-order approximation is perceived to be small with no practical significance. Both perceptions might be inaccurate. This section explores a type of recursive method that simplifies derivation of the second-order Taylor-series approximation to assess the degree of bias in a first-order approximation. If the bias is unacceptably large, then the same methods yield the less biased second-order estimator for the covariance matrix.

For example, continue the relatively complex case of model-based, small-domain volume estimation in Eqs. 115 to 125. Using the methods of Deutsch (1965:Chapter 6) and Särndal and others (1992:173-174, 205-207, 499), the second-order Taylor-series approximation is:

$$\theta_i \approx f\left(\hat{\theta}_i\right) +$$

$$+ \left[d_1 \frac{\partial}{\partial t_1}\left(t_1 \frac{t_{d=i}}{t_2} \right) + \sum_{\substack{j=1 \\ j \neq i}}^{q_D} \left(d_{d=j} \frac{\partial}{\partial t_{d=j}}\left(\frac{t_1 t_{d=i}}{t_{d=j} + \sum_{\substack{k=1 \\ k \neq j}}^{q_D} t_{d=k}} \right) \right) + d_{d=i} \frac{\partial}{\partial t_{d=i}}\left(\frac{t_1 t_{d=i}}{t_{d=i} + \sum_{\substack{k=1 \\ k \neq i}}^{q_D} t_{d=k}} \right) \right] +$$

$$+ \frac{1}{2}\left[\begin{array}{l} d_1^2 \frac{\partial^2}{\partial t_1^2}\left(t_1 \frac{t_{d=i}}{t_2} \right) \\[6pt] + \sum_{\substack{j=1 \\ j \neq i}}^{q_D} \left(d_{d=j} d_1 \frac{\partial^2}{\partial t_{d=j} \partial t_1}\left(\frac{t_1 t_{d=i}}{t_{d=j} + \sum_{\substack{k=1 \\ k \neq j}}^{q_D} t_{d=k}} \right) \right) + d_{d=i} d_1 \frac{\partial^2}{\partial t_{d=i} \partial t_1}\left(\frac{t_1 t_{d=i}}{t_{d=i} + \sum_{\substack{k=1 \\ k \neq i}}^{q_D} t_{d=k}} \right) + \\[6pt] + d_{d=i}^2 \frac{\partial^2}{\partial t_{d=i}^2}\left(\frac{t_1 t_{d=i}}{t_{d=i} + \sum_{\substack{k=1 \\ k \neq i}}^{q_D} t_{d=k}} \right) + \sum_{\substack{m=1 \\ m \neq i}}^{q_D} \left(d_{d=i} d_{d=m} \frac{\partial^2}{\partial t_{d=i} \partial t_{d=m}}\left(\frac{t_1 t_{d=i}}{t_{d=i} + t_{d=m} + \sum_{\substack{k=1 \\ k \neq i \\ k \neq m}}^{q_D} t_{d=k}} \right) \right) + \\[6pt] + \sum_{\substack{j=1 \\ j \neq i}}^{q_D} \left(d_{d=j}^2 \frac{\partial^2}{\partial t_{d=j}^2}\left(\frac{t_1 t_{d=i}}{t_{d=j} + \sum_{\substack{k=1 \\ k \neq j}}^{q_D} t_{d=k}} \right) \right) + \sum_{\substack{j=1 \\ j \neq i}}^{q_D} \sum_{\substack{m=1 \\ m \neq i \\ m \neq j}}^{q_D} \left(d_{d=j} d_{d=m} \frac{\partial^2}{\partial t_{d=j} \partial t_{d=m}}\left(\frac{t_1 t_{d=i}}{t_{d=j} + t_{d=m} + \sum_{\substack{k=1 \\ k \neq j \\ k \neq m}}^{q_D} t_{d=k}} \right) \right) \end{array} \right]$$

(127)

where

$$d_1 = t_1 - \hat{t}_1$$

$$d_{d=i} = t_{d=i} - \hat{t}_{d=i}$$

$$d_{d=j} = t_{d=j} - \hat{t}_{d=j}$$

$$d_{d=k} = t_{d=k} - \hat{t}_{d=k}$$

$$d_{d=m} = t_{d=m} - \hat{t}_{d=m}$$

are evaluated at

$$t_1 = \hat{t}_1$$

$$t_{d=i} = \hat{t}_{d=i}$$

$$t_{d=j} = \hat{t}_{d=j}$$

$$t_{d=k} = \hat{t}_{d=k}$$

$$t_{d=m} = \hat{t}_{d=m}$$

The second-order partial derivatives in Eq. 127, analogous to Eq. 121, are:

$$\left(\frac{\partial^2}{\partial t_1 \partial t_{d=i}}\right)\theta_{d=i}\Bigg|_{\left(\begin{array}{c} t_1 = \hat{t}_1 \\ t_{d=i} = \hat{t}_{d=i} \end{array}\right)} = \frac{1}{\hat{t}_2}\left(1 - \frac{\hat{t}_{d=i}}{\hat{t}_2}\right)$$

$$\left(\frac{\partial^2}{\partial t_{d=j}\partial t_1}\right)\theta_{d=i}\Bigg|_{\left(\begin{array}{c} t_1 = \hat{t}_1 \\ t_{d=j \atop d\neq i} = \hat{t}_{d=j \atop d\neq i} \end{array}\right)} = \frac{-\hat{t}_1\hat{t}_{d=i}}{\hat{t}_2^2}$$

$$\left(\frac{\partial^2}{\partial t_{d=i}\partial t_{d=m}}\right)\theta_{d=i}\Bigg|_{\left(\begin{array}{c} t_{d=i} = \hat{t}_{d=i} \\ t_{d=m \atop m\neq i} = \hat{t}_{d=m \atop m\neq i} \end{array}\right)} = \frac{\hat{t}_1\hat{t}_{d=i}}{\hat{t}_2^2} \qquad (128)$$

$$\left(\frac{\partial^2}{\partial t_{d=i}^2}\right)\theta_{d=i}\Bigg|_{t_{d=i} = \hat{t}_{d=i}} = \frac{\hat{t}_1\hat{t}_{d=i}}{\hat{t}_2^2}$$

where the remaining partial derivatives from Eq. 127 equal zero and do not appear in Eq. 128. Combining terms in Eqs. 127 and 128, the terms that are part of the second-order Taylor-series expansion are:

$$\theta_i \approx f(\hat{\theta}_i) + \left[\left(\frac{\hat{t}_{d=i}}{\hat{t}_2} \right)(t_1 - \hat{t}_1) - \left[\left(\frac{\hat{t}_1 \hat{t}_{d=i}}{\hat{t}_2^2} \right)(d_2) \right] + \left(\frac{\hat{t}_1}{\hat{t}_2} \right)(t_{d=i} - \hat{t}_{d=i}) \right] +$$

$$+ \frac{1}{2} \left[\begin{array}{l} \sum_{j=1}^{q_D} \left((t_1 - \hat{t}_1)(t_{d=j} - \hat{t}_{d=j}) \frac{-\hat{t}_1 \hat{t}_{d=i}}{\hat{t}_2^2} \right) + (t_{d=i} - \hat{t}_{d=i})(t_1 - \hat{t}_1)\left(\frac{1}{\hat{t}_2} \right) + \\ + \sum_{j=1}^{q_D} \frac{\hat{t}_1 \hat{t}_{d=i}}{\hat{t}_2^2}(t_{d=i} - \hat{t}_{d=i})(t_{d=j} - \hat{t}_{d=j}) \end{array} \right]$$

$$\approx f(\hat{\theta}_i) + \left[\frac{\hat{t}_{d=i}}{\hat{t}_2}(t_1 - \hat{t}_1) - \frac{\hat{t}_1 \hat{t}_{d=i}}{\hat{t}_2^2}(t_2 - \hat{t}_2) + \frac{\hat{t}_1}{\hat{t}_2}(t_{d=i} - \hat{t}_{d=i}) \right] +$$

$$+ \frac{1}{2} \left[\begin{array}{l} \frac{-\hat{t}_1 \hat{t}_{d=i}}{\hat{t}_2^2}(t_1 - \hat{t}_1)(t_2 - \hat{t}_2) + \frac{1}{\hat{t}_2}(t_{d=i} - \hat{t}_{d=i})(t_1 - \hat{t}_1) + \\ + \frac{\hat{t}_1 \hat{t}_{d=i}}{\hat{t}_2^2}(t_{d=i} - \hat{t}_{d=i})(t_2 - \hat{t}_2) \end{array} \right]$$

(129)

As in Eqs. 123 to 125, Eq. 129 may be expressed in matrix format for domains $i = 1, \ldots, q_D$ as:

$$\boldsymbol{\theta}_D \approx \hat{\boldsymbol{\theta}}_D + \mathbf{A} \left[\begin{array}{c} \begin{array}{c} \hat{t}_1 - t_1 \\ \hline \hat{t}_2 - t_2 \\ \hline \hat{\mathbf{t}}_3 - \mathbf{t}_3 \end{array} \\ \hline \begin{array}{c} (\hat{t}_2 - t_2)(\hat{\mathbf{t}}_3 - \mathbf{t}_3) \\ \hline (\hat{t}_1 - t_1)(\hat{t}_2 - t_2) \\ \hline (\hat{t}_1 - t_1)(\hat{\mathbf{t}}_3 - \mathbf{t}_3) \end{array} \end{array} \right]$$

(130)

$$\hat{\mathbf{V}}\left[\hat{\boldsymbol{\theta}}_D\right]_{s=1,2,3} \approx \mathbf{A} \left(\hat{\mathbf{V}} \left[\begin{array}{c} \hat{t}_1 \\ \hline \hat{t}_2 \\ \hline \hat{\mathbf{t}}_3 \\ \hline \hat{t}_2 \hat{\mathbf{t}}_3 \\ \hline \hat{t}_1 \hat{t}_2 \\ \hline \hat{t}_1 \hat{\mathbf{t}}_3 \end{array} \right] \right) \mathbf{A}'$$

$$\mathbf{A} = \left[\left[\frac{1}{\hat{t}_2}\hat{\mathbf{t}}_3 \;\middle|\; \frac{-\hat{t}_1}{\hat{t}_2^2}\hat{\mathbf{t}}_3 \;\middle|\; \frac{\hat{t}_1}{\hat{t}_2}\mathbf{I} \right] \;\middle|\; \left[\frac{\hat{t}_1}{2\hat{t}_2^2}\mathbf{I} \;\middle|\; \frac{-\hat{t}_1}{2\hat{t}_2^2}\hat{\mathbf{t}}_3 \;\middle|\; \frac{1}{2\hat{t}_2}\mathbf{I} \right] \right]$$

An empirical estimate of the covariance matrix in Eq. 130 is possible from the sample by adding the appropriate product transformations to form the second partition (Ahmed and Al-Khasawneh 2005). In this example, let the V subscript denote a volume measurement applicable to either the "less-expensive" M = 2 protocol or the "more-expensive" M = 3 protocol, with the domain indicator variable I_i defined in Eqs. 113 and 114. Equation 131 augments the Phase 2 ($s = 2$) estimator (Eq. 113) and Phase 3 ($s = 3$) estimator (Eq. 114), with the additional variables necessary to apply the second-order Taylor-series linear approximation in Eq. 130:

$$
\begin{bmatrix}
\hat{\mathbf{t}}_{M=1} \\
\hline
\hat{\mathbf{t}}_{M=2} \\
\hline
\hat{t}_2\hat{\mathbf{t}}_3
\end{bmatrix}_{s=2}
= \frac{A}{n_{s=2}} \sum_{i\in(s=2)}
\begin{bmatrix}
\mathbf{y}_{M=1} \\
\hline
\mathbf{y}_{M=2} \\
\hline
(y_{M=2})_V I_1 (y_{M=2})_V \\
\vdots \\
(y_{M=2})_V I_i (y_{M=2})_V \\
\vdots \\
(y_{M=2})_V I_{q_D} (y_{M=2})_V
\end{bmatrix}_i
= \frac{A}{n_{s=2}} \sum_{i\in(s=2)}
\begin{bmatrix}
\mathbf{y}_{M=1} \\
\hline
\mathbf{y}_{M=2} \\
\hline
0 \\
\vdots \\
(y_{M=2})_V I_i (y_{M=2})_V \\
\vdots \\
0
\end{bmatrix}_i
$$

and

$$
\begin{bmatrix}
\hat{\mathbf{t}}_{M=1} \\
\hline
\hat{\mathbf{t}}_{M=2} \\
\hline
\hat{t}_2\hat{\mathbf{t}}_3 \\
\hline
\hat{\mathbf{t}}_{M=3} \\
\hline
\hat{t}_1\hat{t}_2 \\
\hline
\hat{t}_1\hat{\mathbf{t}}_3
\end{bmatrix}_{s=3}
= \frac{A}{n_{s=3}} \sum_{i\in(s=3)}
\begin{bmatrix}
\mathbf{y}_{M=1} \\
\hline
\mathbf{y}_{M=2} \\
\hline
(y_{M=2})_V I_1 (y_{M=2})_V \\
\vdots \\
(y_{M=2})_V I_i (y_{M=2})_V \\
\vdots \\
(y_{M=2})_V I_{q_D} (y_{M=2})_V \\
\hline
\mathbf{y}_{M=3} \\
\hline
(y_{M=3})_V (y_{M=2})_V \\
(y_{M=3})_V I_1 (y_{M=2})_V \\
\vdots \\
(y_{M=3})_V I_i (y_{M=2})_V \\
\vdots \\
(y_{M=3})_V I_{q_D} (y_{M=2})_V
\end{bmatrix}_i
= \frac{A}{n_{s=3}} \sum_{i\in(s=3)}
\begin{bmatrix}
\mathbf{y}_{M=1} \\
\hline
\mathbf{y}_{M=2} \\
\hline
0 \\
\vdots \\
(y_{M=2})_V I_i (y_{M=2})_V \\
\vdots \\
0 \\
\hline
\mathbf{y}_{M=3} \\
\hline
(y_{M=3})_V (y_{M=2})_V \\
0 \\
\vdots \\
(y_{M=3})_V I_i (y_{M=2})_V \\
\vdots \\
0
\end{bmatrix}_i
\tag{131}
$$

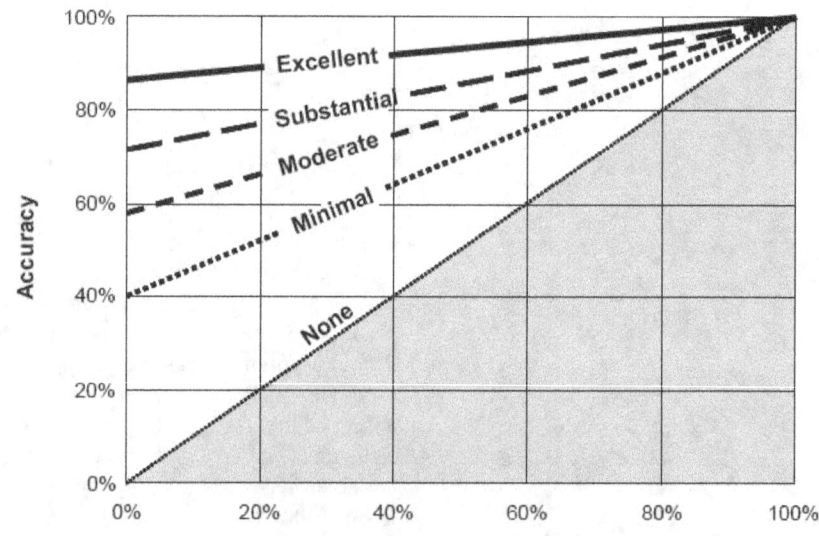

Figure 2. Accuracy required from a remotely sensed, binary variable for gains in precision from stratification (Czaplewski and Patterson 2003). Gains use the metric of design effect (Särndal and others 1992:54) with a design effect of 0.25 for "Excellent," 0.50 for "Substantial," 0.67 for "Moderate," and 0.75 for "Minimal." The required accuracy is highest for common categories and lowest for rare categories. For example, a "Substantial" gain in precision requires an accuracy of 77 percent if the prevalence of a category is 20 percent of the population, but it requires 94 percent accuracy if the prevalence is 80 percent (Czaplewski and Patterson 2003:Table 2).

Therefore, the variances of quadratic terms in Eq. 130, such as $\hat{V}\left[\hat{t}_2 \hat{t}_3\right]$, may be estimated from the realized sample with Eq. 131. However, this may lead to multivariate estimators of high dimension, which can cause numerical problems. Therefore, second-order Taylor-series approximations might be more suitable to occasional assessments of the accuracy of first-order Taylor-series approximations rather than daily application in production settings.

Recall that the first major partition of the matrices in Eq. 130 is from the first-order Taylor-series approximation (Eqs. 120 to 125), and the second partition is from the second order approximation (Eqs. 127 to 129). If the covariance matrix for the model-based estimates $V[\theta_D]$ with both first- and second-order partitions (Eqs. 130 and 131) is approximately the same magnitude (e.g., trace of the covariance matrix) as the covariance matrix without the second-order partitions (Eq. 125), then there is evidence that the bias from the first-order approximation is relatively small, and more confidence may be placed in the simpler first-order approximation. Otherwise, the more complex approximation in Eq. 130 is available in empirical applications, assuming that the extra $(2q_D + 1)$ dimensions of the estimated vector and its covariance matrix allow numerically feasible and stable results. Equation 130 may provide alternative insights into the magnitude of the bias in the first-order Taylor-series approximation of the covariance matrix if realistic assumptions are possible for the relative magnitudes of the second-order terms. Of course, all of this assumes that the third- and higher-order terms in the Taylor-series are negligibly small.

In addition to the Taylor-series method, Wolter (2007:Chapter 9) evaluates alternative estimators of the covariance matrix, including the random group method, the balanced half sample method (pseudo-replication), the jackknife method, the method of generalized variance functions, and the bootstrap method. All these methods generally have identical asymptotic properties, so the concern is with smaller sample sizes. No one estimator is the most accurate or best overall. However, Wolter (2007:363-365) concludes that the

> Taylor-series method is good, perhaps best in some circumstances, in terms of the (mean squared error) and bias criteria, but (other methods) are preferable form the point of view of confidence interval coverage probabilities. … The (Taylor-series) method can generally accommodate any survey estimator (that is a non-linear transformation of the population vector estimate), which includes most statistics used in survey sampling practice. It may be difficult to apply for very complex (transformations), but such statistics do not often occur in practice. … The (Taylor-series) method can deal with any sample design for which an estimator or the covariance matrix can be given.

Accuracy and Registration of Remotely Sensed Data

The success of the statistical estimators presented above depends on the strength of the associations among the remotely sensed auxiliary variables and the study variables. Czaplewski and Patterson (2001, 2003) investigated the gains in statistical efficiency as a function of classification accuracy for categorical variables that are used for stratification (Figure 2). These guidelines are extrapolated through heuristics to RRE and model-based estimators.

The required accuracy is highest for common categories and lowest for rare categories. For example, a substantial gain in statistical efficiency requires an accuracy of 77 percent if the prevalence of a category is 20 percent of the population, but 94 percent accuracy is required if the prevalence is 80 percent (Czaplewski and Patterson 2003:Table 2). In detailed classification systems with many different categories, most categories are relatively rare (e.g., prevalence less than 10 percent).

Because RRE can accommodate categorical variables that are not mutually exclusive and classification systems that are not exhaustive or complete, classification algorithms for remotely sensed data may be separately optimized for each category. For example, a separate dichotomous thematic map may be optimized for each individual category of land cover (e.g., predominantly deciduous forest, predominantly coniferous forest, and mixed forest), which can increase statistical efficiency with remotely sensed data (King 2002). Certain spectral conditions, such as cloud shadows, need not be classified into any category of land cover. This would avoid dilution of accurate predictions with inaccurate predictions.

Czaplewski and Patterson (2001) consider the effects of misclassification error caused by changes in land cover and land use between the acquisition date of the remotely sensed data and the measurement date for the field data. The loss in statistical efficiency is rapid as the agreement deteriorates (Czaplewski and Patterson 2001, 2003; Fattorini and others 2004), regardless of the cause, be it either misclassification error or change in land cover. This is especially true in dynamic landscapes, which are the domains that often have the greatest demand for current monitoring data (Smith 2002; USDA Forest Service 2007).

It is feasible to frequently monitor major changes in land cover with spaceborne sensor data (e.g., Healey and others 2005; Sader and others 2005), and these measurements might substantially improve statistical reliability (e.g., Czaplewski 1999). One might use the post-stratification estimator, but this uses cross-classification of annual, remotely sensed data with relatively rare land cover changes, along with remotely sensed data on more static forest conditions. Extensive cross-classification produces many small strata with few PSUs, especially with annual panel designs. Hence, FIA uses post-stratification solely in the context of the temporally indifferent estimator (Patterson and Reams 2005), which is not amiable to use of remotely sensed estimates of changes in forest cover. Therefore, the post-stratification estimator constrains the potential for using relatively inexpensive time-series of spaceborne, remotely sensed data to improve statistical reliability. For example, Van Deusen (2005) recommends that a single thematic map is best with post-stratification and time-invariant panel estimators. However, RRE can combine remotely sensed data with panel data from the same year without cross-classification over multiple years. Hence, RRE is more amenable to true annual estimation in panel designs that have a time-series of remotely sensed data. In this sense, RRE is much like regression estimation, in which categorical auxiliary data are treated as dichotomous predictor variables rather than strata. RRE does use linear models that might unintentionally introduce model bias. Future research should be designed to evaluate the magnitude of the potential bias and investigate diagnostic tools that detect model bias.

For univariate continuous variables, Särndal and others (1992:250) demonstrate that, under certain assumptions, the correlation between a univariate predictor variable and a univariate population parameter must be 0.5 or higher for the ratio estimator to be more efficient than the Horvitz and Thompson estimator. With very high correlations, e.g., 0.95, the gain in efficiency with the difference estimator is eight-fold (Särndal and others 1992:224). However, similar guidance for multivariate predictors with multiple responses is less well known, and further research is required in the context of FIA applications.

Misregistration between sites measured in the field and measured with remote sensing will degrade associations among remotely sensed and field data, especially in heterogeneous, fine-grained landscapes (McRoberts 2010). Halme and Tomppo (2001), Czaplewski (2005), Magnussen (2007), and Nelson and others (2009) offer methods to improve registration accuracy between Landsat pixel data and field plots.

Discussion

This report presents the static Kalman filter and multivariate pseudo-estimators as a fully integrated and consistent approach to statistical estimation in the FIA program. The Kalman filter is a sophisticated mathematical tool for performing estimation and prediction when data are observed sequentially. In typical applications of the dynamic Kalman filter, this sequence generally follows a time-series. However, in the case of RRE, which is equivalent to the static Kalman filter, the sequence is defined as levels in a hierarchy of data collection. At its roots, Kalman filtering is closely related to Best Linear Unbiased Prediction (BLUP), hence it relies on correlations between variables observed at the different levels to perform predictions. Because the variances and covariances are not observed, they are replaced by estimated moments, so that the resulting estimation approach is Empirical BLUP (EBLUP).

Calibration estimators, which include generalized regression estimators (GREG) as a special case, are widely used in large government sample surveys to gain efficiency and reduce nonresponse bias (Deville and Särndal 1992; Lundström and Särndal 1999). However, Lundström and Särndal caution

> In some surveys, there is an abundance of auxiliary information, so that a selection of the most relevant variables would have to precede the start of the calibration process. We do not necessarily recommend that the totality of the information be used. To blindly add auxiliary information, over and beyond a set of crucial variables, might do more harm than good. These problems are indicated in Nascimento Silva and Skinner (1997) and Lundström (1997). The selection of an 'optimal' set of auxiliary variables is thus not a trivial problem, and will in many cases require the judgment of an experienced survey statistician.

Calibration uses a sub-optimal transformation of multivariate auxiliary information that is invariant for each study variable. Certain auxiliary variables might be well correlated with some study variables but poorly correlated with other study variables. In order to follow the advice of Lundström and Särndal fully, the set of core auxiliary variables must be well correlated with each study variable. This requires prudent intervention by an experienced survey statistician.

In contrast, RRE automatically produces optimal linear weights tailored to each survey variable. If an auxiliary variable is not well correlated with a specific study variable, then it receives little weight. If the same auxiliary variable is highly correlated with a different study variable, then it is heavily weighted. In the worst case, if a certain auxiliary variable is not well correlated with any study variable, it never receives much weight. This integral weighting is achieved through the optimal properties of the RRE, without routine maintenance by an experienced survey statistician. Compared to calibration estimators, RRE is expected to be more robust in the routine production of FIA sample survey statistics, especially if correlations significantly vary over time between FIA study variables and different remotely sensed auxiliary variables.

The statistical estimation methods given in this report accommodate a wide range of estimation scenarios, including multiphase and multistage designs, calibration, nonlinear estimation, and small-area estimation. All of these scenarios use a fully integrated paradigm, which is particularly attractive for a large, multifaceted sample survey. Furthermore, the Kalman filter is a mature field of statistics, and RRE is a special case of the Kalman filter. Solutions to associated numerical hazards are well developed. In addition, the Kalman filter is a well-established time-series estimator. The combination of the static Kalman filter (i.e., RRE) for remotely sensed data with the dynamic Kalman filter for the time-series of FIA panel data is a unified and consistent solution to a complex sample survey design in FIA.

Limitations of the post-stratification estimator

RRE has potential advantages compared to post-stratification used by FIA. RRE correctly accommodates support-regions for sample points (e.g., FIA plots) that straddle strata boundaries (e.g., remotely sensed stand conditions and geopolitical units, such as counties and ownerships) because RRE does not require independent strata to utilize categorical census variables. Similar to a linear calibration estimator or generalized regression estimator (Zhang 2000), RRE treats these variables as dichotomous auxiliary variables. This is similar to regression estimation, in which categorical auxiliary data are treated as dichotomous predictor variables rather than strata.

RRE might be less vulnerable to sampling zeros (e.g., Agresti 1984:54), empty sample post-strata (Zhang 2000), and small, within-stratum sample sizes. These problems can be addressed through merging strata with small sample sizes into similar strata with larger sample sizes. However, this not only reduces statistical efficiency, it is also inappropriate for inference unless the stratum means are expected to be equal (Cochran 1977:134; Särndal and others 1992:411; Knottnerus 2003:169). In a citation to Jagers (1986), Zhang (2000) observes that "post-stratified estimation that ignores the empty sample post-strata is downward biased for non-negative (study-variables)." In contrast, RRE can use the full sample size of annual field plots for a sampled population (e.g., a state with 1000 FIA sample points measured each year) in order to utilize auxiliary data, rather than partition the full sample into numerous small and pseudo-independent strata (e.g., counties separated into major land ownership categories and remotely sensed categories, with as few as four sample points per stratum). In this sense, RRE is similar to a linear calibration estimator or generalized regression estimator (Zhang 2000).

RRE can separately use many different census variables (e.g., separate classifications of land cover, land use, forest type, stand development, and multiple sources, such as several independent land cover maps produced by different agencies or programs, possibly with different legends). Furthermore, there is no need to segment continuous variables (e.g., predicted biomass) into ordinal categories, as in stratification. Moreover, there is no need to cross-classify all such categorical variables into a single, detailed classification system, which is necessary to apply post-stratification. This also reduces problems with small sample sizes in very detailed strata. More important, it opens the door to more complete use of available remotely sensed auxiliary variables.

Problems associated with the post-stratification estimator are avoided with RRE. This is also true with GREG and calibration estimators, which are much less constrained than the post-stratification estimator. With RRE, GREG, and calibration estimators, the strata used with post-stratification estimator are simply replaced with dichotomous categorical predictor variables. The amount and detail of the auxiliary variables is adjusted relative to the available sample size with any of these estimators. Compared to the calibration estimator, RRE and the regression estimators are less vulnerable to poorly correlated auxiliary variables. The RRE has advantages over all these alternatives. RRE can combine data from many different sources and at different scales within a prediction-based framework. In doing so, a number of previously disparate estimation problems are unified, such as small-area estimation, domain estimation, and calibration (Opsomer, personal communication). This unified approach harmonizes the broad array of estimates produced by FIA.

Multivariate estimates

The vast majority of statistical literature in sample surveys deals with estimates of univariate population parameters. However, large government statistical programs, like FIA, estimate thousands of variables from the same sample. This has been successfully accomplished with repetitive application of univariate estimators (e.g., Scott and others 2005). However, simultaneous estimation of multiple population variables is necessary to estimate the covariance matrix for multivariate estimates. This covariance matrix is an integral component to the pseudo-estimators in Eqs. 89 to 131 above, which are used to estimate covariance matrices for rates, ratios, proportions, and products. They also serve at the core of variance estimators that accommodate missing data and small-area estimation with certain model-based approaches. They are even capable of variance estimation in the context of standard linear programming applications from operations research (Knottnerus 2003:354). Therefore, RRE is relevant to core needs in programs like FIA.

Independence among sampling phases

RRE assumes that all phases in a multiphase design are mutually independent. However, often times one phase is a sub-sample of another phase. Recall that the estimators assume an infinite population, and the joint inclusion probabilities are zero among any units in the realized sample. Even if the population is assumed to be finite, the joint inclusion probabilities are very small whenever the sampling fraction is small, in which case multiple phases may be considered "almost-independent" (Knottnerus 2003:258, 262). This condition is true for FIA. If the finite population model is used with a large sampling fraction, then Eq. 9 may be used with the non-null cross-covariance matrix $\mathbf{C}$ between different phases, an estimator for which is given by Knottnerus (2003:316, 375, 389). Similar methods (Knottnerus 2003:392) might be used to combine different annual panels in FIA.

Risk management with complex sampling designs

The traditional FIA system uses a very simple sampling design: simple systematic sampling with equal selection probabilities and the post-stratification estimator. However, more complex sampling designs are needed to fully accommodate multiple remote sensing technologies. Databases need embellishment. New estimators must be assimilated into the information management system. This complexity is accompanied by risk, but risks can be managed.

In general, RRE equals the design-based estimator $\hat{\mathbf{t}}_X$ plus an adjustment (e.g., Eqs. 2, 12, 22, and 132). The adjustment vector is the matrix-weighted ($\mathbf{K}$) difference between the more precise ancillary vector estimate $\hat{\mathbf{t}}_Z$ of a partition of the population vector and the relatively less precise estimate of a larger partition of the population vector, or the full population vector, from a more detailed stage or phase $\left(\mathbf{H}\,\hat{\mathbf{t}}_X\right)$. In a recursive application of RRE, multiple adjustment vectors are generated. These may be grouped into a single term. The following is a generic representation of RRE after the jth recursion:
where

$$\left(\hat{\mathbf{t}}_{\text{RRE}}\right)_j = \hat{\mathbf{t}}_X + \mathbf{K}_j\left[\left(\hat{\mathbf{t}}_Z\right)_j - \mathbf{H}_i\left(\hat{\mathbf{t}}_{\text{RRE}}\right)_{j-1}\right] + \cdots + \mathbf{K}_2\left[\left(\hat{\mathbf{t}}_Z\right)_2 - \mathbf{H}_2\left(\hat{\mathbf{t}}_{\text{RRE}}\right)_1\right] + \mathbf{K}_1\left[\left(\hat{\mathbf{t}}_Z\right)_1 - \mathbf{H}_1\,\hat{\mathbf{t}}_X\right]$$

$$= \hat{\mathbf{t}}_X + \left(\mathbf{t}_{\text{adj}}\right)_j \tag{132}$$

$$\left(\mathbf{t}_{\text{adj}}\right)_j = \sum_{i=j,j-1,\cdots 1} \mathbf{K}_i\left[\left(\hat{\mathbf{t}}_Z\right)_i - \mathbf{H}_i\left(\hat{\mathbf{t}}_{\text{RRE}}\right)_{i-1}\right] \text{ and } \left(\hat{\mathbf{t}}_{\text{RRE}}\right)_0 = \hat{\mathbf{t}}_X$$

Therefore, RRE can be readily separated into two additive terms: (1) the traditional FIA design-based vector estimate $\left(\hat{\mathbf{t}}_X\right)$ for a single panel without post-stratification, and (2) a vector of adjustments $\left(\mathbf{t}_{\text{adj}}\right)_j$ that improve statistical efficiency through the recursive filtering of all auxiliary information. Even the

RRE and calibration weights in Eq. 43 at the PSU level are conveniently factored into the sum of two terms: the simple, design-based π expanded value (i.e., a_k in Särndal and others 1992:43), and a term that fully captures the residual difference between the simple π estimator and the more efficient RRE estimator. This structure might reduce the complexities of temporally dynamic state-space estimates or plot expansion factors. If there are concerns with the reliability of FIA estimates that use auxiliary, remotely sensed information, then the adjustment term may be simply omitted, leaving only a design-based π panel estimate based on the simple random sample of FIA plots in that panel.

Furthermore, $(\mathbf{t}_{adj})_j$ equals the residual difference between the simple FIA panel estimate and RRE that contains all auxiliary information. If the size of $(\mathbf{t}_{adj})_j$ is large relative to its covariance matrix, then there is empirical evidence of an anomaly that requires investigation. This form of quality assurance should be an integral part of the FIA data processing procedures.

Non-sampling errors are always a concern in any large government survey. They include measurement and numerical round-off errors and mistakes in data transcription, computer programming, and sampling frame construction. Non-sampling errors can introduce unrecognized bias into estimators of population totals and variance estimators. FIA already uses extensive edits to detect certain measurement and transcription errors. FIA also conducts thorough tests of computer programs and algorithms. Analyses of residuals that are discussed above can further reduce risk of more subtle biases for some variables (Francisco 2003:71; Estevao and Särndal 2006). For example, Knottnerus (2003:255) uses a runs test that might be applied to residuals for study variables that are sorted on their corresponding residuals for auxiliary variables.

Design-based and **design-consistent** estimators are the least risky. These include estimators previously used by FIA for decadal periodic surveys and estimators for a single panel of annual FIA data[1]. RREs in Eqs. 21 to 70 are design-consistent, similar to ratio and regression estimators. These introduce little incremental risk if implementation and auxiliary estimates are reliable. Residual analyses further mitigate any remaining risk.

The small-area, missing data, and prediction estimators in Eqs. 82 to 131 are model-based methods. They assure internal consistency to maintain credibility. However, these are more risky because they depend upon the reliability of the model (Schreuder and others 1993). Furthermore, they are used to compensate for small sample sizes, which limits the power of residual analyses to detect model prediction bias and non-sampling errors. These latter risks are unavoidable. They are part of the cost of maximizing the utility of expensive field data to estimate small segments of the sampled population. These risks should be clearly communicated to users of such estimates.

FIA already improves data quality through external reviews of new statistical reports by State Forest Service agencies and other external users. This requires routine intervention by FIA staff. RRE might increase the amount of quality assurance procedures conducted by FIA staff. Some of this could require the expertise a senior statistician. These procedures include residual analyses, diagnosis of the cause for suspicious residuals, and elimination of the source of any anomalies. Some unexpectedly large residuals might be caused by bias in model predictions. Other suspicious residuals might be caused by non-random errors, such as systematic errors in computer programs or data collection. Residual analyses could be automated and made more user friendly for FIA staff.

---

[1] Scott and others (2005) treat segments of a single FIA field plot that contains multiple stratification conditions as independent in the variance estimator for a single panel. They acknowledge that this will bias the variance estimator, but they assume the bias is inconsequential. This assumption might be considered model-based. FIA estimators, which use the moving average or temporally indifferent estimator (Patterson and Reams 2005) to combine multiple panels, might also be considered model-based. They are unbiased for the model that assumes a static population among panels. FIA uses volume equations that predict tree volume based on measurements of DBH and tree height. These models are fit to historical, off-frame, purposive samples of trees. Therefore, FIA volume estimates are model-based.

Concerns may arise about the data quality of remotely sensed auxiliary information. If left unattended, measurement bias in auxiliary data can propagate into bias in population estimates. Coulston (2008) provides an example that involves FIA's Phase 1 photo-interpretation. Other concerns may arise during analysis of RRE residuals. In the worst case, RRE auxiliary adjustments, i.e., the $\mathbf{H}\hat{\mathbf{t}}_x$ term in $[\hat{\mathbf{t}}_z - \mathbf{H}\hat{\mathbf{t}}_x]$ from Eq. 132, may be omitted. This leaves the purely design-based estimate, i.e., $\hat{\mathbf{t}}_z$, which is the least risky. This retreat from the RRE estimator obviates risks to data quality caused by anomalies with the remotely sensed or other geospatial sources of auxiliary data, although it also foregoes any gains in efficiency through RRE. The sequential, object-oriented nature of RRE readily permits retention of reliable auxiliary data sets and omission of suspect sets.

Seminal Literature

The RRE estimators used in this report are special cases of the Kalman filter, which originated and matured within the discipline of aerospace engineering during the 1960s and 1970s. The original applications were primarily for astronavigation in the Apollo lunar mission and the Mariner interplanetary space probes. The astrionics of that era used 8-bit digital processors, which are primitive by today's 32- and 64-bit standards. Astronautical navigation systems assimilate time-series of imperfect predictions from linearized astrophysical models plus "noisy" measurements from diverse sensor arrays. Aerospace engineers developed model-based statistical estimators to process this multivariate time-series of stochastic inputs to produce estimates of spacecraft location and trajectory. Mission success demanded efficient and unbiased statistical estimators with accurate covariance matrices from the model-based approach. The consequences of failure were unpleasant, such as reports on the evening news and Congressional inquiries, or truly tragic in the case of manned space exploration.

Statisticians addressed these challenges through theoretical and applied techniques, including the Kalman filter and numerical analysis. One comprehensive and rigorous treatise is Peter Maybeck's (1979) book, *Stochastic Models, Estimation, and Control*. Maybeck covers relevant mathematical statistics, probability theory, linear time-series models, and numerically robust variations of the Kalman filter.

Another contemporaneous source is Gerald J. Bierman's (1977) book, *Factorization Methods for Discrete Sequential Estimation*. Bierman provides a concise description of the mathematical statistics that relates the Kalman filter to linear models that are more familiar to statisticians who are not involved with aerospace engineering. More importantly, Bierman thoroughly covers the problem of divergence, solutions to which are critically important to successful applications of the Kalman filter. Aerospace engineers use the term divergence when their navigation system misdirects a missile, spacecraft, or aircraft to miss the target. Statisticians consider the same phenomenon as an unrecognized bias in a model-based estimator. The source of the bias is often misspecification of the model, and Bierman covers embellishments of the Kalman filter that estimate biases caused by inaccurate or incomplete models or parameters. Divergence may also be caused by numerical errors, and Bierman develops numerically robust versions of the Kalman filter that remain important in applications to spacecraft navigation (e.g., Garcia-Yarnoz and others 2006).

Andrew Jazwinski's (1970) treatise, *Stochastic Processes and Filtering Theory*, is another key reference. He tends to cover the detailed mathematic statistics in more depth than Bierman and Maybeck, but the latter authors provide a more useful perspective for applications.

None of these three seminal references, which are in Academic Press's series on Mathematics in Science and Engineering, seem to be well recognized in the sample survey literature. Anyone interested in applications of RRE or the Kalman filter to complex sample surveys would be well served by thoroughly studying these references.

More current references are available. *Kalman Filtering: Theory and Practice Using MATLAB* by Grewal and Andrews (2001) is a comprehensive and concise reference. It includes computer code for numerous algorithms. The 2001 comprehensive treatise by Yaakov Bar-Shalom, Xiao-Rong Li, and Thiagalingam Kirubarajan covers material relevant to sample survey estimation with RRE, despite its application-oriented title, *Estimation with Applications to Tracking and Navigation: Theory Algorithms and Software*. Charles K. Chui and Guanrong Chen's (2009) heavily cited treatise *Kalman Filtering with Real-Time Applications* is an excellent source for theoretical and applied details.

Knottnerus' (2003) book, *Sample Survey Theory: Some Pythagorean Perspectives,* makes the first direct connection between the static Kalman filter and Pythagorean regression. He uses the latter as the basis for his standard sampling model as a unifying approach to estimation for complex sample surveys. Knottnerus (2003:50) shows how the recursive methods from the Kalman filter can use "additional information … (to improve) an initial estimate or, in general, how the estimator from the previous step can be improved by using new information." Knottnerus also incorporates auxiliary information as constraints. However, Knottnerus does not use the state space model, which I frequently use to further simply complex estimators, and Knottnerus does not emphasize importance of numerical risks and residual analysis.

Finally, many of Knottnerus' sample survey concepts are derived from Särndal and others' (1992) book, *Model Assisted Survey Sampling*. While the authors use finite population sampling theory in their book, it remains influential to this report, in which the infinite population perspective is used.

Future Research and Development

The estimators introduced above are merely examples of many types of complex sampling designs that may be accommodated with sequential application of RREs and subsequent non-linear, multivariate pseudo-estimators. These examples represent basic modules that may be assembled in various ways to incorporate complex sample survey data generated by diverse remote sensing technologies and administrative census statistics. Some of the more obvious opportunities will be touched upon here. These may be the subject of future research.

The two-phase design with cluster plots (Eqs. 62 to 70) may be expanded to include remotely sensed predictions of continuous and categorical variables from full-coverage, wall-to-wall Landsat data (i.e., $M = 0$ and $s = U$). Multivariate predictions for an individual pixel, or a small window of pixels covering a support-region (Czaplewski 2005; McRoberts 2010), can be registered to the location of the FIA plot that is also measured with the photo-interpretation protocol ($M = 1$). Census statistics from all pixels could improve estimated population totals from the photo-interpretation and FIA field protocols.

Summary statistics from a larger support-region of contiguous Landsat pixels can be matched with summary statistics from a photo-interpreted cluster plot. Then, census statistics from Landsat could improve estimated population totals for variables photo-interpreted over the cluster plots, which, in turn, could improve estimated population totals from the FIA field protocol. Likewise, remotely sensed measurements and predictions from coarser-resolution satellites, such as MODIS, could be assimilated at the scale of a larger support-region, analogous to a cluster plot that is also measured with a sample or local census of photo-interpreted observations. A similar approach might be best for spaceborne LiDAR data if they can be registered to a relatively large cluster plot (e.g., 25 to 1000 acres) with sufficient accuracy, but those data cannot be adequately registered to the relatively small support-regions (e.g., 0.05 to 1 acre) for photo-interpretation or FIA field measurements.

A Phase 2 sub-sample of airborne LiDAR data could be registered to photo-interpreted data and FIA field data, and a much larger Phase 1 sample of airborne LiDAR data could be used to improve estimates of forest biomass. Or airborne LiDAR could be acquired for a relatively large support-region (cluster plot), including the FIA plot as a sub-set, and used like the photo-interpreted data for a cluster plot in Eqs. 57 to 61. Other design modules might include collocating samples of spaceborne and airborne LiDAR data, which might be facilitated by collocated, high-resolution aerial photography that support other remote sensing protocols. The model-based methods in Eqs. 115 to 125 can use the association between spaceborne and airborne LiDAR data at the population level to improve precision of estimates for small domains.

Knottnerus (2003:325) uses RRE to assure logical correspondence among study variables. For example, the difference in the areas of forest cover at two different times should agree with a separate estimate of the annual net rate of change in forest extent. Mandallaz (2008:188) calls this time additivity. Knottnerus and van Duin (2006) cover recursive restriction methods to assure additivity among complex statistical tables. Another example is the difference between estimates of timber removals from FIA field plots and estimates of timber consumption from the independent FIA Timber Products Output (TPO) survey (Smith 2002). The state vector in a Kalman filter might be configured to achieve these types of compatibilities. This will likely involve non-null cross-covariances $\mathbf{C}$ among estimates of the state vector and a separate measurement vector, which may be accommodated with the gain matrix $\mathbf{K}$ in Eq. 9. The variance estimate for external estimates, such as TPO, might be problematic; sub-optimal methods might be appropriate (e.g., Knottnerus 2003:334).

FIA field data may be missing because of denied access to private lands or unsafe field conditions. These areas are in the target population, but not the sampled population. In addition, an FIA field plot might not exist in certain known, rare, analytically important conditions, such as the area of a county with state-managed public lands, or lands enrolled in the USDA Conservation Reserve Program. Such conditions are part of the sampled population, but they represent sampling zeros. These anomalies might be addressed through purely model-based pseudo-estimators for missing field data (e.g., Eqs. 91 to 99). Estimates for missing-data domains might be improved with photo-interpretation of high-resolution aerial photography that covers FIA plots that are not measured because of denied access or hazardous field conditions. It might be possible to join together one or more model-based estimators for missing data and the design-based estimator for the remainder of the target population. Other complex estimators might be possible through other methods developed in this paper and elsewhere (e.g., Särndal and Lundström 2008). Further study should assess feasibility.

There are different approaches to small-area estimation. Inverse calibration in Eqs. 82 to 86 and RE in Eq. 88 are examples of different alternatives. While the literature in small-area estimation is large, very little of it covers opportunities offered by the multivariate vector response in RRE. Further research is needed, which might lead to improvements in internal consistency and variance estimators that combine design-based estimates for the sampled population and model-based estimates for the target population that cannot be sampled.

In all cases, it is important to use numerically stable methods with RRE. The special case of RRE as a calibration estimator is considered by Czaplewski (in prep.[b]). Bierman's (1977) factorization methods use and preserve triangular square roots of the covariance matrices, which would reduce storage requirements and numerical errors in a database. Bierman's UD decomposition is a modified form of the Gram-Schmidt orthogonalization. These methods generally replace matrix inverses with element-by-element scalar division. A matrix language is not necessary. Numerical studies are required to understand better the dimensions of the matrix equations that can be reliably processed with a digital computer. Future development should consider implementation of these powerful algorithms in database software, such as Oracle™, which should facilitate transfer of related research to the FIA production environment.

Robust RRE requires an accurate estimate of the covariance matrix. However, the sample covariance matrix is not necessarily an accurate estimator whenever the number of variables is large relative to the sample size (Ledoit and Wolf 2004). Dimensions for the auxiliary variables increase multiplicatively with cross-classification of polychotomous categorical variables. However, cross-classification might not substantively increase statistical efficiency with remotely sensed, auxiliary data (Czaplewski in prep.[b]). Furthermore, covariance shrinking can improve reliability of Kalman filtering with high-dimension state vectors (Furrer and Bengtsson 2007) and other applications that face similar challenges (e.g., Schafer and Strimmer 2005; Bickel and Levina 2008). Ledoit and Wolf (2003) provide a relatively straightforward algorithm. Furthermore, orthogonalization and factorization methods (e.g., Bierman 1997) might mitigate impacts of estimation error with these covariance matrices. Monitoring of residuals might detect consequences of imprecise estimates of the covariance matrix. Further research can reveal the best compromise between reliability of RRE and the detail of remotely sensed, auxiliary data and FIA study variables that are incorporated into the state vector.

Prudent applications of RRE strongly depend upon analyses of recursive residuals, which are called the innovation sequence in the Kalman filter literature. Additional research is required for residual analyses in the context of the recursive static Kalman filter as applied to complex sample surveys, such as FIA. This research might be facilitated with the robust methods with census data and other numerically stable methods. These methods sequentially apply orthogonally transformed auxiliary variables one at a time. Each has a corresponding variance estimate, which can standardize the scalar residual difference between the auxiliary measurement datum and its estimate from the state vector. Standardized residuals that are unexpectedly large offer a powerful diagnostic. The auxiliary variable associated with a large residual may be omitted from the final RRE. Further study is needed to determine the order in which scalar auxiliary variables enter the RRE. There might be opportunities to use a stepwise approach to this order to improve estimates of FIA study variables and avoid over-zealous application of remotely sensed auxiliary variables (Eq. 38).

FIA statistical reports can be more conveniently produced with a vector of unique RRE expansion values for each individual PSU (see "Optimal PSU Expansion Valuesfor Each FIA Plot"). The section "Robust Numerics" also introduces practical methods to mitigate numerical errors inherent with RE. In order to ensure numerical stability of matrix inversions, these methods decompose the problematic covariance matrix for the estimates of the auxiliary data. The result is an upper triangular and diagonal matrix. This structure differs from the assumptions used for the expansion values in Eqs. 76 and 81. Further research is needed to express the results from robust RRE as plot expansion values. In addition, it would be convenient from the analysis perspective to express results from pseudo-estimators as expansion values (see "A Model-Based Estimator for Small-Domain Predictions"). This too requires further research.

As an alternative, Sõstra and Traat (2009) use Knottnerus' RRE to derive simpler scalar weights that depend solely on the auxiliary variables; the same scalar weight applies to all study variables measured at a sampled PSU. These weights are sub-optimal, meaning they do not replicate the minimum variance linear estimator. However, scalar weights are more compatible with the current FIA database, which uses scalar expansion factors for area and volume. Additional research would evaluate the compromise between statistical efficiency and database convenience.

Further research is needed to develop fully the equivalency of the RRE with complex sample survey estimators that are available in the statistical literature (e.g., Eqs. 39 to 43). This will better define the statistical properties of the RRE in the context of sample survey estimators, and it might suggest algebraic identities that allow the RRE to be better expressed as analytical sampling weights (e.g., Eq. 43). The view of complex sample survey estimation from the perspective of the RRE and the Kalman filter might pave the way for rapid development of relatively simple survey estimators.

RRE applies the static Kalman filter to complex sampling designs for data gathered at one point in time. The Kalman filter is most often applied to dynamic systems that change over time. Therefore, the Kalman filter provides a unified approach to processing complex sample survey panel data. Future research will study the Kalman filter as a recursive, object-oriented approach to assimilating the time-series of FIA field data, both the Phase 2 and Phase 3 sub-samples for forest health monitoring, with multiple asynchronous time-series of remotely sensed data from different sensors.

Future research should focus on the object-oriented approaches of recursive estimation for population parameters and recursive Taylor series approximations for variance estimation. Not only will these approaches simplify complex estimation problems, they might also facilitate adaptation of estimators, software, and databases to future remote sensing and other technologies, while minimizing impact on database maintenance and development.

Conclusions

By an Act of Congress (Gillespie 1999), FIA began the transition from a state-by-state, decadal, periodic survey to an annual panel survey in all states. The transition is nearly complete. The only limitation is a modest increase in annual funding. The current statistical methods used with FIA panel data are essentially identical to those used for the FIA period surveys in the 1950s to 1990s. The most current data for PSUs from different panels, which are measured in different years, are treated as though they were measured at the same instant, hence the term temporally indifferent estimation (Patterson and Reams 2005). Efficiency is improved with post-stratification based on remotely sensed classifications of forest and non-forest cover at one point in time. The next era of FIA will build on this foundation by more fully incorporating different types of remotely sensed data (USDA Forest Service 2007). In anticipation of this corporate strategy, reliable and practical statistical methods must be developed and thoroughly tested in the near future so that they can be confidently incorporated into FIA production procedures.

This report is merely an initial step needed to satisfy this requirement. It represents one possible blueprint for a consistent and unified statistical engine within the FIA production system for national statistics on forest ecosystems. It portrays a design intended to be a reliable, adaptable, cohesive, and comprehensive mathematical system for improving FIA estimates with diverse, remote sensing technologies. The same mathematical paradigm is directly extendable to time-series of FIA panel data. Future research must rigorously test this integrated design. There are viable alternatives under development (e.g., Roesch 1999, 2008). Future research will need to compare alternatives to the current FIA methods.

Use of complex, remotely sensed data requires a more complex statistical system. Introduction of additional statistical complexity into an already complex production system incurs some risk. Comprehensive pilot tests are critical before implementation is attempted. Numerous pilot studies have already investigated innovative uses of remotely sensed data relevant to FIA (Czaplewski in prep.[b]). These have involved challenges in acquisition and use of remotely sensed data. Database management has also presented demanding challenges. Development of the necessary statistical estimators has been especially elusive in these pilot studies because statistical complexities are inseparably associated with the technologies and logistics of remote sensing. No amount of innovation in remote sensing has full value to FIA statistical products until statistically combined with field data to form better population estimates. The statistical estimators introduced above appear capable of accommodating many types of remotely sensed data. However, they must be thoroughly tested with realistic numerical datasets and published in a journal with sufficient statistical expertise in the peer-review and editorial processes.

Post-stratification is a common and simple approach in large government survey programs of natural resources, such as FIA (Mandallaz 2008). Its results are conveniently captured in the large FIA database (McRoberts and others 2004) with relative ease, and it poses no extraordinary risk. However, its potential for improving population estimates with remotely sensed data is limited. RRE is more complex, but it can improve accuracy and efficiency by assimilating larger quantities of auxiliary remotely sensed information. This might reduce the sample size needed to achieve a minimum accuracy criterion. A decision to convert from post-stratification to RRE depends on the compromise among implementation costs, risks, efficiency, accuracy, and long-term cost savings. The decision is reversible. If the costs of implementation and risk management with RRE are unacceptable in FIA, then RRE might remain an attractive choice for special analytical studies whenever extra accuracy merits extra effort.

RRE offers opportunities to improve detailed sample survey products with remotely sensed and other geospatial auxiliary data known as complex auxiliary information (Estevao and Särndal 2006). However, judicious applications require attention to numerical problems and monitoring for other anomalies. Otherwise, results are not necessarily reliable. These problems are not well recognized in the sample survey literature, which might explain the paucity of survey applications that use RRE, especially given widespread popularity of the closely related Kalman filter in engineering, econometrics, atmospheric sciences, and physical oceanography.

Given existing and emerging remote sensing technologies, each with their own unique capabilities and limitations, and the inherent complexity of large statistical monitoring programs with diverse objectives, design modules may be added and removed in the FIA sampling and estimation processes. New types of relatively inexpensive, remotely sensed measurements can be used to improve precision and efficiency of estimates made with FIA field data. The value of all these complex design modules depends on strong empirical correlations and associations between measurements made with different protocols, different support-regions (e.g., cluster plots), the incremental cost of adding these modules, and support from a flexible information management system that can readily process and distribute statistical estimates.

RRE is a powerful solution to difficult sample survey problems. It separates a large complex sampling design into small modules, each of which is more easily addressed. These modules are sequentially reassembled into more efficient and accurate population estimates. RRE offers the opportunity to consider complex sampling designs that would otherwise be too intimidating. The dynamic Kalman filter further extends closely related opportunities with the time-series of FIA panel data. Särndal (2007) hypothesizes that calibration estimation might offer the potential to "generalize earlier theories or approaches." Based on the insights offered in this report, RRE might provide an even more complete foundation to make further advances in complex sample survey estimation.

References

Achard, F., R. Defries, H. Eva, M. Hansen, P. Mayaux, and H.J. Stibig. 2007. Pan-tropical monitoring of deforestation. Environmental Research Letters 2:1-11.

Agresti, A. 2007. An introduction to categorical data analysis. Hoboken, NJ: John Wiley & Sons. 400 p.

Ahmed, M.S. and M. Al-Khasawneh. 2005. Ratio and regression type estimators using higher order moments. Statistics in Transition 7(1):13-20.

Aldrich, R. 1979. Remote sensing of wildland resources: a state-of-the-art review. Gen. Tech. Rep. RM-71. Fort Collins, CO: U.S. Department of Agriculture, Forest Service, Rocky Mountain Forest and Range Experiment Station. 56 p.

American Forest Council. 1992. First report of the blue ribbon panel on forest inventory and analysis. Washington, DC: U.S. Department of Agriculture, Forest Service, Forest Inventory, Economics, and Recreation Research. 10 p.

Anderson, E., Z. Bai, C. Bischof, S. Blackford, J. Demmel, J.J. Dongarra, J. Du Croz, A. Greenbaum, S. Hammarling, A. McKenney, and D. Sorensen. 1999. LAPACK Users' Guide, 3rd ed. Philadelphia, PA: Society for Industrial and Applied Mathematics. 397 p.

Ashok, S., K. Varshney Pramod, and K. Arora Manoj. 2007. Robustness of change detection algorithms in the presence of registration errors. Photogrammetric Engineering and Remote Sensing 73(4):375-383.

Baffetta, F., L. Fattorini, S. Franceschi, and P. Corona. 2009. Design-based approach to k-nearest neighbours technique for coupling field and remotely sensed data in forest surveys. Remote Sensing of Environment 113(3):463-475.

Bailey, R. 2004. Identifying ecoregion boundaries. Environmental Management. 34:S14-S26.

Bailey, R.G. 1995. Description of the ecoregions of the United States. 2nd ed. Misc. Publ. No. 1391. Washington, DC: U.S. Department of Agriculture, Forest Service. 108 p.

Bar-Shalom, Y., X.-R. Li, and T. Kirubarajan. 2001. Estimation with applications to tracking and navigation. New York, NY: John Wiley & Sons. 584 p.

Bauer, M., T. Burk, A. Ek, P. Coppin, S. Lime, T. Walsh, D. Walters, W. Befort, and D. Heinzen. 1994. Satellite inventory of Minnesota forest resources. Photogrammetric Engineering and Remote Sensing 60(3):287-298.

Bauer, M.E., M.M. Hixson, and B.J. Davis. 1978. Area estimation of crops by digital analysis of Landsat data. Photogrammetric Engineering and Remote Sensing 44:1033-1043.

Bechtold, W. and C. Scott. 2005. The Forest Inventory and Analysis plot design. In: Bechtold, W. and P.L. Patterson, eds. The enhanced Forest Inventory and Analysis program—national sampling design and estimation procedures. Gen. Tech. Rep. SRS-80. Asheville, NC: U.S. Department of Agriculture, Forest Service, Southern Research Station: 27-42.

Bickel, P.J. and E. Levina. 2008. Regularized estimation of large covariance matrices. Annals of Statistics 36:199-227.

Bickford, A., C. Mayer, and K. Ware. 1963. An efficient sampling design for forest inventory: the northeastern forest resurvey. Journal of Forestry 826-833.

Bierman, G. 1977. Factorization methods for discrete sequential estimation. New York, NY: Academic Press. 241 p.

Binder, D.A. and M.A. Hidiroglou. 1988. Sampling in time. In: Krishnaiah, P.R. and C.R. Rao, eds. Handbook of statistics, vol. 6: sampling. Elsevier, Amsterdam: 187-211.

Blackard, J.A., M.V. Finco, E.H. Helmer, G.R. Holden, M.L. Hoppus, D.M. Jacobs, A.J. Lister, G.G. Moisen, M.D. Nelson, R. Riemann, B. Ruefenacht, D. Salajanu, Weyermann, K.C. Winterberger, T.J. Brandeis, R.L. Czaplewski, R.E. McRoberts, P.L. Patterson, and R.P. Tymcio. 2008. Mapping U.S. forest biomass using nationwide forest inventory data and moderate resolution information. Remote Sensing of Environment 112(4):1658-1677.

Blundell, R. and J.M. Robin. 1999. Estimation in large and disaggregated demand systems: an estimator for conditionally linear systems. Journal of Applied Econometrics 14:209-232.

Boggs, D., M. Ghil, and C. Keppenne. 1995. A stabilized sparse-matrix U-D square-root implementation of a large-state extended kalman filter. Proceedings: WMO second international symposium on assimilation of observations in meteorology and oceanography; Tokyo, Japan; WMO/TD No. 651: 219-224.

Brandtberg, T., T.A. Warner, R.E. Landenberger, and J.B. McGraw. 2003. Detection and analysis of individual leaf-off tree crowns in small footprint, high sampling density LiDAR data from the eastern deciduous forest in North America. Remote Sensing of Environment 85(3):290-303.

Breidt, J. and J. Opsomer. 2008. Endogenous post-stratification in surveys: classifying with a sample-fitted model. Annals of Statistics 36(1):403-427.

Breiman, L., J. Friedman, C.J. Stone, and R.A. Olshen. 1984. Classification and regression trees. Belmont, CA: Wadsworth International Group. 368 p.

Brown, P.J. 1982. Multivariate calibration. Journal of the Royal Statistical Society. Series B (Methodological) 44(3):287-321.

Card, D. 1982. Using known map category marginal frequencies to improve estimates of thematic map accuracy. Photogrammetric Engineering and Remote Sensing 48(3):431-439.

Carmel, Y., D. Dean, and C. Flather. 2001. Combining location and classification error sources for estimating multi-temporal database accuracy. Photogrammetric Engineering and Remote Sensing 7:865-872.

Casady, R.J. and R. Valliant. 1993. Conditional properties of post-stratified estimators under normal theory. Survey Methodology 19:183-192.

Catts, G., N. Cost, R. Czaplewski, and P. Snook. 1987. Preliminary results from a method to update timber resource statistics in North Carolina. In: Everitt, J. and P. Nixon, eds. Color aerial photography and videography in the plant sciences and related fields: proceedings of the eleventh biennial workshop on color aerial photography in the plant sciences: American Society for Photogrammetry and Remote Sensing; Hoblitzelle Auditorium; Agricultural Experiment Station; Weslaco, TX: 39-52.

Chrisman, N.R. 1983. Beyond accuracy assessment: correction of misclassification. In: Proceedings: 5th international symposium on computer assisted cartography and the International Society of Photogrammetry and Remote Sensing Commission IV; 1982 August 22-28; Crystal City, VA: 123-132.

Chui, C.K. and G. Chen. 2009. Kalman filtering with real-time applications. Springer series in information sciences, vol. 17. 4th ed. Berlin, Germany: Springer-Verlag. 229 p.

Cochran, W. 1977. Sampling techniques, 3rd ed. Hoboken, NJ: John Wiley & Sons. 448 p.

Cohen, W. 2003. Comparisons of land cover and LAI estimates derived from ETM+ and MODIS for four sites in North America: a quality assessment of 2000/2001 provisional MODIS products. Remote Sensing of Environment 88(3):233-255.

Cohen, W.B., T.K. Maiersperger, T.A. Spies, and D.R. Oetter. 2001. Modelling forest cover attributes as continuous variables in a regional context with thematic mapper data. International Journal of Remote Sensing 22(12):2279-2310.

Cohen, W.B., T.A. Spies, and M. Fiorella. 1995. Estimating the age and structure of forests in a multi-ownership landscape of western Oregon, U.S.A. International Journal of Remote Sensing 16(4):721-746.

Coulston, J. 2008. Forest inventory and stratified estimation: a cautionary note. Res. Note SRS-16. Asheville, NC: U.S. Department of Agriculture, Forest Service, Southeastern Forest Experiment Station. 8 p.

Czaplewski, R. 2000. Accuracy assessment and areal estimates using two-phase stratified random sampling, cluster plots and the multivariate composite estimator. In: Mowrer, T. and R. Congalton, eds. Quantifying spatial uncertainty in natural resources: theory and applications for GIS and remote sensing. Chelsea, MI: Ann Arbor Press: 79-100.

Czaplewski, R. 2001. Areal control using generalized least squares as an alternative to stratification. In: Reams, G., R. McRoberts, and P. Van Deusen, eds. Proceedings of the second annual Forest Inventory and Analysis symposium; 2000 October 17-18; Salt Lake City, UT. Gen. Tech. Rep. SRS-47. Asheville, NC: U.S. Department of Agriculture, Forest Service, Southern Research Station: 63-65.

Czaplewski, R. 2005. Re-sampling remotely sensed data to improve national and regional mapping of forest conditions with confidential field data. In: Marsden, M., M. Downing, and M. Riffe, eds. Workshop proceedings: quantitative techniques for deriving national-scale data; Westminster, CO; July 26-28. FHTET-05-12. Fort Collins, CO: U.S. Department of Agriculture, Forest Service, Forest Health Technology Enterprise Team: 262-284.

Czaplewski, R. In prep.[b] Recursive restriction estimation: an alternative to post-stratification in surveys of land and forest cover. Fort Collins, CO: U.S. Department of Agriculture, Forest Service, Rocky Mountain Research Station.

Czaplewski, R. In prep.[a]. Time-series analysis of panel data with an empicrical Bayes estimator. Forest Science.

Czaplewski, R. In prep.[b] Remote sensing strategies for the Forest Inventory and Analysis program. Fort Collins, CO: U.S. Forest Service, Rocky Mountain Research Station.

Czaplewski, R. and G. Catts. 1992. Calibration of remotely sensed proportion or area estimates for misclassification error. Remote Sensing of Environment 39(1):29-43.

Czaplewski, R. and P. Patterson. 2001. Accuracy of remotely sensed classifications for stratification of forest and nonforest lands. In: Reams, G., R. McRoberts, and P. Van Deusen, eds. Proceedings of the second annual Forest Inventory and Analysis symposium; 2000 October 17-18; Salt Lake City, UT. Gen. Tech. Rep. SRS-47. Asheville, NC: U.S. Department of Agriculture, Forest Service, Southern Research Station: 32-42.

Czaplewski, R.L. and P.L. Patterson. 2003. Classification accuracy for stratification with remotely sensed data. Forest Science 49(3):402-408.

Czaplewski, R. and M. Thompson. 2009. Opportunities to improve monitoring of temporal trends with FIA panel data. In: McWilliams, W., G. Moisen, and R. Czaplewski, comps. Forest Inventory and Analysis (FIA) symposium 2008; October 21-23; Park City, UT. Proc. RMRS-P-56CD. Fort Collins, CO: U.S. Department of Agriculture, Forest Service, Rocky Mountain Research Station. 55 p.

Czaplewski, R.L. 1989. Combining inventories of land cover and forest resources with prediction models and remotely sensed data. In: Lund, G. and G. Preto, tech. coords. Global natural resource monitoring and assessment: preparing or the 21st century. Proceedings of the international conference and workshop; September 24-30; Venice, Italy. Bethesda, MD: American Society for Photogrammetry and Remote Sensing: 1079-1089.

Czaplewski, R.L. 1990. Kalman filter to update forest cover estimates. In: Labau, V.J. and T. Cunia, tech. eds. State-of-the-art methodology of forestry inventory: a symposium proceedings. Gen. Tech. Rep. PNW-GTR-263. Portland, OR: U.S. Department of Agriculture, Forest Service, Pacific Northwest Research Station: 457-465.

Czaplewski, R.L. 1992. Misclassification bias in areal estimates. Photogrammetric Engineering and Remote Sensing 58:189-192.

Czaplewski, R.L. 1996. Continuous adaptive monitoring of status and trends in ecosystem. In: Sustaining forests, sustaining people: proceedings of the 1995 Society of American Foresters convention; 1995 October 28-November 1; Portland, ME. SAF-96-01. Bethesda, MD: Society of American Foresters: 80-85.

Czaplewski, R.L. 1999. Multistage remote sensing—toward an annual national inventory. Journal of Forestry 97(12):44-48.

Czaplewski, R.L., R.J. Alig, and N.D. Cost. 1988. Statistical monitoring of changes in land/forest cover over large regions using the Kalman filter. In Ek, A.R., S.R. Shifley, and T.E. Burk, eds. International IUFRO conference on forest growth modeling and prediction, volume 2. Gen. Tech. Rep. NC-120. Minneapolis, MN: U.S. Department of Agriculture, Forest Service, North Central Forest Experiment Station: 1089-1096.

Czaplewski, R., J. Rack, V. Lessard, D. Heinzen, S. Ploetz, T. Schmidt, and E. Leatherberry. 2005. Coordination, cooperation, and collaboration between FIA and NRI. In: McRoberts, R.E., G.A. Reams, P.C. Van Deusen, W.H. McWilliams, C.J. Cieszewski, eds. Proceedings of the fourth annual Forest Inventory and Analysis symposium; 2002 November 19-21; New Orleans, LA. Gen. Tech. Rep. NC-252. St. Paul, MN: U.S. Department of Agriculture, Forest Service, North Central Research Station: 141-148.

de Gruijter, J., D. Brus, M. Bierkens, and M. Knotters. 2006. Sampling for natural resource monitoring. Berlin: Springer-Verlag. 332 p.

Deville, J.C. and C.E. Särndal. 1992. Calibration estimators in survey sampling. Journal of the American Statistical Association 87(418):376-382.

Deutsch, R. 1965. Estimation theory. Englewood Cliffs, NJ: Prentice-Hall. 269 p.

Diderrich, G.T. 1985. The Kalman filter from the perspective of Goldberger-Theil estimators. The American Statistician 39:193-198.

Doran, H. 1997. Applying linear time-varying constraints to econometric models: with an application to demand systems. Journal of Econometrics 79(1):83-95.

Duncan, D.B. and S.D. Horn. 1972. Linear dynamic recursive estimation from the viewpoint of regression analysis. Journal of the American Statistical Association 67(340):815-821.

Dymond, J.R. 1992. How accurately do image classifiers estimate area? International Journal of Remote Sensing 13(9):1735-1742.

Estevao, V. and C.-E. Särndal. 2004. Borrowing strength is not the best technique within a wide class of design-consistent domain estimators. Journal of Official Statistics 20(4):645-669.

Estevao, V. and C.-E. Särndal. 2006. Survey estimates by calibration on complex auxiliary information. International Statistical Review 74(2):127-147.

Fattorini, L., M. Marcheselli, and C. Pisani. 2004. Two-phase estimation of coverages with second-phase corrections. Environmetrics 15(4):357-368.

Flewelling, J., R. Ernst, and L. Raynes. 2000. Use of three-point taper systems in timber cruising. In: Hansen, M., and T. Burk, (eds.). Integrated tools for natural resources inventories in the 21st century. Gen. Tech. Rep. NC-212. St. Paul, MN: U.S. Department of Agriculture, Forest Service, North Central Forest Experiment Station: 364-371.

Francisco, J. 2003. Small area estimation: an overview of existing methodologies with application to the estimation of unemployment rates in the Philippines. Quebec City, Quebec: Laval University. 104 p. Thesis.

Frayer, W.E. and G. Furnival. 1999. Forest survey sampling designs: a history. Journal of Forestry 12(1):4-10.

Frees, E. 2004. Longitudinal and panel data: analysis and applications in the social sciences. New York, NY: Cambridge University Press. 484 p.

Frescino, T., G. Moisen, K. Megown, V. Nelson, E. Freeman, P. Patterson, M. Finco, K. Brewer, and J. Menlove. 2009a. Nevada photo-based inventory pilot (NPIP) photo sampling procedures. Gen. Tech. Rep. RMRS-GTR-222. Fort Collins, CO: U.S. Department of Agriculture, Forest Service, Rocky Mountain Research Station. 30 p.

Frescino, T., G. Moisen, W. McWilliams, and R. Czaplewski. 2009b. Using interpreted large scale aerial photo data to enhance satellite-based mapping and explore forest land definitions. In: McWilliams, W., G. Moisen, and R. Czaplewski, comps. Forest Inventory and Analysis (FIA) Symposium 2008; October 21-23; Park City, UT. Proc. RMRS-P-56CD. Fort Collins, CO: U.S. Department of Agriculture, Forest Service, Rocky Mountain Research Station. 16 p.

Fuller, W.A. 2009. Sampling statistics. Hoboken, NJ: John Wiley & Sons. 454 p.

Fuller, W.A. and J. N. K. Rao. 2001. A regression composite estimator with application to the Canadian labour force survey. Survey Methodology 27:45-51.

Furrer, R. and T. Bengtsson. 2007. Estimation of high-dimensional prior and posterior covariance matrices in Kalman filter variants. Journal of Multivariate Analysis 98:227-255.

Gallego, F.J. 2004. Remote sensing and land cover area estimation. International Journal of Remote Sensing 25(15):3019-3047.

Gallego, J. and C. Bamps. 2008. Using CORINE land cover and the point survey LUCAS for area estimation. International Journal of Applied Earth Observation and Geoinformation 10(4):467-475.

Garcia-Yarnoz, D., R. Jehn, and M. Croon. 2006. Interplanetary navigation along the low-thrust trajectory of BepiColombo. Acta Astronautica 59(1-5):284-293.

Gillespie, A. 1999. Rationale for a national annual forest inventory program. Journal of Forestry 97(12):16-20.

Gillespie, A.J.R. 2000. Pros and cons of continuous forest inventory: customer perspectives. In Hansen, M. and T. Burk, eds. Integrated tools for natural resources inventories in the 21st century. Gen. Tech. Rep. NC-212. St. Paul, MN: U.S. Department of Agriculture, Forest Service, North Central Forest Experiment Station: 60-66.

Gillis, M.D., A.Y. Omule, and T. Brierley. 2005. Monitoring Canada's forests: the national forest inventory. The Forestry Chronicle 81(2):214-221.

Goeking, S. and G. Liknes. 2009. The role of pre-field operations at four forest inventory units: we can see the trees, not just the forest. In: McWilliams, W., G. Moisen, and R. Czaplewski, (eds.). Forest Inventory and Analysis (FIA) symposium 2008; October 21-23; Park City, UT. Proc. RMRS-P-56CD. Fort Collins, CO: U.S. Department of Agriculture, Forest Service, Rocky Mountain Research Station. 12 p.

Golub, G. and C. Van Loan. 1996. Matrix computations, 3rd ed. Baltimore, MD: The Johns Hopkins University Press. 694 p.

Gregoire, T. and D. Walters. 1988. Composite vector estimators derived by weighting inversely proportional to variance. Canadian Journal of Forest Research 18(2):282-284.

Gregoire, T.G. and H.T. Valentine. 2007. Sampling strategies for natural resources and environment. London, England: Chapman and Hall/CRC Press. 496 p.

Grewal, M. and A. Andrews. 2001. Kalman filtering: theory and practice using MATLAB. John Wiley & Sons. 416 p.

Gupta, N. 2008. Constrained Kalman filtering and predicting behaviour in agent-based financial market models. Oxford, United Kingdom: University of Oxford. Dissertation.

Gupta, N. and R. Hauser. 2007. Kalman filtering with equality and inequality state constraints. Oxford University Computing Laboratory, Numerical Analysis Group. 26 p.

Guttman, I. and D. Lin. 1995. Robust recursive estimation for correlated observations. Statistics & Probability Letters 23(1):79-92.

Hahn, J., C. Maclean, S. Arner, and W. Bechtold. 1995. Procedures to handle inventory cluster plots that straddle two or more conditions. Forest Science Monograph 31:12-25.

Halme, M. and E. Tomppo. 2001. Improving the accuracy of multisource forest inventory estimates to reducing plot location error—a multicriteria approach. Remote Sensing of Environment 78:321-327.

Hansen, M. and D. Wendt. 2000. Using classified Landsat thematic mapper data for stratification in a statewide forest inventory. In: McRoberts, R., G. Reams, and P. Van Deusen, (eds.). Proceedings of the first annual Forest Inventory and Analysis symposium. Gen. Tech. Rep. NC-213. St. Paul, MN: U.S. Department of Agriculture, Forest Service, North Central Research Station: 20-27.

Härdle, W. 1990. Applied nonparametric regression. New York, NY: Cambridge University Press. 352 p.

Harvey, A. 1978. The estimation of time-varying parameters from panel data. Annales de L'Inséé (30/31):203-226.

Harvey, A.C. and P.H.J. Todd. 1983. Forecasting economic time series with structural and Box-Jenkins models: a case study. Journal of Business & Economic Statistics 1(4):299-307.

Haslett, S. and G. Jones. 2005. Small area estimation using surveys and censuses: some practical and statistical issues. Statistics in Transition 7(3):541-555.

Hay, A.M. 1988. The derivation of global estimates from a confusion matrix. International Journal of Remote Sensing 9(8):1395-1398.

Healey, S., W. Cohen, Y. Zhiqiang, and O. Krankina. 2005. Comparison of tasseled cap-based Landsat data structures for use in forest disturbance detection. Remote Sensing of Environment 97(3):301-310.

Helms, J., ed. 1998. The dictionary of forestry. Bethesda, MD: Society of American Foresters. 224 p.

Higham, N.J. 2002. Accuracy and stability of numerical algorithms, 2nd ed. Society for Philadelphia, PA: Industrial and Applied Mathematics. 680 p.

Holmgren, P. and T. Thuresson. 1998. Satellite remote sensing for forestry planning: a review. Scandinavian Journal of Forest Research 13(1):90-110.

Holthausen, R., R. L., Czaplewski, D. Delorenzo, G. Hayward, W. B., Kessler, P. Manley, K. S., Mckelvey, D. S., Powell, L. F., Ruggiero, M. K., Schwartz, B. Van Horne, and C.D. Vojta. 2005. Strategies for monitoring terrestrial animals and habitats. Gen. Tech. Rep. RMRS-GTR-161. Fort Collins, CO: U.S. Department of Agriculture, Forest Service, Rocky Mountain Research Station. 34 p.

Hoppus, M. and A. Lister. 2002. A statistically valid method for using FIA plots to guide spectral class rejection in producing stratification maps. In: McRoberts, R., G. Reams, P. Van Deusen, and J. Moser, (eds.). Proceedings of the third annual Forest Inventory and Analysis symposium. Gen. Tech. Rep. NC-230. St. Paul, MN: U.S. Department of Agriculture, Forest Service, North Central Research Station: 44-49.

Horler, D.N.H. and F.J. Ahern. 1986. Forestry information content of thematic mapper data. International Journal of Remote Sensing 7:405-428.

Householder, A. 1964. The theory of matrices in numerical analysis. Dover Publications.

Houston, A.G. and F.G. Hall. 1984. Use of satellite data in agricultural surveys. Communications in Statistics—Theory and Methods 13(23):2857-2880.

Huete, A., K. Didan, T. Miura, E.P. Rodriguez, X. Gao, and L.G. Ferreira. 2002. Overview of the radiometric and biophysical performance of the MODIS vegetation indices. Remote Sensing of Environment 83(1-2):195-213.

Iles, K. 2010. Nearest neighbor bias: A simple example. Mathematical and Computational Forestry & Natural-Resource Sciences 2:18-19.

Jagers, P. 1986. Post-stratification against bias in sampling. International Statistical Review 54:159-167.

Jazwinski, A. 1970. Stochastic processes and filtering. San Diego, CA: Academic Press. 376 p.

Jiang, S. and M. Ghil. 1993. Dynamical properties of error statistics in a shallow-water model. Journal of Physical Oceanography 23(12):2541-2566.

Jones, R. 1993. Longitudinal data with serial correlation. London, England: Chapman and Hall/CRC Press. 225 p.

Justice, C.O., J.R.G. Townshend, E.F. Vermote, E. Masuoka, R.E. Wolfe, N. Saleous, D.P. Roy, and J.T. Morisette. 2002. An overview of MODIS Land data processing and product status. Remote Sensing of Environment 83:3-15.

Kalman, R.E. 1960. A new approach to linear filtering and prediction problems. Transactions of the ASME. Journal of Basic Engineering 82(Series D):35-45.

Kalman, R.E. and R.S. Bucy. 1961. New results in linear filtering and prediction theory. Transactions of the ASME. Journal of Basic Engineering 83(Series D):95-107.

Kalman, R.E., P.L. Falb, and M.A. Arbib. 1969. Topics in mathematical system theory, vol. 8. McGraw-Hill. 358 p.

Katila, M. and E. Tomppo. 2001. Selecting estimation parameters for the Finnish multisource national forest inventory. Remote Sensing of Environment 76(1):16-32.

King, R.B. 2002. Land cover mapping principles: a return to interpretation fundamentals. International Journal of Remote Sensing 23(18):3525-3545.

Knottnerus, P. 2003. Sample survey theory: some Pythagorean perspectives. New York, NY: Springer-Verlag. 415 p.

Knottnerus, P. and C. van Duin. 2006. Variances in repeated weighting with an application to the Dutch labour force survey. Journal of Official Statistics 22:565-584.

Krewski, D. and J.N.K. Rao. 1981. Inference from stratified samples: properties of the linearization, jackknife and balanced repeated replication methods. The Annals of Statistics 9(5):1010-1019.

Lawson, C.L. and R.J. Hanson. 1974. Solving least squares problems. In: Lawson, C.L. and R.J. Hanson, eds. Prentice-Hall series in automatic computation. 3rd ed. Englewood Cliffs, NJ: Prentice-Hall. 337 p.

Ledoit, O. and M. Wolf. 2003. Honey, I shrunk the sample covariance matrix. The Journal of Portfolio Management 30(4):110-119.

Ledoit, O. and M. Wolf. 2004. A well-conditioned estimator for large-dimensional covariance matrices. Journal of Multivariate Analysis 88:365-411.

Lefsky, M.A., W.B. Cohen, and T.A. Spies. 2001. An evaluation of alternate remote sensing products for forest inventory, monitoring, and mapping of Douglas-fir forests in western Oregon. Canadian Journal of Forest Research 31:78-87.

Lehtonen, R., C.-E. Särndal, and A. Veijanen. 2003. The effect of model choice in estimation for domains including small domains. Survey Methodology 29(1):33-44.

Lister, T., A. Lister, E. Alexander, W. McWilliams, G. Moisen, and R. Czaplewski. 2009. Estimating fine-scale land use change dynamics using an expedient photointerpretation-based method. In: McWilliams, W., G. Moisen, and R. Czaplewski, comps. Forest Inventory and Analysis (FIA) symposium 2008; October 21-23; Park City, UT. Proc. RMRS-P-56CD. Fort Collins, CO: U.S. Department of Agriculture, Forest Service, Rocky Mountain Research Station. 10 p.

Longford, N. 1999. Multivariate shrinkage estimation of small area means and proportions. Journal of the Royal Statistical Society. Series A (Statistics in Society) 162(2):227-245.

Lowe, R. and C. Cieszewski. 2005. Comparison of programs used for FIA inventory information dissemination and spatial representation. In: McRoberts, R.E., G.A. Reams, P.C. Van Deusen, and W.H. McWilliams, eds. Proceedings of the fifth annual forest inventory and analysis symposium; 2003 November 18-20; New Orleans, LA. Gen. Tech. Rep. WO-69. Washington, DC: U.S. Department of Agriculture Forest Service. 222 p.

Lui, K.-J. and W. G. Cumberland. 1991. A model-based approach: composite estimators for small area estimation. Journal of Official Statistics 7(1):69-76.

Lund, G., W. Befort, J. Brickell, W. Ciesla, E. Collins, R. Czaplewski, A. Disperati, R. Douglass, C. Dull, J. Greer, R. Hershey, V. Labau, H. Lachowski, P. Murtha, D. Nowak, M. Roberts, Pierre, A. Singh, K. Winterberger, and W. Philipson. 1997. Forestry. In: Philipson, W.R., ed. Manual of photographic interpretation, 2nd ed. Bethesda, MD: American Society for Photogrammetry and Remote Sensing: 399-440.

Lundström, S. 1997. Calibration as a standard method for treatment of nonresponse. Stockholm, Sweden: Stockholm University. Dissertation.

Lundström, S. and Särndal, C.-E. 1999. Calibration as a standard method for treatment of nonresponse. Journal of Official Statistics 15:305-327.

Magnussen, S. 2003. Stepwise estimators for three-phase sampling of categorical variables. Journal of Applied Statistics 30(5):461-475.

Magnussen, S. 2007. A method for estimation of a land-cover change matrix from error-prone unit-level observations. Canadian Journal of Forest Research 37:1501-1517.

Magnussen, S., P. Boudewyn, M. Gillis, M. Hansen, and T. Burk. 2000. Towards a plot size for Canada's national forest inventory. In: Hansen, M. and T. Burk, eds. Integrated tools for natural resources inventories in the 21st century. Gen. Tech. Rep. NC-212. St. Paul, MN: U.S. Dept. of Agriculture, Forest Service, North Central Forest Experiment Station: 116-128.

Magnussen, S., R. McRoberts, and E. Tomppo. 2009. Model-based mean square error estimators for k-nearest neighbour predictions and applications using remotely sensed data for forest inventories. Remote Sensing of Environment 113(3):476-488.

Magnussen, S., Tomppo, E., and McRoberts, R. E. 2010. A model-assisted k-nearest neighbour approach to remove extrapolation bias. Scandinavian Journal of Forest Research 25:174-184.

Mandallaz, D. 2008. Sampling techniques for forest inventories. CRC Press. 272 p.

Martinussen, T., T. Nord-Larsen, and V. Johannsen. 2008. Estimating forest cover in the presence of missing observations. Scandinavian Journal of Forest Research 23(3):266-271.

Maybeck, P. 1979. Stochastic models, estimation, and control. New York, NY: Academic Press. 423 p.

McRoberts, R. 2005. The enhanced forest inventory and analysis program. In: Bechtold, W.A., and P.L. Patterson, eds. The enhanced forest inventory and analysis program—national sampling design and estimation procedures. Gen. Tech. Rep. SRS-80. Asheville, NC: U.S. Department of Agriculture, Forest Service, Southern Research Station: 11-20.

McRoberts, R. 2006. A model-based approach to inventory stratification. In: McRoberts, R.E., G.A. Reams, P.C. Van Duesen, and W.H. McWilliams, eds. Proceedings of the sixth annual forest inventory and analysis symposium; 2004 September 21-24; Denver, CO. Gen. Tech. Rep. WO-70. Washington, DC: U.S. Department of Agriculture Forest Service. 126 p.

McRoberts, R.E. 2008. Using satellite imagery and the k-nearest neighbors technique as a bridge between strategic and management forest inventories. Remote Sensing of Environment 112:2212-2221.

McRoberts, R. and E. Tomppo. 2007. Remote sensing support for national forest inventories. Remote Sensing of Environment 110(4):412-419.

McRoberts, R. E. 2010. The effects of rectification and global positioning system errors on satellite image-based estimates of forest area. Remote Sensing of Environment 114:1710-1717.

McRoberts, R. and G. Liknes. 2005. Assessing the effects of forest fragmentation using satellite imagery and forest inventory data. In: McRoberts, R., G. Reams, P. Van Deusen, W. McWilliams, and C. Cieszewski, (eds.).Proceedings of the fourth annual Forest Inventory and Analysis symposium. Gen. Tech. Rep. NC-252. St. Paul, MN: U.S. Department of Agriculture, Forest Service, North Central Research Station: 117-120.

McRoberts, R., E. Tomppo, A. Finley, and J. Heikkinen. 2007. Estimating areal means and variances of forest attributes using the k-nearest neighbors technique and satellite imagery. Remote Sensing of Environment 111(4):466-480.

McRoberts, R., W. McWilliams, G. Reams, T. Schmidt, J. Jenkins, K. O'Neill, P. Miles, and G. Brand. 2004. Assessing sustainability using data from the Forest Inventory and Analysis Program of the United States Forest Service. Journal of Sustainable Forestry 18(1):23-46.

McRoberts, R.R.E., D.G. Wendt, M.D. Nelson, and M.H. Hansen. 2002. Using a land cover classification based on satellite imagery to improve the precision of forest inventory area estimates. Remote Sensing of Environment 81(1):36-44.

Means, J.E., S.A. Acker, D.J. Harding, J.B. Blair, M.A. Lefsky, W.B. Cohen, M.E. Harmon, and W.A. McKee. 1999. Use of large-footprint scanning airborne LiDAR to estimate forest stand characteristics in the western Cascades of Oregon—biomass distribution and production budgets. Remote Sensing of Environment 67(3):298-308.

Meinhold, R. and N. Singpurwalla. 1983. Understanding the Kalman filter. The American Statistician 37(2):123-127.

Militino, A., M. Ugarte, and B. Ibáñez. 2008. Longitudinal analysis of spatially correlated data. Stochastic Environmental Research and Risk Assessment 22:49-57.

Montanari, G. 2000. Conditioning on auxiliary variable means in finite population inference. Australian & New Zealand Journal of Statistics 18:407-421.

Montanari, G.E. 1998. On regression estimation of finite population means. Survey Methodology 24(1):69-77.

Montanari, G.E. and M.G. Ranalli. 2002. Asymptotically efficient generalized regression estimators. Journal of Official Statistics 18:559-589.

Morin, R., T. Prichard, V. Everson, J. Westfall, C. Scott, W. McWilliams, G. Moisen, and R. Czaplewski. 2009. Wisconsin State Forests continuous forest inventory: a look at the first year. In: McWilliams, W., G. Moisen, and R. Czaplewski, comps. Forest Inventory and Analysis (FIA) symposium 2008; October 21-23; Park City, UT. Proc. RMRS-P-56CD. Fort Collins, CO: U.S. Department of Agriculture, Forest Service, Rocky Mountain Research Station. 10 p.

Nascimento Silva, P.L.D. and C. J. Skinner. 1997. Variable selection for regression estimation in finite populations. Survey Methodology 23:23-32.

Nelson, M., G. Moisen, M. Finco, and K. Brewer. 2007. Forest inventory and analysis in the United States: remote sensing and geospatial activities. Photogrammetric Engineering and Remote Sensing 73(7):729-732.

Nelson, M.D., R.E. McRoberts, G.R. Holden, and M.E. Bauer. 2009a. Effects of satellite image spatial aggregation and resolution on estimates of forest land area. International Journal of Remote Sensing 30(8):1913-1940.

Nelson, R., J. Boudreau, T. Gregoire, H. Margolis, E. Naesset, T. Gobakken, and G. Stahl. 2009b. Estimating Quebec provincial forest resources using ICESat/GLAS. Canadian Journal of Forest Research 39(4):862-881.

Nusser, S.M., F.J. Breidt, and W.A. Fuller. 1998. Design and estimation for investigating the dynamics of natural resources. Ecological Applications 8(2):234-245.

Opsomer, J. 2010. [Personal communication]. Professor, Statistics Department, Colorado State University, Fort Collins, CO.

Opsomer, J. D., Breidt, J. F., Moisen, G. G., and Kauermann, G. 2007. Model-assisted estimation of forest resources with generalized additive models. Journal of the American Statistical Association 102:400-409. Oswald, D. 1988. Use of sample photo-plot data for forest resource mapping. Western Journal of Applied Forestry 3(2):52-54.

Oud, J. 2004. SEM state space modeling of panel data in discrete and continuous time and its relationship to traditional state space modeling. In: In van Montfort, K., J. Oud, and A. Satorra, eds. Recent developments on structural equation models. Springer: 13-40.

Patterson, P. and G. Reams. 2005. Combining panels for forest inventory and analysis estimation. In: Patterson, B.A. and L. Paul, eds. The enhanced forest inventory and analysis program—national sampling design and estimation procedures. Gen. Tech. Rep. SRS-80. Asheville, NC: U.S. Department of Agriculture, Forest Service, Southern Research Station: 79-84.

Pfeffermann, D. and R. Tiller. 2006. Small-area estimation with state-space models subject to benchmark constraints. Journal of the American Statistical Association 101(476):1387-1397.

Piepho, H.-P. and J. Ogutu. 2007. Simple state-space models in a mixed model framework. The American Statistician 61(3):224-232.

Pollock, D.S.G. 2003. Recursive estimation in econometrics. Computational Statistics and Data Analysis 44(1-2):37-75.

Pontius, G. 2000. Quantification error versus location error in comparison of categorical maps. Photogrammetric Engineering and Remote Sensing 66(8):1011-1016.

Pope, K., J. Reybenayas, and J. Paris. 1994. Radar remote sensing of forest and wetland ecosystems in the Central American tropics. Remote Sensing of Environment 48:205-219.

Popescu, S., R. Wynne, and R. Nelson. 2003. Measuring individual tree crown diameter with LiDAR and assessing its influence on estimating forest volume and biomass. Canadian Journal of Remote Sensing 5:564-577.

Ranson, K.J. and S. Guoqing. 1997. An evaluation of AIRSAR and SIR-C/X-SAR images for mapping northern forest attributes in Maine, USA. Remote Sensing of Environment 59(2):203-222.

Ranson, K.J. and G. Sun. 1994. Mapping biomass of a northern forest using multifrequency SAR data. Geoscience and Remote Sensing, IEEE Transactions on 32(2):388-396.

Ranson, K.J., G. Sun, J.F. Weishampel, and R.G. Knox. 1997. Forest biomass from combined ecosystem and radar backscatter modeling. Remote Sensing of Environment 59:118-133.

Rao, J.N.K. 2003. Small area estimation. Hoboken, NJ: John Wiley & Sons. 313 p.

Rao, J.N.K. 2005. Inferential issues in small area estimation: some new developments. Statistics in Transition 7(3):513-526.

Reams, G. and J. McCollum. 2000. The use of multiple imputation in the southern annual forest inventory system. In: Hansen, M. and T. Burk, eds. Integrated tools for natural resources inventories in the 21st century: an international conference on the inventory and monitoring of forested ecosystems; 1998 August 16-19; Boise, ID. Gen. Tech. Rep. NCRS-212. St. Paul, MN: U.S. Department of Agriculture, Forest Service, North Central Research Station: 228-233.

Reams, G., W. Smith, M. Hansen, W. Bechtold, F. Roesch, G. Moisen, and P. Patterson. 2005. The forest inventory and analysis sampling frame. In: Bechtold, W.A. and P.L. Patterson, eds. The enhanced forest inventory and analysis program—national sampling design and estimation procedures. Gen. Tech. Rep. SRS-80. Asheville, NC: U.S. Department of Agriculture, Forest Service, Southern Research Station: 31-36.

Roesch, F. 2009. Spatial-temporal models for improved county-level annual estimates. In: McWilliams, W., G. Moisen, and R. Czaplewski, comps. Forest Inventory and Analysis (FIA) symposium 2008; October 21-23; Park City, UT. Proc. RMRS-P-56CD. Fort Collins, CO: U.S. Department of Agriculture, Forest Service, Rocky Mountain Research Station. 20 p.

Roesch, F.A. 1999. Analytical alternatives for an annual inventory system. Journal of Forestry 97:33-37.

Roesch, F.A. 2008. An alternative view of continuous forest inventories. Forest Science 54:455-464.

Rosenbrock, H.H. and A.G.J. Macfarlane. 1972. State-space and multivariable theory. Systems, Man and Cybernetics, IEEE Transactions on 2(2):295-296.

Sader, S., M. Hoppus, J. Metzler, and S. Jin. 2005. Perspectives of Maine forest cover change from Landsat imagery and Forest Inventory Analysis (FIA). Journal of Forestry 103(6):299-303.

Särndal, C.-E. 2007. The calibration approach in survey theory and practice. Survey Methodology 33(2):99-119.

Särndal, C.-E. and Lundström, S. 2008. Assessing auxiliary vectors for control of nonresponse bias in the calibration estimator. Journal of Official Statistics 24:167-191.

Särndal, C.-E., B. Swensson, and J.H. Wretman. 1992. Model assisted survey sampling. New York, NY: Springer-Verlag. 694 p.

Schafer, J. and Strimmer, K. 2005. A shrinkage approach to large-scale covariance matrix estimation and implications for functional genomics. Statistical Applications in Genetics and Molecular Biology 4:1175-1189.

Schaible, W.L. 1978. Choosing weights for composite estimators for small area statistics. In: Proceedings of the section on survey research methods, American Statistical Association: 741-746.

Schott, J. 2005. Matrix analysis for statistics. John Wiley & Sons. 456 p.

Schreuder, H., G. Wood, and T. Gregoire. 1993. Sampling methods for multiresource forest inventory. John Wiley & Sons. 446 p.

Scott, C.T., W.A. Bechtold, G.A. Reams, W.D. Smith, J.A. Westfall, M.H. Hansen, and G.G. Moisen. 2005. Sample-based estimators used by the forest inventory and analysis national information management system. In: Bechtold, W.A. and P.L. Patterson, eds. The enhanced forest inventory and analysis program— national sampling design and estimation procedures. Gen. Tech. Rep. SRS-80. Asheville, NC: U.S. Department of Agriculture, Forest Service, Southern Research Station: 53-77.

Simon, D. and T. Chia. 2002. Kalman filtering with state equality constraints. Aerospace and Electronic Systems, IEEE Transactions on 38(1):128-136.

Smith, W. 2002. Forest inventory and analysis: a national inventory and monitoring program. Environmental Pollution 116:S233-S242.

Sõstra, K. 2007. Restriction estimator for domains. Tartu, Estonia: University of Tartu. Dissertation.

Sõstra, K. and I. Traat. 2009. Optimal domain estimation under summation restriction. Journal of Statistical Planning and Inference 139:3928-3941.

Stengel, R. 1986. Stochastic optimal control: theory and application. New York, NY: John Wiley & Sons. 638 p.

Story, M. and R. Congalton. 1986. Accuracy assessment—a user's perspective. Photogrammetric Engineering and Remote Sensing 52(3):397-399.

Sugden, R.A. and T. M. F. Smith. 2002. Exact linear unbiased estimation in survey sampling. Journal of Statistical Planning and Inference 102:25-38.

Sun, G., K. Ranson, D. Kimes, J. Blair, and K. Kovacs. 2008. Forest vertical structure from GLAS: an evaluation using LVIS and SRTM data. Remote Sensing of Environment 112(1):107-117.

Tam, S.M. 1987. Analysis of repeated surveys using a dynamic linear model. International Statistical Review/Revue Internationale de Statistique 55(1):63-73.

Tenenbein, A. 1972. A double sampling scheme for estimating from misclassified multinomial data with applications to sampling inspection. Technometrics 14(1):187-202.

Tepping, B.J. 1968. Variance estimation in complex surveys. In: Proceedings of the social statistics section, American Statistical Association: 11-18.

Theil, H. and A.S. Goldberger. 1961. On pure and mixed statistical estimation in economics. International Economic Review 2(1):65-78.

Tian, Y., C.E. Woodcock, Y. Wang, J.L. Privette, N.V. Shabanov, L. Zhou, Y. Zhang, W. Buermann, J. Dong, B. Veikkanen, T. Hame, K. Andersson, M. Ozdogan, Y. Knyazikhin, and R.B. Myneni. 2002. Multiscale analysis and validation of the MODIS LAI product—II. Sampling strategy. Remote Sensing of Environment 83(3):431-441.

Tiller, R. 1992. Time series modeling of sample survey data from the U.S. current population survey. Journal of Official Statistics 8(2):149-166.

Trotter, C.M., J.R. Dymond, and C.J. Goulding. 1997. Estimation of timber volume in a coniferous plantation forest using Landsat TM. International Journal of Remote Sensing 18(10):2209-2223.

Tucker, C. 1979. Red and photographic infrared linear combinations for monitoring vegetation. Remote Sensing of Environment 8(2):127-150.

USDA Forest Service. 1998. Strategic plan for forest inventory and monitoring. Washington, DC: U.S. Department of Agriculture, Forest Service. 48 p. Online: http://fia.fs fed.us/documents/pdfs/Mandate%203a-%20FIA%20 1st%20Strat%20Plan%2099-03.pdf.

USDA Forest Service. 2007. Forest inventory and analysis strategic plan: a history of success, a dynamic future. FS-865. Washington, DC: U.S. Department of Agriculture, Forest Service. 20 p. Online: http://fia fs.fed.us/documents/pdfs/ Mandate%203b-FIA%202nd%20Strat%20Plan%2008-12.pdf.

Valliant, R., A. Dorfman, and R. Royall. 2000. Finite population sampling and inference: a prediction approach. John Wiley & Sons. 504 p.

Van Deusen, P.C. 2002. Issues related to panel creep. In: McRoberts, R.E., G.A. Reams, P.C. Van Deusen, and J.W. Moser, eds. Proceedings of the third annual Forest Inventory and Analysis symposium; Gen. Tech. Rep. NC-230. St. Paul, MN: U.S. Department of Agriculture, Forest Service, North Central Research Station: 31-35.

Van Deusen, P.C. 2005. Stratified forest inventory estimation with mapped plots. Canadian Journal of Forest Research 35(10):2382-2386.

Van Deusen, P., S. Prisley, and A. Lucier. 1999. Adopting an annual inventory system: user perspectives. Journal of Forestry 97(12):11-14.

Verbyla, D.L. and S.H. Boles. 2000. Bias in land cover change estimates due to misregistration. International Journal of Remote Sensing 21(18):3553-3560.

Wikle, C.K. and N. Cressie. 1999. A dimension-reduced approach to space-time Kalman filtering. Biometrika 86(4):815-829.

Williams, M.S., K.L. Cormier, R. G., Briggs, and D. L. Martinez. 1999. Evaluation of the barr & stroud fp15 and criterion 400 laser dendrometers for measuring upper stem diameters and heights. Forest Science 45:53-61.

Wilson, T. and W. Ibes. 2005. Forest inventory and analysis information delivery architecture. In: Proceedings, 16th annual workshop on database and expert systems applications (DEXA), 5th FEIDSS workshop; Copenhagen, Denmark. Los Alamitos, CA: Institute of Electrical and Electronic Engineers Computer Society Press: 706-710.

Wolter, K. 2007. Introduction to variance estimation. New York, NY: Springer. 427 p.

Woodruff, R. 1971. A simple method for approximating the variance of a complicated estimate. Journal of the American Statistical Association 66(334):411-414.

Wynne, R. and D. Carter. 1997. Will remote sensing live up to its promise for forest management? Journal of Forestry 95(10):23-26.

Xu, Y., B. G., Dickson, H. M., Hampton, T. D., Sisk, J. A., Palumbo, and J. W. Prather. 2009. Effects of mismatches of scale and location between predictor and response variables on forest structure mapping. Photogrammetric Engineering and Remote Sensing 75:313-322.

Zarnoch, S.J. and W.A. Bechtold 2000. Estimating mapped-plot forest attributes with ratios of means. Canadian Journal of Forest Research 30(5):688-697.

Zhan, X., R.A. Sohlberg, J.R.G. Townshend, C. Dimiceli, M.L. Carroll, J.C. Eastman, M.C. Hansen, and R.S. Defries. 2002. Detection of land cover changes using MODIS 250 m data. Remote Sensing of Environment 83(1-2):336-350.

Zhang, L. 2000. Post-stratification and calibration—a synthesis. The American Statistician 54:178-184.

Zhu, Z., L. Yang, S. Stehman, and R. Czaplewski. 2000. Accuracy assessment for the U.S. Geological Survey Regional Land-Cover Mapping Program: New York and New Jersey Region. Photogrammetric Engineering and Remote Sensing 66:1425-1438.

Zimble, D.A., D.L. Evans, G.C. Carlson, R.C. Parker, S.C. Grado, and P.D. Gerard. 2003. Characterizing vertical forest structure using small-footprint airborne LiDAR. Remote Sensing of Environment 87(2-3):171-182.